ARTHUR
RIMBAUD

COMPLETE
WORKS

arthur rimbaud

COMPLETE
WORKS

*Translated from the French
by Paul Schmidt*

HARPER**PERENNIAL** ⬤ MODERN**CLASSICS**

NEW YORK • LONDON • TORONTO • SYDNEY • NEW DELHI • AUCKLAND

HARPER**PERENNIAL** ● MODERN**CLASSICS**

Portions of this work originally appeared in *Arion*, *Delos*, *Prose*, and the *New York Review of Books*.

P.S.™ is a trademark of HarperCollins Publishers.

HarperCollins books may be purchased for educational, business, or sales promotional use. For information, please e-mail the Special Markets Department at SPsales@harpercollins.com.

First Harper Colophon edition published 1976.
First Perennial Classics edition published 2000.
First Harper Perennial Modern Classics edition published 2008.

The Library of Congress has catalogued the previous edition as follows:

Rimbaud, Arthur, 1854–1891.
[Works. English. 2000]
Complete works / Arthur Rimbaud ; translated by Paul Schmidt.—
Perennial Classics ed.
          p. cm.
ISBN 0-06-095550-3
Includes bibliographical references.
1. Rimbaud, Arthur, 1854–1891—Translations into English. I. Title: Arthur Rimbaud, complete works. II. Schmidt, Paul, 1934– . III. Title.
PQ2387.R5 A28   2000
841'.8—dc21   99-057064

ISBN 978-0-06-156177-1 (pbk.)

23 24 25 26 27 LBC 33 32 31 30 29

For Edward, and for Roger and Nora

Contents

THIRD SEASON
War   57

FOURTH SEASON
The Tormented Heart   73

FIFTH SEASON
The Visionary

SIXTH SEASON

The Damned Soul   215

SEVENTH SEASON

A Few Belated Cowardices   245

EIGHTH SEASON
The Man with the Wind at His Heels

Translator's Introduction

For a long time, there was a word in Rimbaud's writing that I never understood. I think perhaps I do now. It is a word he used quite often: season—*saison*.

All periods of time have ends to them, and these fatal endings we anticipate. A period of time—a day, an hour, a year—and this will end, we say; all this will end, the season will turn, and all will be over. We look in vain for some eternal moment, for happiness, felicity, that state of bliss that will go on for ever and ever. Is not happiness defined only when no term to its extent is imagined? So Rimbaud thought, it seems to me. His seasons are those stretches of time that open unawares and close painfully in our lives. That summer, those two years in the city, this love affair, that month in the country—these are the true, the organic epochs of our lives; the dates that mark their endings are our true anniversaries. Are not these the seasons Rimbaud wrote of: the implacable turning of seasons, and the denial of happiness implicit in their movement? Here then are the records of Rimbaud's Seasons—all his poems, his prose, most of his letters.

How does one go about translating a poet's complete writings? I found that I had posed enormous problems for myself. Rimbaud's early poetry is that of a clever schoolboy, very familiar with his literary models and handling them with great sureness. How could this be made clear? And how could the progress of a rapidly maturing poetic genius be presented in translation? Rimbaud's poems had all been written in such a short space of time—five years, perhaps less! How could I assimilate all the experiences that had influenced these writings? How could I make clear the relationship of the work as a whole to the exterior world, to the environment—literary, physical, historical—that had produced it? I felt I could not sit down to translate a series of separate poems, but that I had to find a vocabulary and a voice for all Rimbaud had written.

It was with the sound of a voice that I began—but with my own. I was seduced by false coincidences. Rimbaud seemed to me a kind of mirror, and my early translations of his poems were essays in narcissism. It was a childish preoccupation: I set myself the task of entering his strange world as I perceived it; to seek his path even where the wind at his heels had effaced it. I came at last to see his poems as incidents in a life that we—he and I—somehow, somewhere, shared. My own adolescence was swallowed up in the new one his poems revealed to me. I was out to master his poetry, to grasp his thought—whose record his poems were, that I *knew*—to make it mine, to write his poems myself, as myself, in my own voice, in my own language. I soon found no way within me or without to separate his voice from mine, nor did I want to. My task led me irresistibly from one page to another, and off the page finally altogether. I ran after him. I sought out streets and houses he had lived in. I drank and drugged myself in taverns and in alleys he had known. My derangements went beyond his, on and on. At last, somehow, I stopped, and found that my adolescence had come to an end. "Beware biography," critics had told me. Yes—but whose?

It was only then that I began to listen to Rimbaud, to his voice, to what he himself was saying. His writings are the notes of a quest, a search for a kind of perfection only children believe in, an attempt to find an absolute freedom. That quest moved through time and space as his life did, but it became clear to me that the writing itself was his life, the clear set of objective facts we like to call biography. The events he lived seemed suddenly no more than the fictions of some "artistic" imagination. Had a romantic poet set out to imagine Rimbaud's life, he could never have produced such profusion, such a dazzling luxuriance of events—but in Rimbaud's own imagination, in his poetry, there is only vision, lucidity, clarity, and courage. It is poetry, yes, but it is also process: a poetic, an attempt at a method—"I searched continually to find the place and the formula," he writes. The events of his life were merely the terms of his argument.

And that argument, I realized, is a dramatic one. The record of his search is a drama: the sound of his voice shifts from one tone to another, voices succeed voices, all with irony, sarcasm, delight, despair, clearly marked in them. What poet's work is so full of proper names, of voices speaking, addressing each other, addressing *you*? *"JE est un autre,"* he writes; *"I* is an *other,"* indeed, in all his poems.

And I? My task was clear: I weeded out my youthful identifications and threw them away. What remained for me then was to wrestle with Rimbaud's poetry the way an actor wrestles with a part, to perform what his words revealed. To arrange it? To impose order on his derangements? No. Simply to speak it in my own language, to say what he wrote, to tell what appears to have happened within the periods that Rimbaud himself has set, the seasons that obsessed him. They are the natural acts and scenes of this drama—a drama that Rimbaud has written, and that I now perform. So this is *my* Rimbaud, though I am not Rimbaud, and he is not me. We are both somebody else.

In this book, my performance, I have broken up a kind of ordering imposed long ago on what he wrote. The reader will not find the general title *Illuminations* in this edition, though all the poems variously included under this title in previous editions are here.

Let me explain.

A sticky point of Rimbaud scholarship has always been the problem of dating a group of prose poems usually referred to as *Illuminations*. Were they written before the summer of 1873, the date of *A Season in Hell,* and was the latter then a "farewell to literature"? Or were they written after it, and is the story of the great abandonment thus no more than a critic's fancy? The problem, I think, has always been conditioned by the existence of the title. Having a body of work in hand called *Illuminations,* one was curious to know when Rimbaud had written it. But if there had been nothing but a series of poems, undated, entitled not as a collection, but individually, what then?

It was Paul Verlaine who first used the title, in a letter to his brother-in-law, Charles de Sivry, in 1878. Verlaine's elliptical style in correspondence is difficult to pin down, but it does seem clear from his written references to Rimbaud's writings in prose that he consistently had difficulty with titles. He speaks variously of "prose poems," "prose fragments," "a manuscript whose title escapes us . . . ," "a sealed manuscript entitled *La Chasse Spirituelle* . . . ," "a series of superb fragments, *Les Illuminations,* lost forever, we have reason to fear. . . ." Are these separate works? Or is Verlaine giving various descriptions of the same poems? And are these "fragments" meant to form a whole, or not?

All we can say from the evidence of letters and manuscripts is this:

1. Rimbaud was writing "prose poems" prior to July 1872.

2. With the exception of *A Season in Hell,* whose pieces he referred to as "stories," Rimbaud himself never gave any of his prose poems any general title.

3. The manuscripts of some "prose fragments" and some verses were delivered by Charles de Sivry in 1885, in a "bundle," to Gustave Kahn, to be printed in Kahn's magazine *La Vogue.* This bundle presumably contained forty-eight poems in prose and verse, because that is what *La Vogue* subsequently published. They gave the forty-eight poems the general title *Les Illuminations,* since this was a title Verlaine had once given to some "prose fragments." But it is unclear whether all the poems in the bundle—verse as well as prose—were "Illuminations" or not. Verlaine was never very precise on the subject. The bundle was edited for *La Vogue* by the poet Felix Féneon, who described it later thus: "The manuscript I was given was a bundle of sheets of the kind of ruled paper you find in school notebooks. Loose pages, without page numbers, a pack of cards—otherwise why would I have thought of arranging them in some kind of order, as I remember doing?"

Clearly, then, the title, the actual contents, and the order of any collection of poems called *Illuminations* are all hypothetical, and cannot be traced to Rimbaud himself. The prose poems further seem to me of diverse inspiration, as well as of uneven quality, and they are clearly varied in style and in theme. As for dating them, deciding whether they came before *A Season in Hell,* the summer of 1873, or after, I think all in all that we must agree with the opinion of Mme.

Suzanne Bernard, and of Miss Enid Starkie in her latest edition of *Arthur Rimbaud,* that those "prose fragments" usually called *Illuminations* were written over a period of time that may well have begun before July of 1872 and may possibly have continued until 1875, or perhaps even after that.

And so I have taken the liberty in this edition of Rimbaud's writings of completely discarding Verlaine's title. In ordering Rimbaud's prose poems I have maintained the sequences that the manuscripts impose because of runovers from page to page, and beyond that have arranged them according to thematic considerations as suggested by Yves Bennefoy. But the ordering and the inevitably implied dating of these poems are my own.

In the course of the twelve years I have worked at these translations, I have been very much aware of developments in poetics, broadly defined, that link us to some of Rimbaud's perceptions. In certain of his poetic modes we recognize structures and metaphors that are familiar to us in our own experience of a certain kind of contemporary American poetry. Certain American poets, crucial in the development of contemporary American poetic style, seem clearly influenced by Rimbaud; I think of the work of Frank O'Hara and John Ashbery. Surely the fascination of contemporary artists with the syntax and imagery of the drug experience and their use of commercial and industrial terminology and forms reflect the work of Rimbaud. In these preoccupations he was our precursor, and by a century.

He was, more, rigorously preoccupied with himself as a poet—in the strictest technical sense of the word, a craftsman. His innovations in versification and the theory of poetry, though stated clearly only in his poetry, were radical, and remain influential. His poems are a study in the styles of nineteenth-century French poetry: the often breathtakingly swift development from one form to another, and into new forms, is one of his greatest accomplishments as a poet. It is because of this aspect of Rimbaud's work that I have been most centrally concerned about the form of the prose poem in translation. While it would seem on the surface to pose fewer problems than verse, it has had little currency until recently in English, and what use has been made of it seems very much influenced by French examples—and by far the greatest influence on the French prose poem has been Rimbaud's work in the genre.

How can this French prose best be presented as poetry in English? The prose poem seems possible in French partly because the canons of French prose style are so strictly defined. A piece of writing that seriously distorts the norms of French sentence and paragraph structure is no longer prose, though it may well be poetry. But English prose structure is not so rigidly codified; so poetic a style as James Joyce's we easily define as prose. A prose poem in French is poem first and prose secondarily; a prose poem in English is in the opposite case. Do we falsify this French poetry by presenting it as English prose?

Contemporary American poets have developed a sense of equation between the syntactic unit and the line of verse, an equation held in balance by the notion of the poet's voice: what is written is presented as a reflection of some acoustical presence. Now, these prose poems of Rimbaud's have a number of formal characteristics, but the major one seems to concern the arrangement of syntactic units on the page. It is in the density of their language on the page that these poems reveal their structure; they are arrangements of blank spaces and words. This also helps us to imagine their acoustical dimension—and this seems to me so close in intention to the form of most modern American poetry that I have generally tried to make an equation between sentence and line the major formal device of my translations of these poems.

It is further evident that divisions between prose and poetry nowadays are not nearly so clear-cut as traditional scholarship has had them. Nor are they in Rimbaud's work. At least two poems that have always been considered prose poems ("Veillées" and "Départ") are now generally recognized as traditional verse forms. And in the chronological course of Rimbaud's writing as a whole, there seems to be a clear movement from very strict observance of traditional forms to abandonment of them entirely. But I find no good reasons for defining very precise points at which a form was abandoned or innovation introduced; certainly the hypothetical datings of many of Rimbaud's poems discourage such precision. Thus, rather than emphasize the radical nature of writing prose poems, I have preferred to try to make clear the relationship of these poems to Rimbaud's previous work by concentrating on factors such as line length, syntactic parallelism, and the typographical arrangement of lines on a page, when it is in fact these elements that determine the shape of a particular poem.

My tendency has been to discount information provided by most of the early biographers of Rimbaud who knew him: his high school teacher Georges Izambard, his friend Ernest Delahaye, his sister Isabelle and her husband Paterne Berrichon. They were all clearly writing reports in retrospect, reminiscences of a familiar and therefore largely unperceived individual who had become suddenly famous; with the best wills in the world, they all had axes to grind: Izambard had to justify his inability to recognize in his pupil a great poet of the nineteenth century; Delahaye had to prove himself an intellectual intimate of a great poet, without too much incriminating himself in some of the more sordid experiences of the poet's life; Isabelle, a woman of somewhat hysterical comportment, to judge by her letters, was concerned to present the great poet as a good Catholic and a credit to a bourgeois family; while Berrichon corrected the great poet's grammar and his public figure in general. The various testimonies of the poet Paul Verlaine, though much more difficult to disentangle in his idiosyncratic prose, seem to me more reliable, if only because they are indeed fragments, and because they refer to Rimbaud as a poet primarily, and not as a pupil, friend, brother, or lover.

This edition contains all of Rimbaud's poetry written in French, and all of his prose writings with two exceptions. The first exception is a short school composition written at the age of fifteen, "Charles d'Orléans à Louis XI," a pastiche of medieval French. The second is "La Lettre du Baron de Petdechèvre," a short political satire found in

Le Nord-Est, a radical newspaper published in Charleville in the 1870s. It is signed with a pseudonym, and its authenticity is not certain. The selection of letters and documents is intended to present as complete as possible a picture of Rimbaud's attitudes and preoccupations. Omissions mainly concern letters from his later years that seemed to me to repeat others.

In the poem "Parisian Orgy," whose text was probably constituted from memory by Verlaine, I have taken the liberty, on a cue from Mme. Suzanne Bernard, of reversing the usual order of the last four stanzas.

I owe a grateful debt to the scholars who have preceded me. My working texts have been the critical editions of Henri Bouillane de Lacoste (*Poésies,* 1939; *Une Saison en Enfer,* 1941; *Illuminations,* 1949; Mercure de France), of J. Mouquet and Rolland de Renéville (*Oeuvres Complètes,* Bibliothèque de la Pléiade, 1954) and of Suzanne Bernard (*Oeuvres,* Classiques Garnier, 1960). The admirable completeness of the Pléiade edition, the impeccable care of Bouillane de Lacoste's edition, and the brilliantly perceptive textual notes of Mme. Bernard have provided me with inspiration as well as information.

The best biography of Rimbaud is in English, *Arthur Rimbaud,* by Enid Starkie (New Directions, 1968). The staggering iconoclastic work of Etiemble on Rimbaud and Rimbaud studies (*Le Mythe de Rimbaud,* Gallimard, 1954) is fundamental to any study of the poet— and a refreshing douse of cold water for students of literature in general. The most valuable studies of Rimbaud that I know are two: *The Design of Rimbaud's Poetry* by John Porter Houston (Yale University Press, 1963) and *Rimbaud* by Yves Bonnefoy (Editions du Seuil, 1961), which I have translated into English (Harper & Row, 1973). These two critics address themselves to what Rimbaud wrote: Houston with a sensitive formalist critic's intelligence, and Bonnefoy with instinctive intelligence and the perception of one poet into another's poetry.

I owe thanks to Louis Keith Nelson for his patient assistance on this book, to my teacher Roman Jakobson, whose lectures inspired much of my work on it, and to the late Frank O'Hara, whose criticisms and suggestions are reflected many times here. And most especially I owe thanks to Roger Shattuck, whose encouragement began all this, and whose friendship kept me at it.

Austin, Texas
1973

FIRST SEASON

Childhood

"Once, if my memory serves me well, my life
was a banquet where every heart revealed itself,
where every wine flowed."

A SEASON IN HELL

His father was a captain in the army; a garrison soldier, full of dreams, a translator of the Koran, a wanderer. In 1853 he was stationed near Charleville in northeastern France, near the Belgian border. There he married Vitalie Cuif, the daughter of a well-to-do farmer who had moved to town. Arthur Rimbaud was born on October 20, 1854. He was the second of four children, two boys and two girls.

Captain Rimbaud deserted his family because he could not get along with his wife; from the age of three Arthur was left in the hands of his mother. "Shadow-mouth," he called her later. Tall, severe, and proud, forever in black, an aspiring bourgeoise and a bigot. A perfect opponent for her son. He could do nothing right, his two young sisters could do nothing wrong; his brother Frédéric, older by a year, couldn't have cared less. Whatever the bitterness of Vitalie Cuif Rimbaud, whatever her rancor at the failures of love, whatever she may have suffered, what we know of her is somehow monstrous. The repressions she arranged for her son brought him soon to wish himself an orphan, then to hypocrisies in an attempt to deceive her, finally to frantic attempts to escape from her tall black silhouette.

But in the beginning, it seemed that she had shaped her "poor Arthur" as she wanted him: quiet, studious, bright, forever combed and brushed: the perfect first Communicant that we see in the photograph. Precocious in school, he took prize after prize in Composition, in Latin, and in French. That he was a brilliant Latinist his school verses attest: his examination hexameters on a theme from Horace are a marvel of facility and pastiche.

In his earliest writings we find clearly announced the themes and intentions that will dominate all his poetry. Rimbaud brought to his work an astonishing sense of the directions the poetry of his time was to take, and of the new attitudes that would be possible in poetry: ugliness, violence, realism, and finally, as he wrote, "something new—in ideas and forms." These, he was eventually to provide. But consider his first poem in Latin, his first poem in French; both these schoolroom exercises already show clearly the hallmarks of all his writing: an idea or a treatment taken from another poet, an astonishing technical virtuosity in composition, and a preoccupation with a limited core of themes: a child, a child as poet, and the absence of a mother's love. Love was denied by his own mother, and we find it denied by women again and again in his poems. Few poets have restricted themselves so steadfastly to a few crucial subjects.

But what seems clearest in all Rimbaud's work is his overwhelming consciousness of himself as a poet. His first poems are strongly influenced by the popular poets of his day: Victor Hugo, Alfred de Musset, Charles Leconte de Lisle, François Coppée, Théodore de Banville. Their tropes, their allusions, their subjects, are his; later we shall see him turn against them in parody. But at this time they were Rimbaud's ideal of poetic creation. At the age of fifteen he wrote to Banville, editor of *Le Parnasse Contemporain,* house organ for the brightest young men in French poetry; Parnassians, they called themselves. Rimbaud presents himself as a new member of their fraternity: "*Anch'io,* gentlemen of the press, I will be a Parnassian! I don't know what it is I have inside me . . . something that wants to come out. . . ."

If poetry might be a way to undo the unhappiness he found with his mother and with women, and a way to find that happiness he imagined, and that all other poets seemed to know, then he would work at it with fervor. And as a poet, a child-poet, he might someday see what men had only dreamed they saw.

Prologue

The sun was hot; and yet it scarcely lighted the earth any longer; as a torch placed within a gigantic vault lights it by only a feeble gleam, so the sun, the earthly torch, extinguished itself while letting escape from its fiery body a final and feeble gleam, that nonetheless still showed the green leaves of the trees, the little flowers beginning to fade, and the gigantic summits of the pines, the poplars, and the century-old oaks. The cooling wind, that is to say a cool breeze, moved the leaves of the trees with a rustling somewhat similar to the sound that came from the silvery waters of the stream at my feet. The ferns bent their green faces before the wind. I fell asleep, having first quenched my thirst with the water of the stream.

I dreamed that . . . I had been born in Rheims, in the year 1503.

Rheims was then a small city, or better yet a town, nevertheless renowned because of its beautiful cathedral, a reminder of the coronation of King Clovis.

My parents were not rich, but very respectable: all they owned was a little house which had always belonged to them and, in addition, a few thousand francs to which must be added the small sums derived from my mother's economies.

My father was an officer* in the King's Army. He was a tall man, thin, with dark hair, and beard, eyes and skin of the same color. Although he was barely forty-eight or fifty years old when I was born, one would have certainly said that he was sixty or fifty-eight. His character was quick, fiery, and he was often angry and would not stand for anything that displeased him.

My mother was quite different: a sweet, quiet woman, upset at very little, and yet maintaining perfect order in the house. She was so quiet

*A colonel in the Royal Guard.

that my father used to make her laugh like a young lady. I was the one they loved most. My brothers were not so brave as I was, and yet they were bigger. I did not much like to study, that is to say to learn to read, to write, and to count. But to help around the house, to work in the garden or to do errands, that was something different, I liked that.

I remember that one day my father promised me twenty sous if I did well on a long-division problem for him; I started it, but I couldn't finish it. Oh! How many times he promised me money, toys, treats, once even five francs, if I could read something for him. In spite of that, my father put me in school as soon as I was ten. Why—I used to ask myself—learn Greek and Latin? I don't know. After all, nobody needs it. What do I care if I get promoted, what good does it do to get promoted, none, right? Oh, yes; they say you can't get a job if you don't get promoted. But I don't want a job; I'm going to be a rich man. And even if you did want one, why learn Latin? Nobody speaks that language. Sometimes I see some in the newspapers, but I'm not going to be a newspaper writer, for godsakes. And why study history and geography? It's true that you have to know that Paris is in France, but nobody asks at what latitude. In history, learning the life of Chinaldon, of Nabopolasser, of Darius, of Cyrus, of Alexander, and their other remarkable buddies with the long names is a torture.

What do I care if Alexander was famous? What do I care. . . . Who even knows whether the Latins existed? Maybe their language is just something made up, or even if they did exist, why don't they leave me alone to be rich and keep their language to themselves? What did I ever do to them that they have to make me go through all that? Let's consider Greek. That stupid language isn't spoken by anybody, anybody in the world! . . .

Oh! Damn, Damn, Damn, Damn! Damn! I'm going to be a rich man; it's no good wearing out the seat of your pants in school, for godsakes!

To shine shoes, to get a job shining shoes, you have to pass an exam, and the jobs that you get are either to shine shoes, or to herd cows, or to tend pigs. Thank God, I don't want any of that! Damn it! And besides that they smack you for a reward; they call you an animal and it's not true, a little kid, etc. . . .

Oh! Damn Damn Damn Damn Damn! . . .

> To Be Continued,
> Arthur
> Age 10

Examination in Latin Composition
November 6, 1868
Develop in Latin verses the theme outlined by Horace in the follow-
ing lines from Ode IV, Book III:

Me fabulosae, Vulture in Apulo,
Altricis extra limen Apuliae,
Ludo fatigatumque somno
Fronde nova puerum palumbes
Texere. . . .
. . . Ut premerer sacra
Lauroque collataque myrto
Non sine Dis. . . .

(As a boy, once, beside the Vultur
In Apulia, not far from my house,
Tired of games and of sleep,
Wonderful doves covered me
With new leaves. . . .
. . . I was crowned with sacred laurel
And with myrtle, not without
Divine intent. . . .)

Note: Three and a half hours are allowed for the examination in composition.

"VER ERAT"

Ver erat, et morbo Romae languebat inerti
Orbilius: diri tacuerunt tela magistri
Plagarumque sonus non jam veniebat ad aures,
Nec ferula assiduo cruciabat membra dolore.
Arripui tempus: ridentia rura petivi
Immemor; a studio moti curisque soluti
Blanda fatigam recrearunt gaudia mentem.
Nescio qua laeta captum dulcedine pectus
Taedia jam ludi, jam tristia verba magistri
Oblitum, campos late spectare juvabat
Laetaque vernantis miracula cernere terrae.
Nec ruris tantum puer otia vana petebam:
Majores parvo capiebam pectore sensus:
Nescio lymphatis quae mens divinior alas
Sensibus addebat: tacito spectacula visu
Attonitus contemplabar: pectusque calentis
Insinuabat amor ruris: ceu ferreus olim
Annulus, arcana quem vi Magnesia cautes
Attrahit, et caecis tacitum sibi colligat hamis.

Interea longis fessos erroribus artus
Deponens, jacui viridanti in fluminis ora
Murmure languidulo sopitus, et otia duxi,
Permulsus volucrum concentu auraque Favoni.
Ecce per aetheream vallem incessere columbae,
Alba manus, rostro florentia serta gerentes
Quae Venus in Cypriis redolentia carpserat hortis.
Gramen, ubi fusus recreabar turba petivit
Molli remigio: circum plaudentibus alis
Inde meum cinxere caput, vincloque virenti
Devinxere manus, et olenti tempora myrto
Nostra coronantes, pondus per inane tenellum

"IT WAS SPRINGTIME"

It was springtime; a malady immobilized Orbilius
In Rome; the weapons of a terrible teacher were stilled.
The sound of slaps no longer reached my ears;
The whipping-stick no longer kept me in continual pain.
I took my advantage, sought the smiling countryside,
Forgetting all; free from studies and free from care,
Sweet blandishments restored my wearied mind.
A certain florid rapture seized my breast;
Boring classes, the teacher's harsh lectures
Were blotted out of mind; I rejoiced in the fields afar,
In the florid wonders of the burgeoning earth.
Nor did I, childishly, seek empty rural idleness:
I was filled with feelings greater than my small breast;
An unknown intent more divine added wings
To these exalted feelings: I watched what I saw,
Marveling silently, and in my breast was born
A love for the warm countryside: like an iron
Ring the Magnesian rock by some mysterious force
Attracts, and silently binds to itself with invisible hooks.

Meanwhile my limbs were fatigued from my long wanderings,
And I lay down on the green-growing bank of a stream;
Lulled by its languishing murmur, I lay and took my ease,
Charmed by the songs of birds and the breath of the Western wind.
And lo, through the airy valley doves approached,
White flock that bore in their beaks fragrant crowns,
Flowers that Venus had gathered in her Cyprian gardens.
The swarm approached the grassy ground I lay upon
With a soft beating of wings, and hovering above me
Thereupon they bound my head and my hands
With green-growing garlands, and with sweet myrtle
Crowning my temples, they bore me, delicate weight,

Erexere. . . . Cohors per nubila celsa vehebat
Languidulum rosea sub fronde: cubilia ventus
Ore remulcebat molli nutantia motu.
Ut patrias tetigere domos, rapidoque volatu
Monte sub aerio pendentia tecta columbae
Intravere, breve positum vigilemque reliquunt.
O dulcem volucrum nidum! . . . Lux candida puri.
Circumfusa humeros radiis mea corpora vestit:
Nec vero obscurae lux illa similima luci,
Quae nostros hebebat mixta caligine visus:
Terrenae nil lucis habet caelestis origo!
Nescio quid caeleste mihi per pectora semper
Insinuat, pleno currens ceu flumine, numen.

Interea redeunt volucres, rostroque coronam
Laurea serta gerunt, quali redimitus Apollo
Argutas gaudet compellere pollice chordas.
Ast ubi laurifera frontem cinxere corona,
Ecce mihi patuit caelum, visuque repente
Attonito, volitans super aurea nubila, Phoebus
Divina vocale manu praetendere plectrum.
Tum capiti inscripsit caelesti haec nomina flamma:
Tu vates eris. . . . In nostros se subjicit artus
Tum calor insolitus, ceu, puro splendida vitro,
Solis inardescit radiis vis limpida fontis.
Tunc etiam priscam speciem liquere columbae:
Musarum chorus apparet, modulamina dulci
Ore sonans, blandisque exceptum sustulit ulnis,
Omina ter fundens ter lauro tempora cingens.

First Prize in Latin Composition

November 6, 1868

Rimbaud, Arthur, Age 14

Born Charleville, October 20, 1854

Through the empty air. . . . The flock through lofty clouds
Conveyed me, drowsing beneath a branch of roses: the wind
With its breath caressed my gently swaying bed.
When the doves in rapid flight had reached their habitat
Beneath a lofty cliff, and gained their hanging
Homes, they set me down and left me there, awake.
O ineffable nest! . . . A light gleaming with brightness
Poured round my shoulders, wrapping my body in its rays:
Nor was this light at all like the dim light
Mixed with darkness that obscures our eyes:
Its heavenly origin bears no trace of earthly light!
And within my breast rose something celestial, godlike
Power, that flows forever like a stream in flood.

Meanwhile the doves returned; in their beaks they bore
A crown, a laurel garland: crowned thus, Apollo
Delights to strike with his finger the sounding strings.
And when they had bound my brows with the laurel crown,
Lo, the heavens opened before me and suddenly
To my astonished eyes, hovering on a golden cloud,
Phoebus! His divine hand offered me the sounding lyre,
And with fire from heaven he traced these words on my brow:
YOU WILL BE A POET. . . . Through all my veins, then,
Heavenly warmth flowed, just as a fountain,
Pure shining crystal, flames in the light of the sun.
And then the doves their former shapes dissolved:
The Muses in chorus appear, singing sweet songs
With melodious voices; in their caressing arms
They caught me up and carried me away,
Three times uttering omens, three times crowning me with laurel.

THE ORPHANS' NEW YEAR

I

The room is full of shadows; vaguely heard,
The soft, sad whispers of two tiny babes.
Their faces, heavy still with sleep, peek out
Through long white curtains that shake and swirl . . .
—Outside, the shivering birds hop near;
Their wings are numb beneath the dark gray sky;
And New Year's Day, with all her foggy troop,
Dragging along the folds of her snowy gown,
Smiles through tears, and, shivering, sings her song.

II

And the little children behind the flapping curtain
Speak soft and low as in the dark of night.
They listen, sunk in thought, to a distant hum . . .
They tremble often at the golden voice
Of the morning bell, which strikes and strikes again
Its metal chime within a globe of glass . . .
And oh, the room is cold . . . in heaps about the floor
Around the bed, we see black mourning clothes:
The bitter wind that howls before the door
Sighs round about the house with gloomy breath!
We feel, in all of this, a certain lack—
Do these small children have no mother, then,
No smiling mother, with triumphant eyes?
She must that night have forgotten, bending alone,
To blow the naked coals again to flame,
To tuck the blanket and the quilt around them
Before she left them, saying "pardon me."
Could she not have foreseen the morning's cold,
Nor closed the door against the wintry blast? . . .

A dream of mother is a cozy comforter,
A cotton-covered nest where snuggling children lie,
As pretty drowsing birds in swaying branches
Sleep their sweet sleep, their soft white dreams!
But here—this is some cheerless, featherless nest
Where the young are cold, afraid, and cannot sleep;
A nest quite frozen by the bitter wind . . .

III

Your heart tells you the truth—they have no mother.
No mother in the house! And a father far away!
An old housekeeper, then, took them in charge.
The children are alone in the icy house:
Orphans at four, now in their hearts and minds
A happy memory by degrees revives,
As bead by bead, we tell a rosary:
Ah! What a wondrous morning, New Year's Day!
Each one, that night, had dreamed a dream of gifts,
The strangest dream, where he saw heaps of toys
That whirled about, dancing a noisy dance,
Then hid behind the curtain, then appeared once more!
And in the morning they would hop from bed
With a foretaste of sugarplums, rubbing their eyes . . .
They would go, hair tousled on their heads,
Their eyes shining brightly, as on holidays,
Their bare little feet skimming the floor,
To tap very softly at their parents' door . . .
They let them in! Then came greetings, laughing loud,
And kisses upon kisses, and happiness allowed!

IV

Ah! How lovely, those words said over and over!
But how that house of long ago has changed!

A huge fire once burned brightly on the hearth,
And lit up every corner of the room;
The red reflections coming from the fire
Would dance upon the polished furniture . . .
The cabinet's keys were gone! No cabinet keys!
They kept on glancing at its dark old doors . . .
No keys! How strange it was! They often thought
Of mysteries waiting in its wooden heart
And thought they heard, beyond the beckoning
Keyhole, a distant sound, a distant happy hum . . .
Their parents' room is quite empty today:
No red reflections come from beneath the door:
There are no parents, hearth, or hidden keys,
And hence no kisses and no sweet surprises!
Oh, how sad their New Year's Day will be!
And thoughtfully, while from their big blue eyes
Begins to fall a silent bitter tear,
They murmur: "When will we see our mother dear?"

        V

Now the little ones are sadly fast asleep:
You would say, to see them, that, slumbering, they wept.
Their eyes are swollen so, their breathing heavy!
The hearts of little children are so sensitive!
—But a guardian angel wipes away their tears
And to their heavy slumber brings a happy dream,
A dream so happy that their parted lips,
Smiling, seem to murmur something out loud . . .
They dream that from under their small round arms,
—Sweet gesture of awakening—they peep out;
Their sleepy eyes begin to look around them—
They think they have slept in a rosy paradise!
In the bright reflecting hearth a fire sings.
Beyond the window shines a bright blue sky;

Nature awakes and bathes in shining rays . . .
The half-bare earth, happy to be revived,
Shivers with joy at the kisses of the sun,
And in the old house all is warm and red:
The somber clothes no longer lie about,
The biting wind has finally died away—
You would think a good fairy had just passed by!
The children, happy, cried for delight, for there,
Beside the bed, in a beautiful rosy light,
There, on the carpet, something wondrous shone:
Two silvery medallions, black and white,
Of shining mother-of-pearl and glittering jet;
Little black frames whose covers of glass unfold,
And the words "To Our Mother" engraved in gold.

THE BLACKSMITH

The Tuileries Palace,
about August 10, 1792

One hand on a giant hammer, frightening,
Enormous, drunk, a massive face, and laughing
With all his strength, like a great bronze trombone,
Fixing the fat man with a threatening look:
A Blacksmith spoke to King Louis the Sixteenth, once,
When the People were present, shoving their way in,
Dragging their dirty clothes across the golden floor.
King Louis, standing behind his stomach, grew pale
As a convict on his way to be hanged,
And like a beaten dog he never moved,
For the blacksmith with the enormous shoulders
Kept talking, using old words, saying funny things
That hit him hard, like a fist in the face!

"Well, King, you know we used to sing tra la
And drive our teams in someone else's field:
The Pastor said his Paternoster in the sun,
On bright beads strung top to bottom with gold.
The Lord of the Manor rode by us with his hounds,
And between the noose and the riding crop they beat us
Down, into the ground. Our eyes grew dull as cows' eyes
And forgot how to cry. We just kept on, and on,
And when we had furrowed up the land of France,
When we had sown our flesh in that black earth,
We got a little present in return:
They burned our rotten houses down at night—
Our kids were roasted to a turn. Oh, look,
I'm not complaining. I say what I have to;
Just tell me I'm wrong if you think so, go ahead.
Look now, isn't it nice, in June, to see
The haywagons drive into the enormous barns?
To smell the smell of growing things, of the new grass?
The odor of orchards after the rain?
To watch the wheat, the ripe wheat full of grain,
And think of all the bread that it will make?
Oh, we'd go off more surely to the glowing forge
And sing our heads off, hammering the anvil,
If we were sure we'd get a bit—we're only men,
After all!—of the stuff that God provides!
But you know, it's always the same routine!
I know what's happening now! No one has the right
When I've got two hands, my head, and my hammer,
To come up to me with a weapon in his hand
And tell me: Boy, go out and plant my field;
Or come up when there's a war on and grab
My only son from right before my eyes!
All right! So I'm a man; all right, so you're a king;
You say to me: I WANT . . . You see how dumb that is . . .
You think I like to see your golden dump, Versailles,

Your gilded officers, your fat officials,
Your goddamn bastards parading like peacocks?
Your nest was filled with the smell of our daughters,
Your little tickets locked us up in the Bastille—
And we should say, all right! We'll all bow down!
We'll drown your Louvre in gold, we'll give you our last cent,
And you'll get drunk and have a big old time,
And your nobles will laugh and step all over us!

"No. That was the shit our fathers had to take.
Oh, the people are no longer whores. One, two, three,
And your stinking Bastille came tumbling down!
Those stones sweat blood, it made us sick to see it
Hiding the sky: its rotten walls said everything
And always kept us cowering in the dark!
Citizens! That was the shadowy past that fell,
That screamed and fell the day we took the tower!
We felt within our hearts something like love.
We embraced our sons, and one another, that day.
And just like your horses, flaring our nostrils,
We walked around, strong and proud, and felt good right *here!*
We walked in sunshine, heads held high, like this,
Across Paris! They bowed before our dirty clothes!
Well, we were finally *men* that day! We were pale,
King, we were drunk with a terrible hope:
And when we gathered before the black towers
Waving our bugles and branches of oak,
Pikes in our hands, we felt no hate, we felt ourselves
So strong, we wanted only to be gentle!

"And ever since that day, we've been like madmen!
The hordes of workers grew, down in the streets,
And those black hordes wandered, swollen always
With dark apparitions, to howl at rich men's gates,
And I went with them, beating up your spies;

I went to Paris, black from work, with my hammer
On my shoulder, killing a rat at every step!
And if you'd laughed at me I'd have killed you.
And then, believe me, you made yourself well liked
With your men in black, who took our petitions
And tossed them back and forth, and underneath
Their breath, the bastards! smiled and said: 'What fools!'
To brew up laws, to plaster all the walls
With pretty pink edicts and trash like that,
To get their kicks by cutting people down to size
And then to hold their noses when they pass us by!
Our great representatives think we're filthy!
And not afraid of anything—but bayonets . . .
That's wonderful. The hell with all their speeches.
We've had enough of that, those empty heads
And god-bellies. Oh, that's the stuff you feed us,
You bourgeois, when we're already running wild
And croziers and scepters have already been smashed!"

He takes him by the arm, and tears the curtain
Back, and shows him the courtyard down below
Where the mob mills about, seething beneath them,
The awful mob that makes a roaring like the surf,
A howling like a bitch, a howling like the sea,
With their heavy sticks and iron pikes,
Their drums, their cries from markets and from slums,
A dark heap of rags bleeding with Liberty caps:
The Man from the open window shows it all
To the pale-faced king who sweats and can barely stand,
Sick to his stomach at the sight!
                              "That's Shit,
King, out there. It slobbers over the walls,
It boils, it moves about. They're hungry, King,
So they're beggars. I'm a blacksmith; my wife's down there,

Crazy-mad. She thinks the palace is full of bread.
We aren't exactly welcome in the bakeries.
I've got three kids. I'm shit. I know old women
Who cry beneath their funny faded hats
Because they've had a son or daughter taken off:
They're shit. One man was in the Bastille, another
In the galleys: they were both of them citizens,
And honest. Freed, they were worse than dogs.
People used to laugh at them! Well, there's something there,
Inside them, and it hurts! It's a terrible thing,
They feel put down, they feel their lives have been destroyed,
And that's why they're out there screaming at you!
They're shit! There are women out there, dishonored
Because—well, women, they're weak, you knew that,
You Gentlemen from Court—they always want to please—
You spit into their souls, and laughed at it!
Your pretty tricks are all down there today. They're shit.

"Oh, all the Poor, the ones whose backs are burned
By the angry sun, the ones who do your work,
Who feel their bones begin to crack as they work—
Take off your hats, all you rich people! These are Men!
We are Workers, King! Workers! We're the ones
Made for the time to come, the New Day dawning,
When Man will work his forge from dawn to dusk,
—Seeker after great causes, great effects—
When he will finally bend all things to his will
And mount Existence as he mounts a horse!
Oh, the gleam of fires in forges! Evil destroyed,
Forever! The Unknown may be terrible:
Still we will know it! Let us examine
All that we know: then onward, Brothers, onward!
We sometimes dream a moving dream
Of living simply, fervently, without a word

Of Evil spoken, laboring beneath the smile
Of a wife we love with an elevated love:
Then we would labor proudly all day long,
With duty like a trumpet ringing in our ear!
Then would we think ourselves happy, and no one,
No one, ever, could make us bend a knee!
For a rifle would hang above the hearth . . .

"Oh, The air is full of the smell of battle!
What was I saying? I'm part of the rabble!
We still have your informers, sneaks, and profiteers—
But we are free! There are terrible moments
When we feel ourselves tower over all! I told you
Back a bit about tranquil duty, and a home . . .
Just look at the sky! It's too small for us,
We'd suffocate, we'd live forever on our knees!
Just look at the sky! I'm going back to the mob,
To the endless rabble, the dirt, the ones who roll
Your cannons, King, across the slimy cobblestones;
Oh, when we're dead, then we'll have washed them clean!
And if in the face of our howling vengeance
The claws of bronzed old kings across our France
Push their regiments in their fancy dress-up clothes,
Well, then, all you out there, what then? We'll give them shit!"

He swung his hammer over his shoulder.
                                                        The crowd
In that man's presence felt their souls catch fire,
And in the palace courtyard, through the palace halls,
Where Paris panted, howling all the while,
A shiver ran through the enormous mob.
And then he clapped his hand, his splendid Blacksmith's hand,
Upon the shaken, sweating, fat king's head,
And crowned him with the cap of Revolution!

CREDO IN UNAM

I

The Sun, the source of tenderness and life,
Pours burning love upon a ravished land,
And we who lie upon her slopes can feel
The earth below us, ripe and rich with blood;
We feel her bosom that a spirit formed
Of love like God, and flesh like any woman,
That swells with moisture and the sun's rays,
Enclosing the endless movement of all embryos!
Everything grows, mounts up!
                                    O Venus, goddess sure!

Bring back those ancient days when all was young;
Days of lascivious satyrs, animal fauns,
Of Gods whose love-bites broke the bark of trees,
Who kissed blond nymphs among the waterflowers!
Bring back the days when the world's sweet sap—
Rivers and streams, the pink blood of young trees,
Poured through the universal veins of Pan!
When the green earth beat beneath his goat-feet,
When his breath, in shining Syrinx' soft embrace,
Brought forth beneath the sky the hymn of love;
When standing in the plain, he heard about him
Living Nature answer to his call;
When the silent trees cradling the singing birds,
The great earth cradling man, the azure Ocean,
And animals all, still loved in the power of God!
Bring back the days of almighty Cybele—
Gigantically beautiful, once she rode
A chariot of bronze through the glittering cities,
Her great breasts pouring through the universe
The streaming purity of boundless life.

Then Man sucked happy at her nourishing bosom
And like a tiny child played at her feet;
—Since he was strong, Man was pure and good.
Ah, wretch! Today he says: I know it all,
And goes away, closing his eyes and ears.
And the gods are no more! Mankind is King,
And Man is God! But Love is the only faith . . .
Ah! If man again drew life from thy breast,
Great Mother of gods and men, Cybele!
If he had not abandoned bright Astarte
Who once emerged into unending daylight
From the blue waves, flower of flesh by seas perfumed,
Her rosy-hued navel sparkling with foam,
Awakening, Goddess of dark compelling eyes,
Nightingales in groves, and love in human hearts!

II

I believe! I believe in Thee, Divine Mother,
Aphrodite of the sea! Oh, the way is hard;
That other God has bound us to his cross!
Flesh, Marble, Flower, Venus—in thee I believe!
Yes, Man is sad beneath the echoing sky;
He clothes himself, he is no longer chaste,
He has soiled his splendid body, gift of the gods,
And, like an idol to the fire, consigned
His Olympian body to filthy servitude!
Yes, even after death, in pallid skeletons
He hopes to live, insulting the beauty he once owned!
And that Shrine where you enthroned virginity,
Woman, in whom you made our clay divine,
So Man could lighten his puny soul
And slowly, in a swell of endless love,
Rise from an earthly prison into light—
She can no longer even be a courtesan!

—A true farce! And now the whole world sneers
At the sweet, the great, the sacred name of Venus!

III

If that age could come again, that age gone by!
For Man is finished! Man has played his roles!
Now in daylight, tired of smashing idols,
He will arise again, freed from his Gods,
And, child of heaven, will contemplate the skies!
Ideal, invincible, eternal Thought,
The god within, beneath his mortal clay,
Will then arise, will shine upon his brow!
And when you see him scan the wide horizon,
Despising his ancient yoke, free from all fear,
Come to him then, and bring divine Redemption!
Radiant, upon the bosom of the broad sea
Arise, and cast upon the Universe
Infinity of Love in Love's infinite smile!
The World will resound like some vast lyre
That trembles in some endless vast embrace!

The world thirsts after love: you will assuage it!

Oh! Man again has raised his proud free head!
The sudden sight of beauty he once owned
Will make the god within him rise on his altar of flesh;
Happy in present good, pale from evil past,
Man wishes to forget all—and to know!
Thought, so long, so long in him put down
Springs to his brow! He will know why!
Let thought rise free, and man will soon find Faith!
—Why is the azure mute, and space unfathomable?
Why do the golden planets swarm like sand?
If we could pierce that height, what would we find?

Does some great Shepherd lead that endless flock
Of worlds wandering in abhorrèd vastness?
And all those worlds, within the airy heavens—
Do they move to the sound of some eternal voice?
—And Man; can he see? Can he say: I believe?
And is the voice of thought more than mere dream?
If Man was born so late, if life is short,
Whence does he come? Do the depths of Ocean hide
A nest of fetuses, of Embryos,
A teeming Vortex from whose depths Nature
Will summon him, a living creature,
To love among roses, to grow in fields of grain?
We cannot hope to know! We are weighed down
With ignorance and narrow fantasies!
Men are monkeys, dropped from maternal wombs;
Our faded reason hides the Absolute!
We wish to look: Doubt is our punishment!
Doubt, somber bird, blinds us with his wing . . .
And the horizon fades, in an eternal flight! . . .

The skies have opened! Mystery is dead
Before Man, erect, who folds his strong arms
In the endless splendor of abundant nature!
He sings . . . and the woods, the rivers round him sing
A song of hope that seeks the skies above!
It is Redemption! It is Love! Love! Love!

IV

O glory of the flesh! O splendor! O ideal!
Rebirth of Love, O bright triumphant dawn
When at their feet both Gods and Heroes kneel:
White Kallipyge and her immortal son
Stand smiling in a snowy shower of roses,
As women and flowers spring up beneath their feet!

—Great Ariadne weeps upon the shore
As in the watery distance, white in sunlight,
Theseus' shining vessels disappear.
O virgin child, broken in a single night,
Be calm! In a golden car wound with black vines,
Lysios comes through the tawny Phrygian fields,
Drawn by amorous tigers stained with wine;
Along blue streams he turns the mosses red.
—Zeus the Great Bull cradles on his back
Europa, naked; her white arm lies along
The neck of God, and trembles in the wave . . .
He slowly turns his vacant gaze toward her;
She lays her bloodless, burning cheek upon
The brow of Zeus; her eyes begin to close;
She dies in his divine embrace, and the waves
Leave golden foam upon her floating hair.
—Past laurel flowers and murmuring lotuses
The sleepy swan moves sensual and slow,
Enfolding Leda in his gleaming wings.
—And while the Cyprian Queen in her strange beauty
Walks, bending the splendid roundness of her loins,
Parading the gold of her enormous breasts,
Her snowy stomach laced with soft black moss,
—The hero Hercules, as in a cloud of glory,
Enfolds his body in the lion's skin
And strides off, terrible and calm, toward the stars!
And in the watery beams of the summer moon,
Naked, dreaming, her gilded pallor stained
By the heavy flood of her long blue hair,
In a dark grove of mosses stuck with stars,
The Dryad stares at silent, empty skies . . .
—White Selene drops her floating veil
Faintly on Endymion's beautiful feet,
And sends him kisses in a ray of light.
—A distant fountain weeps in endless ecstasy:

A Nymph who leans upon her vase and dreams
Of the pale young man who dove beneath her wave.
—The winds of love have passed us in the night . . .
Yet in the sacred grove, that threatening shade,
They stand in majesty, those marble forms:
The Gods, whose eyes the ivy tries to hide . . .
The Gods stand watching Man and the unending World.

FEELINGS

On a blue summer night I will go through the fields,
Through the overgrown paths, in the soft scented air;
I will feel the new grass cool and sharp on my feet,
I will let the wind blow softly through my hair.

I will not say a word, I will not think a thing,
But an infinite love will set my heart awhirl,
And I will wander far, like a wild vagabond,
Throughout Nature—happy as if I had a girl.

OPHELIA

I

Where the stars sleep in the calm black stream,
Like some great lily, pale Ophelia floats,
Slowly floats, wound in her veils like a dream.
—Half heard in the woods, halloos from distant throats.

A thousand years has sad Ophelia gone
Glimmering on the water, a phantom fair;

A thousand years her soft distracted song
Has waked the answering evening air.

The wind kisses her breasts and shakes
Her long veils lying softly on the stream;
The shivering willows weep upon her cheeks;
Across her dreaming brows the rushes lean.

The wrinkled water lilies round her sigh;
And once she wakes a nest of sleeping things
And hears the tiny sound of frightened wings;
Mysterious music falls from the starry sky.

II

O pale Ophelia, beautiful as snow!
Yes, die, child, die, and drift away to sea!
For from the peaks of Norway cold winds blow
And whisper low of bitter liberty;

For a breath that moved your long heavy hair
Brought strange sounds to your wandering thoughts;
Your heart heard Nature singing everywhere,
In the sighs of trees and the whispering of night.

For the voice of the seas, endless and immense,
Breaks your young breast, too human and too sweet;
For on an April morning a pale young prince,
Poor lunatic, sat wordless at your feet!

Sky! Love! Liberty! What a dream, poor young
Thing! you sank before him, snow before fire,
Your own great vision strangling your tongue,
Infinity flaring in your blue eye!

III

And the Poet says that by starlight you came
To pick the flowers you loved so much, at night,
And he saw, wound in her veils like a dream,
Like some great lily, pale Ophelia float.

THE HANGED MEN DANCE

On old one-arm, black scaffolding,
The hanged men dance;
The devil's skinny advocates,
Dead soldiers' bones.

Beelzebub jerks ropes about the necks
Of small black dolls who squirm against the sky;
With slaps, with whacks and cuffs and kicks
He makes them dance an antique roundelay!

Excited jumping jacks, they join thin arms;
Black organ lofts, their fretwork breasts
That once beat fast at beauteous damsels' charms
Now clack together in a perverse embrace.

Hurrah the jolly dancers, whose guts are gone!
About the narrow planks they jerk and prance!
Beelzebub roars the rasping fiddles' song!
Hop! They cannot tell the battle from the dance!

Hard heels, that never wear out shoes!
They've all put off their overcoat of skin;
What's left beneath is hardly worth excuse—
Their skulls are frail and white beneath the rain.

A crow provides a crest for these cracked heads,
A strip of flesh shakes on a skinny chin;
They swing about in somber skirmishes
Like heroes, stiff, their armor growing thin.

And the breeze blows for the skeletons' ball!
The gibbet groans like an organ of iron;
In violet forests the wolves wail;
The distant sky flames with hell's own fires!

Oh, shake me these dark commanders down!
Who slyly rake through broken fingertips
Love's rosary across their pale ribs:
This is no monastery, you dead men!

And there in the midst of the danse macabre
One wild skeleton leaps in the scarlet clouds,
Stung with madness like a rearing horse
With the rope pulled stiff above his head.

He tightens bony fingers on his cracking knees
With squeals that make a mock of dead men's groans,
And, like a puppet flopping in the breeze,
Whirls in the dance to the sound of clacking bones.

> On old one-arm, black scaffolding,
> The hanged men dance;
> The devil's skinny advocates,
> Dead soldiers' bones.

KIDS IN A DAZE

Black against the fog and snow,
Against a grating all aglow,
Their asses spread,

Five kids—poor things!—squat and shake,
To watch a happy Baker bake
Hot golden bread.

They watch his white arms beat
The dough, and feel the heat
Of the bright stoves.

They hear the Baker softly hum
And hear a crackling sound come
From the baking loaves.

They are transfixed; they do not dare
Disturb the fragrant glowing air,
Warm as a mother's breast.

For a rich man's holiday he bakes
Golden rolls and pies and cakes—
A sugary feast!

And then beneath the smoky roof
They hear a song from a savory loaf
—Just like a bird!

The warm window steams and glows,
And they squat in their ragged clothes,
Their senses blurred—

They even think that they're rich, too—
Poor Baby Jesuses in a row
As the snow falls;

They stick their little noses in
Through the grating, moaning something
Through the holes

In a daze, saying prayers
And bending toward the lights
Of paradise,

So hard they split their pants,
And their shirttails dance
In a wind like ice.

TARTUFE CHASTISED

Fanning flames in a lovesick heart beneath
His chaste black robe, content, and hand in glove,
One day he went to church smirking with love,
Gray, dribbling faith from a mouth without teeth;

One day he went to church, "to pray"; a crook
Grabbed him and whispered some dirty words in
His holy ear, and with a nasty look
Removed his chaste black robe from his damp skin!

Chastisement! With all his buttons undone
And the list of indulgences he'd won
Unraveling on his breast, Tartufe went white!

He prayed and confessed in an awful fright!
But the man ran away with all his clothes—
Ugh! Tartufe stood naked from head to toes!

FIRST EVENING

Her clothes were almost off;
Outside, a curious tree

Beat a branch at the window
To see what it could see.

Perched on my enormous easy chair,
Half nude, she clasped her hands.
Her feet trembled on the floor,
As soft as they could be.

I watched as a ray of pale light,
Trapped in the tree outside,
Danced from her mouth
To her breast, like a fly on a flower.

I kissed her delicate ankles.
She had a soft, brusque laugh
That broke into shining crystals—
A pretty little laugh.

Her feet ducked under her chemise;
"Will you please stop it! . . . ."
But I laughed at her cries—
I knew she really liked it.

Her eyes trembled beneath my lips;
They closed at my touch.
Her head went back; she cried:
"Oh, *really!* That's too much!

"My dear, I'm warning you . . ."
I stopped her protest with a kiss
And she laughed, low—
A laugh that wanted more than this . . .

Her clothes were almost off;
Outside, a curious tree

Beat a branch at the window
To see what it could see.

ROMANCE

I

Nobody's serious when they're seventeen.
On a nice night, the hell with beer and lemonade
And the café and the noisy atmosphere!
You walk beneath the linden trees on the promenade.

The lindens smell lovely on a night in June!
The air is so sweet that your eyelids close.
The breeze is full of sounds—they come from the town—
And the scent of beer, and the vine, and the rose . . .

II

You look up and see a little scrap of sky,
Dark blue and far off in the night,
Stuck with a lopsided star that drifts by
With little shivers, very small and white . . .

A night in June! Seventeen! Getting drunk is fun.
Sap like champagne knocks your head awry . . .
Your mind drifts; a kiss rises to your lips
And flutters like a little butterfly . . .

III

Your heart Crusoes madly through novels, anywhere,
When through the pale pool beneath a street light,

A girl goes by with the *most* charming air,
In the grim shadow of her father's dark coat.

And since she finds you marvelously naïve,
While her little heels keep tapping along
She turns, with a quick bright look . . .
And on your lips, despairing, dies your song.

IV

You are in love. Rented out till fall.
You are in love. Poetic fires ignite you.
Your friends laugh; they won't talk to you at all.
Then one night, the goddess deigns to write you!

That night . . . you go back to the café, to the noisy atmosphere;
You sit and order beer, or lemonade . . .
Nobody's serious when they're seventeen,
And there are linden trees on the promenade.

BY THE BANDSTAND

Railroad Square, Charleville

On Railroad Square, laid out in little spots of lawn,
Where all is always order, the flowers and trees,
All the puffing bourgeois, strangling in the heat,
Parade their envious nonsense on Thursday afternoon.

In the middle of the garden a military band is
Playing, helmets jiggling to "Lady of Spain";
By the benches in front dawdle the dandies;
The Notary dangles from his own watch chain.

Retired bourgeois blink through their glasses at the noise;
Fat stuffed clerks drag along their fat stuffed wives;
By them scurry others, fussy elephant boys,
Flapping like signs with nothing to advertise.

On the green benches, clumps of retired grocers
Poke at the sand with their knob-top canes,
Gravely talk of treaties, of war, move closer,
Take snuff from little boxes, then begin: "Which means . . ."

Flattening his global bottom on a bench,
A bourgeois with a shiny-buttoned gut—Flemish, not French—
Sucks his smelly pipe, whose flaky tobacco
Overflows—"It's real imported stuff, you know . . ."

On the green grass, slum kids yell and throw stones;
Chewing on roses, fresh-faced young soldiers
Feel sexy at the sound of slide trombones,
And wink at babies on pretty nurses' shoulders.

—And I go running after girls beneath the trees,
In my messy clothes, just like a student:
They know exactly what I'm after, and their eyes
On me can't hide the things I know they want.

I don't say anything: I just keep staring
At the white skin on their necks, their tousled hair,
At what's beneath the silly dresses they're wearing
That show their backs and leave their shoulders bare.

Pretty soon I see a shoe, then a stocking . . .
I put it all together: shoulders, back, hips;
They think I'm strange; they whisper, laughing, mocking . . .
And my brutal wishes bite their little lips . . .

RIMBAUD TO THÉODORE DE BANVILLE

Charleville
May 24, 1870

To Théodore de Banville
c/o M. Alphonse Lemerre, Publisher
passage Choiseul
Paris

CHER MAÎTRE,

This is the season of love; I'm seventeen years old. The age of hopes and fantasies, as they say, and so I have begun, only a child, but touched by the finger of the Muse (excuse me if this is banal) to write down my dearest beliefs, my hopes, my feelings, all the things that poets do—this is what I call springtime.

Because if I send you some of these verses—through the kindness of the publisher M. Lemerre—it's because I love all poets, all true Parnassians—since the poet is a Parnassian, in love with ideal beauty . . . that's what I admire in you, quite simply; you are a descendant of Ronsard, a brother of the great poets of the thirties, a true romantic, a true poet. That's why. This sounds stupid, I know . . . but what else can I say?

In two years, perhaps in a year, I will be in Paris. *Anch'io*, gentlemen of the press, I will be a Parnassian!

I don't know what it is I have inside me . . . something that wants to come out . . . cher maître, I swear I will always adore two goddesses, Liberty and the Muse.

Don't make too much of a face when you read these verses; you would drive me mad with hope and joy, cher maître, if you were to have them make a little place among the Parnassians for my piece "Credo in Unam" . . . I could get into the last issue of *Le Parnasse;* it would be a Credo for poets! Ambition! Oh, what madness!

ARTHUR RIMBAUD

Do you suppose these verses could find a place in *Le Parnasse Contemporain*? Are they not of the poet's creed?

I am unknown; what does that matter? All poets are brothers. These verses believe; they love; they hope; that is all.

Cher maître, help me: raise me up a little; I am young; hold out your hand to me. . . .

SECOND SEASON

The Open Road

"Ah! My life as a child, the open
road in every weather; I was unnaturally
abstinent, more detached than the best
of beggars, proud to have no country,
no friends. . . ."

A SEASON IN HELL

Whatever it is that drives children out of the house, that makes them run away, Rimbaud had his full share. Official outings were frightening; a school acquaintance describes: ". . . the two little girls, Vitalie and Isabelle, holding hands; in the next line came the two boys, also holding hands; Mme. Rimbaud brought up the parade at a prescribed distance."

His flights from home took place during the disequilibrium attendant on the fall of the Second Empire. Whatever confusions drove him out, the idea of poetry was clearly involved in running away. More than anything, it was a perfect excuse for writing a poem.

The first of these flights was to Paris, in August 1870, and ended in Mazas prison on a vagrancy charge. A scared fifteen-year-old was released by his sympathetic rhetoric professor, Georges Izambard, who had become Arthur's friend and literary mentor, providing him with the kind of books that Mme. Rimbaud disapproved of—Victor Hugo's *Les Misérables,* for one. Izambard took the boy home with him to Douai for a few weeks before returning him to his mother's. He treated him kindly, as an intellectual equal—and so Rimbaud's next flight was in his direction, north toward Belgium. It was a pilgrimage of delight, to judge by the poems it occasioned. For Rimbaud, the vision of happiness was forever connected with Nature, and the women who accompanied him in fantasy were loving and nourishing—his Muse, the smiling waitresses of country inns, the girls who waved from wagons passing on the road.

The final point of his journey was a visit to a friend of Izambard in Brussels, Paul Demeny, a published poet, the author of *Les Glaneuses*. He functions briefly in Rimbaud's career as a recipient of letters—for like Izambard, like Banville, like Verlaine later, he was a poet officially, someone who had preceded Rimbaud into that world where love dwelled with happiness. From Brussels Rimbaud went to stay for a while with Izambard at Douai. From there he was sent back to his mother's—under police escort as she demanded.

FAUN'S HEAD

Among the leaves, green curtain stained with gold,
Among the tremulous leaves, the flowery
Tangled bower, like a sudden kiss revealed,
Bright rent in this exquisite tapestry,

Glitter the eyes of a frightened faun
Who bites the red flowers with his small white teeth.
Brown and bloody as the dregs of wine,
His lips part in laughter beneath a leaf.

Then, like a squirrel, he turns and disappears,
But his laughter lingers still along the leaves,
And, shaken as a startled chaffinch soars,
The Golden Kiss of the Woods is left in peace.

THE SIDEBOARD

It is a high, carved sideboard made of oak.
The dark old wood, like old folks, seems kind;
Its drawers are open, and its odors soak
The darkness with the scent of strong old wine.

Its drawers are full, a final resting place
For scented, yellowed linens, scraps of clothes
For wives or children, worn and faded bows,
Grandmothers' collars made of figured lace;

There you will find old medals, locks of gray
Or yellow hair, and portraits, and a dried bouquet
Whose perfume mingles with the smell of fruit.

—O sideboard of old, you know a great deal more
And could tell us your tales, yet you stand mute
As we slowly open your old dark door.

THE TEASE

In the dark brown dining room, whose heavy air
Had a comfortable smell of fruit and varnish,
I got a plate full of some local Belgian dish
Or other, and stretched out long in my lazy chair.

Content and still, I ate and listened to the clock.
Just then the kitchen door flew open wide
And the servant-girl came in, I don't know why—
The top of her dress undone, her hair pulled back.

And while she put a finger to her cheek,
All rosy-white and velvet, like a peach,
And made a face just like a five-year-old,

To make things easier she shifted the dishes;
And then she said—and I knew she wanted kisses!—
Real low: "Feel *that:* my cheek has got so cold . . ."

AT THE GREEN CABARET

(five in the afternoon)

A week of walking had torn my boots to shreds.
I finally got to Charleroi and came

To the Green Cabaret; I ordered bread
And butter and a piece of half-cold ham.

I felt good, stretched out my legs under
A table and looked at the silly tapestries
Hanging on the wall. And what a wonder,
When a girl with enormous tits and shining eyes

—Hell, a kiss would never scare *her* off!—
Laughed as she brought me the bread and butter
And a fancy platter of ham, half-cold—

Ham, all pink and white, it had a garlic
Taste—and filled my mug with beer, whose froth
A ray of fading sunlight turned to gold.

WANDERING

I ran away, hands stuck in pockets that seemed
All holes; my jacket was a holey ghost as well.
I followed you, Muse! Beneath your spell,
Oh, la, la, what glorious loves I dreamed!

I tore my shirt; I threw away my tie.
Dreamy Hop o' my Thumb, I made rhymes
As I ran. I slept out most of the time.
The stars above me rustled through the sky.

I heard them on the roadsides where I stopped
Those fine September nights, when the dew dropped
On my face and I licked it to get drunk.

I made up rhymes in dark and scary places,
And like a lyre I plucked the tired laces
Of my worn-out shoes, one foot beneath my heart.

DREAM IN WINTERTIME

To . . . her

All winter we'll wander in a red wagon
With cushions of blue.
Nice and warm. With a nest of creepy kisses
Just for us two.

You shut your eyes and won't look out the window
Where shadows lurk:
Hordes of black wolves and black demons and nightmares
Inhabit the dark.

And then in panic suddenly you feel
A little kiss, like a scared spider, crawl
Across your cheek . . .

You turn to me to help you find the beast,
And of course I promise to do my best,
If it takes all week . . .

on the road, October 7, 1870

WHAT NINA ANSWERED

HE: Just the two of us together,
    Okay? We could go
Through the fresh and pleasant weather
    In the cool glow

Of the blue morning, washed in
    The wine of day . . .
When all the love-struck forest
    Quivers, bleeds

From each branch; clear drops tremble,
    Bright buds blow,
Everything opens and vibrates;
    All things grow.

You rush about, and alfalfa
    Stains your white gown,
As the shadows beneath your eyelids
    Fade in the clear dawn.

Madly in love with the country,
    You sprinkle about
Like shining champagne bubbles
    Your crazy laugh:

Laughing at me, and I'd be brutal
    And I'd grab your hair
Like this—how beautiful,
    Oh!—In the air

Your strawberry-raspberry taste,
    Your flowery flesh!
Laughing at the wind that kissed
    You like a thief,

At the eglantine you stumble in
    (It loves you, too!)
Laughing most of all, little dummy,
    At me with you!

Just the two of us together,
    Our voices joined,
Slowly we'd wander farther
    Into the wood . . .

Then, like the girl in the fairy tale
    You'd start to faint;
You'd tell me to carry you
    With half a wink . . .

I'd carry you quivering
    Beneath a tree;
A bird nearby is whistling:
    "Who loves to lie with me . . ."

I'd whisper into your mouth,
    Put you to bed,
Your body curled like a baby's,
    Drunk on the blood

That flows, blue, beneath the softness
    Of skin like snow;
Whispering about those shameless
    Things . . . You know . . .

Our woods smell of springtime,
    And the sun
Powders with gold their vision
    Vermilion and green.

At night? We'll return on the shining
    White road that goes
Idly along, like a flock browsing;
    Around us grows

The blue grass of lovely orchards,
    Their bending trees;
For miles around as you wander
    You smell their scent!

We'll get back to the village
    Just at dusk,
And smell the odor of milking
    On the evening air,

And the warm smell of stables
    Full of manure,
Of a calm rhythm of breathing
    And of broad backs

Pale in the light of a lantern;
    And there below
A cow drops dung, dignified
    And slow.

Grandmother's eyeglasses sparkle
    As she peers
In her prayerbook; a tin bucket
    Of beer

Foams in front of long pipes
    That happily expel
Clouds of smoke; the flapping faces,
    Smoking still,

Shove in ham by forkfuls:
    Lots, then more;
The fire lights the cupboards
    And beds on the floor.

The fat shiny bottom
    Of a husky kid
Crawling to lick the dishes,
    His tow head

Tousled by a huge hound dog
    With a soft growl,
Who licks the round features
    Of the dear child . . .

Dark, on the edge of her chair,
    An arrogant profile—
An old woman spinning
    By the fire.

What things we'll see, my darling,
    In those farms,
By those bright fires sparkling
    In dark windowpanes!

Then, tiny, hidden under
    A lilac bush, fresh
And shady: a little window
    Just for us . . .

I love you! Come! Come for
    A beautiful walk!
You will come, won't you? What's more . . .

SHE: *And be late for work?*

THE CUSTOMS MEN

The redneck cops, the big fat ones who leer,
Retired sailors, soldiers, Legionnaires,

Are nothing next to the Great Concessionaires:
The cops who guard our virginal frontier.

With pipes and knives and clubs—but without fear—
They take their German Shepherds out in pairs
To catch the simple smuggler unawares.
They chuckle in the drooling atmosphere.

They bring forest deities their modern laws.
They round up wandering Fausts and Diavolos.
"The game is up! Let's put those bundles down!"

And when these great men have to search the young,
Watch out! They hate to let "Delinquents" pass—
God help you, when the Customs grabs your ass!

RIMBAUD TO GEORGES IZAMBARD

Paris
September 5, 1870

Dear Sir,

What you advised me not to do, I did: I left the maternal mansion and went to Paris! I did it on the 29th of August.

I was arrested as I got off the train for not having any money and owing thirteen francs on my ticket, and taken to the police station, and now I am in prison at Mazas waiting for trial! Oh! I depend on you as on my mother; you've always been like a brother to me. I ask you immediately for the help you once promised. I wrote to my mother, to the State attorney, to the chief of police in Charleville; if you don't hear anything from me by Wednesday before the train that goes from Douai to Paris, take that train, come here to claim me by letter, or go to the attorney, to intercede, to vouch for me, and pay my debt! Do what you can, and when you get this letter, you write too, I order you to, yes, write to my poor mother (5 Quai de la Madelaine, Charlev.) to console her. Write me too; do everything! I love you like a brother, I will love you like a father.

> Sincerely yours,
> your poor
> ARTHUR RIMBAUD
> Mazas

And if you get me out, take me to Douai with you.

RIMBAUD TO PAUL DEMENY

> [*Douai*
> *September 26, 1870*]

I came to say goodbye, you weren't home.

I don't know if I can come back, I'm leaving tomorrow, first thing in the morning, for Charleville. I have a safe-conduct pass—I am infinitely sorry not to be able to say goodbye to you—especially to you.

Very, very sincerely; all the best.

I will write you. Will you write me? Won't you?

ARTHUR RIMBAUD

RIMBAUD TO GEORGES IZAMBARD

> *Charleville*
> *November 2, 1870*

SIR,

—THIS IS FOR YOU ALONE—

I got back to Charleville a day after I left you. My mother took me back, and here I am . . . with nothing whatsoever to do. My mother won't send me back to school until next January.

Well, I kept my promise.

I am dying, rotting in platitudes, nastiness, and grayness. What do you expect, I persist stubbornly in worshipping free freedom and . . . a lot of things that are "such a pity," aren't they? I should have left again today, I could have: I had new clothes on, I could have sold my watch, and then hurrah for freedom!—Anyway I stayed! I stayed! And there'll be lots of times when I'll want to go—hat, coat, hands in pocket, and take off—But I'll stay, I'll stay. I didn't promise that! But I'll do it to be worthy of your affection. You said I would. And I will.

The gratitude I have for you I can't express today any more than the other day. I shall prove it to you. I would do something for you that I'd have to die to do. I give you my word.

I've still got a lot of things to say. . . .

That "heartless"

A. RIMBAUD

War; but Mezières isn't under siege. When? Nobody talks about it. I gave your message to M. Deverrière, and if there's more to do, I'll do it. Occasional sniping. The mind of the populace is an abominable itch of idiocy. You hear some real gems, believe me! It's a riot!

THIRD SEASON

War

"If only I had a link to some point
in the history of France!
But instead, nothing.
I am well aware that I have always
been of an inferior race. I cannot
understand revolt. My race has
never risen, except to plunder. . . ."

A SEASON IN HELL

July 1870: war between France and Prussia. An iron man in Berlin, an emperor of wax in Paris. Wild enthusiasm in France, among the bourgeois, for war. "Frenchmen of 1870, Bonapartists, Republicans, remember your ancestors of 1792, etc. . . . ." Thus the jingoist newspapers. A silly French victory at Saarebruck—the Germans lost two officers and seventy men. The Prince Imperial received his baptism of fire in the field with his proud papa, who cabled home: ". . . and once, in fact, he calmly picked up a bullet that had suddenly fallen at his feet. The soldiers of the Guard wept to see how calm he was. . . ." But at Sedan on the first of September the Emperor and his army were captured, and the tinsel empire fell apart.

The Germans kept advancing. And now, when Rimbaud's war with his mother had come to an impasse, that struggle exploded into an awesome metaphor for his boy's brain: his country at war, that war came right to his own front door. It closed his school, mobilized his neighbors, dropped bombs in his streets. The Germans bombarded Mezières, the town next door to Charleville, and almost buried his best friend Ernest Delahaye in the cellar of his house.

All that winter the Germans occupied Mezières and Charleville. In January an armistice was signed, and in February Rimbaud ran away again. Once more to Paris, slipping through the German lines. He wandered through the streets of the city still under siege, while the frantic provisional government tried to arrange a peace treaty. He was in Paris on the first of March, when the German armies entered the city to march down a deserted Champs-Élysées. And he was in Paris when the unloved children of the Motherland—the oppressed, the weak, the workers, the poor—rose in revolt against the new government, solidly bourgeois and reactionary, that was meeting at Versailles. The National Guard, the poor, workers, students! Barricades rose in the streets; mobs wheeled about; palaces, buildings burned. The city prepared for revolutionary government, the Commune.

Rimbaud returned to Charleville early in March. Images of the war, of Paris under siege, filled his head and his poetry. Visions of workers and guardsmen on street barricades, of the "gasoline girls," the incendiaries, of flames; in Baudelairean phrases he described the occupied city.

"YOU DEAD OF NINETY-TWO AND NINETY-THREE"

> "Frenchmen of 1870,
> Bonapartists, Republicans, remember
> your ancestors of 1792, etc. . . ."
> PAUL DE CASSAGNAC, in *The Nation*

You dead of ninety-two and ninety-three,
Pale in freedom's powerful embrace,
Whose wooden shoes once crushed a yoke that weighs
On the soul and brow of all humanity;

Men made great by agony, ecstatic men,
Ragged men, hearts moved by love alone,
Soldiers whom Death, unflinching Lover, has sown
In our wasted furrows, to flourish again;

Men whose blood restored our tarnished greatness,
Dead men of Italy, of Valmy, of Fleurus,
A million Christs with somber gentle eyes;

We have let you fall with our Republic, we
Have bent our backs by Imperial decree—
And now our *newspapers* praise you to the skies!

THE BRILLIANT VICTORY OF SAAREBRUCK

> Won to the Accompaniment of Cries of "Long Live the Emperor!"
> *(A Belgian print, in full color,*
> *on sale in Charleroi for 35 centimes)*

In the middle, the Emperor, an apotheosis
Of blue and gold, rides off, stiff as a rod,

Seeing the world through rosy-colored glasses.
Our Dear Old Daddy, glorious as God!

Below, the draftees, waking from their nap
Beside a gilded tent and a great red gun,
Get up politely. Pitou puts on his cap,
And seeing his Chief, he cries with joy: "We've won!"

On the right, Dumanet, leaning on the stock
Of his rifle, rubbing his shivering, shaven neck,
Yells: "The Emperor!" His neighbor's mouth stays shut . . .

A helmet appears—a sunrise out of place;
But Boquillon, in blue, flat on his face,
Heisting his ass, says: "Emperor of *what?*"

EVIL

While the red-stained mouths of machine guns ring
Across the infinite expanse of day;
While red or green, before their posturing King,
The massed battalions break and melt away;

And while a monstrous frenzy runs a course
That makes of a thousand men a smoking pile—
Poor fools!—dead, in summer, in the grass,
On Nature's breast, who meant these men to smile;

There is a God, who smiles upon us through
The gleam of gold, the incense-laden air,
Who drowses in a cloud of murmured prayer,

And only wakes when weeping mothers bow
Themselves in anguish, wrapped in old black shawls—
And their last small coin into his coffer falls.

ASLEEP IN THE VALLEY

A small green valley where a slow stream runs
And leaves long strands of silver on the bright
Grass; from the mountaintop stream the sun's
Rays; they fill the hollow full of light.

A soldier, very young, lies open-mouthed,
A pillow made of ferns beneath his head,
Asleep; stretched in the heavy undergrowth,
Pale in his warm, green, sun-soaked bed.

His feet among the flowers, he sleeps. His smile
Is like an infant's—gentle, without guile.
Ah, Nature, keep him warm; he may catch cold.

The humming insects don't disturb his rest;
He sleeps in sunlight, one hand on his breast,
At peace. In his side there are two red holes.

ANGRY CAESAR

This man, pale, walks the flowering lawns,
Dressed in black, cigar between his teeth.
The pale man thinks about the Tuileries
In flower . . . and at times his dead eye flames.

His twenty years of orgy have made him drink!
He told himself: "I will extinguish Liberty
As I put out a candle—softly, politely . . ."
Liberty lives again! He feels worn out.

They've caught him. Now what name trembles
On his silent lips! What quick regret?
No one will know: the Emperor's eye is dead.

He sees again, perhaps, the man in the pince-nez . . .
And watches drifting from his lighted cigar,
Like evenings at St. Cloud, a thin blue haze.

PARISIAN WAR CRY

Spring is at hand, for lo,
Within the city's garden plots
The government's harvest is beginning to grow—
But the gardeners call the shots!

O May! What bare-assed ecstasy!
Sèvres, Meudon, Bagneux, Asnières,
Hear our Farmer-Generals, busy
Planting in the empty air!

Guns and sabers glitter in parade,
Bright-mouthed weapons pointing straight ahead—
It's a treat for them to beat their feet
In the mud of a river running red!

Never, never now will we move back
From our barricades, our piles of stone;
Beneath their clubs our blond skulls crack
In a dawn that was meant for us alone.

Like Eros, politicians hover overhead,
Their shadows withering the flowers:
Their bombs and fires paint our garden red:
Their beetle-faced forces trample ours . . .

They are all great friends of the Grand Truc!
Their chief in his gladiolus bed blinks
Back his tears, puts on a sorrowful look,
Sniffs smoke-filled air, and winks.

The city's paving stones are hot
Despite the gasoline you shower,
And absolutely, now, right now, we've got
To find a way to break your power!

Bourgeois, bug-eyed on their balconies,
Shaking at the sound of breaking glass,
Can hear trees falling on the boulevards
And, far off, a shivering scarlet clash.

THE HANDS OF JEANNE-MARIE

Jeanne-Marie has powerful hands,
Dark hands summertime has tanned,
Hands pale as a dead man's hands.
Are these the hands of Juana?

Were they rubbed with dark creams
Beside voluptuous lagoons?
Were they dangled in clear streams
To dissipate reflected moons?

Have they drunk from savage
Skies, calm upon quiet knees?
Have they rolled cigars?
Dealt in diamonds?

At the feet of the Madonna
Have they crumpled flowers of gold?
With the black blood of belladonna
Their glistening palms are filled.

Hands that hunt auroral
Beetles, bluenesses bumbling
Over nectaries? Hands
That pour out poison?

Ah, what dream seizes
And convulses them?
Some unimagined dream of Asias,
Khenghavars or Sion?

These are no orange-seller's hands,
Hands darkened as a god's disguise;
These hands have never washed the clothes
Of heavy children without eyes.

These are not like the hands at home,
Nor the hardened hands of girls who work
In factories, whose fat faces burn
In sunlight sick with oily smoke.

These are the benders of backbones,
Hands that have never done wrong,
Hands fatal as machinery,
Strong as a horse is strong!

Shaking like bright furnaces,
Their flesh cries out the "Marseillaise,"
Shakes shivering to silences,
And never quavers Kyries!

They'll break your necks, you whores,
Strangle you, daughters of night;
Crush your hands, you countesses,
Your hands painted red and white.

The brilliance of these hands in love
Dazzles the skulls of baby lambs!
At the joint of each rich knuckle
The bright sun's ruby gleams!

A stain, a splash of populace,
Darkens them like yesterday's breast;
The back of these Hands is the place
All your ardent Rebels have kissed!

Marvelously pale in the sun's
Love-provoking light, they hauled
The bronze barrels of machine guns
Across Paris in revolt!

And sometimes on these sacred Hands,
Hands made fists, where our mouths remain
Trembling, our intoxicated mouths,
Sounds the bright clinking of a chain!

And then how strange, you Angel-hands,
That sudden shudder deep inside,
When they wish to crush your fingers
To drench your Hands in blood!

PARISIAN ORGY

Cowards, behold her now! Pour from your trains!
The fiery breath of the sky sweeps down
Along boulevards barbarians have stained.
Behold the Holy City, in the setting sun!

Go on! Beware of buildings still on fire!
Here are the quais, the boulevards, and here
Are houses, beneath bright streaks of sky
That last night were stuck with stars of fire!

Board up the dying palaces, the empty halls;
The ancient trembling daylight cools your eyes.
Behold this rusty troop of wriggling souls:
Your mad haggard faces and your wild cries!

Hordes of bitches in heat gulp cataplasms;
The scream of houses full of gold commands: Steal!
Gorge! Behold, the joyful night in inky spasms
Descends upon the street. O desolate drinkers,

Drink! And then when mad blinding light stabs
Through the dripping heap of orgy at your sides,
Will you not slaver slowly, silent, still,
Into your glasses, staring at empty distances?

Drink to the Empress and her cascading ass!
Hear the sound of retching, of drunken yells!
Hear burning nights recoil beneath this mass
Of howling idiots, old men, perverted fools!

O filthy hearts, O monstrous stinking mouths,
Perform your functions harder, louder, wilder!

Pour wine, grovel like beasts upon these tables . . .
Your stomachs melt with shame, O Conquerors!

Open your nostrils, smell this maddening stench!
Let poisons soak the channels of your throats!
Over your childish heads, lowering his folded hands,
The Poet speaks: "O cowards, now cry out!

"See how you forage in the belly of Woman,
And still you fear her, wait for her to moan,
For convulsions that will crush the foul nest
You force in crusted slime upon her breast.

"Syphilitics, madmen, kings and fools,
Do you think Paris cares, the monstrous whore?
Cares for your souls, your bodies, poisons, rags?
She will shake you off, rotten, wretched, foul,

"And when you lie crushed, groaning in your bowels,
Dead flesh crying for gold, hysterical,
The scarlet courtesan with battle-swollen tits
Above your groans will clench her fiery fists!"

When your feet have danced in savage anger,
Paris! When so many knives have stabbed your breast,
When you lie prostrate, still in your clear eyes
Shines the innocence of the regenerate beast,

O sorrowful city! O city now struck dumb,
Head and heart stretched out in paleness
In endless doorways thrown wide by Time;
City the dismal Past can only bless:

Body galvanized for sufferings yet to come,
You drink once more the bitter draught that saves!

Within your veins you feel the white worms swarm;
Within your perfect love a freezing finger moves!

And the feeling isn't bad. The worms, the white worms
Cannot pervert the Progress of your mouth,
Nor the Stryx close up the eyes of Caryatids
Whose tears of astral gold rain from the azure South.

The Poet will gather the sobs of monstrous Criminals,
The Convict's hate, the cries of the Accursed;
The streams of his love will flay all womankind.
His poems will soar: Behold, thieves! Do your worst!

Society, all is restored: orgies, the old
Groans choke the lupanars once more,
Maddened gaslight on blood-stained walls
Lights the blue dark with a sinister glare!

And though we shrink to see you thus laid waste,
Though never thus before was a city
Made abominable in Nature's face,
The Poet speaks: "Great is the sight of your Beauty!"

The storm has christened you supreme poetry;
An enormous stirring raises you; death groans.
Your task is lifted from you, Holy City!
Stridencies resound in your trumpet of bronze.

CROWS

Lord, when the open field is cold,
When in the battered villages
The endless angelus dies—

Above the dark and drooping world
Let the empty skies disclose
Your dear, delightful crows.

Armada dark with harsh cries,
Your nests are tossed by icy winds!
Along the banks of yellowed ponds,
On roads where crumbling crosses rise,
In cold and gray and mournful weather
Scatter, hover, dive together!

In flocks above the fields of France
Where yesterday's dead men lie,
Wheel across the winter sky;
Recall our black inheritance!
Let duty in your cry be heard,
Mournful, black, uneasy bird.

Yet in that oak, you saints of God,
Swaying in the dying day,
Leave the whistling birds of May
For those who found, within that wood
From which they will not come again,
That every victory is vain.

RIMBAUD TO PAUL DEMENY

Charleville
April 17, 1871

To Paul Demeny
Rue Jean-de-Bologne
Douai

Your letter arrived yesterday, the 16th. Thank you.—As for what I asked you: that was stupid. Knowing nothing of what I ought to know, resolved to do nothing of what I ought to do, I am condemned; have always been, forever. Well, tomorrow's another day.

Since the 12th, I've been working in the office of the *Progrès des Ardennes:* today, of course, the newspaper is suspended. But I've pacified Shadow-mouth for a while.

Yes, you are happy. I say so.—and that there are unfortunates who will never find their Sister of Charity, be she woman, or idea.

For the rest, for today, I would strongly advise you to steep yourself in these verses from Ecclesiastes chap. 11–12, as wise as they are Romantic: "He hath folly sevenfold within his soul, who, having hung up his garments in the sun, will lament when the rain cometh"; but away with wisdom and the 1830s; let's talk Paris.

I saw some new titles at Lemerre's: two poems by Leconte de Lisle, *Le Sacre de Paris, Le Soir d'une bataille.* By F. Coppée: *Lettre d'un Mobile breton.* Mendès: *Colère d'un franc-tireur.* A. Theuriet: *L'Invasion.*

A. Lacaussade: *Vae victoribus.* Poems by Felix Franck and by Emile Bergerat. A *Siège de Paris,* thick volume, by Claretie.

I read while there *Le Fer Rouge, Nouveaux Châtiments,* by Glatigny, dedicated to Vacquerie; on sale at Lacroix, Paris and Brussels, probably. At La Librairie Artistique—I was trying to get Vermesch's address; they asked me for news of you. You were at Abbeville then as far as I knew.

Every bookstore is selling its book about the Siege, its *News of the*

Siege; the *Siege* by Sarcey is in its fourteenth edition; I saw endless outpourings of photographs and drawings concerning the siege—all as you can well imagine. The etchings of A. Marie, *les Vengeurs, les Faucheurs de la Mort* attracted much attention, and especially the cartoons of Draner and Faustin. What was new were *le Mot d'ordre* and the fantasies, really good, by Vallès and Vermesch in the *Cri du Peuple*.

Such was literature—from the 25th of February to the 10th of March. Anyway, I'm probably not telling you anything you don't already know.

In which case, let us turn our faces to the lances of the storm, and open our souls to the wisdom of the ancients.

And may Belgian literature bear us both beneath its arm.

Goodbye.

A. Rimbaud

FOURTH SEASON

The Tormented Heart

"Hadn't I *once* a youth that was
lovely, heroic, fabulous—something
to write down on pages of gold? . . .
I was too lucky!"

A SEASON IN HELL

Much of what information we have about Rimbaud's early life comes from the reminiscences of Ernest Delahaye, Rimbaud's close friend through school. One has the impression, reading between his lines, that Rimbaud was putting him on much of the time. And his recollections do have an element of hero worship in them that smacks of exaggeration. But the poems Rimbaud wrote in the spring of 1871 will make most any exaggeration believable.

For this is the point they all come to, these adolescent rebels. Defiance of parental authority, rejection of religion, of social conventions—hair down to the shoulders, filthy clothes, smoking too much, shouting obscenities, dropping out of school. Whether any specific incident in Rimbaud's life set off such a full-scale rebellion against convention is unclear; the strictures of his mother and his early docility were likely to have brought him to it sooner or later. Still, few adolescent rebellions have yielded such a harvest of vitriolic verse. Nothing escapes him: God, the Church, the Family, the Nation, the town of Charleville, its citizenry and institutions and, above all, its women. For the main burden of these poems is scatological—the furious boy scrawling "shit on God" on the sidewalks in front of the church is clearly their author. They are full of the bodily functions, of diseased flesh, of the filth and clutter of old age and poverty, of the equivocal role of woman and the image of the "monstrous whore." Much of this is clearly Baudelairean in origin—but the country boy turns a spotlight on it. The details are sharp and clear.

Yet out of all this fury comes a conviction—of what it means to be a poet, and what a poet must do to create poetry. In the two letters of May 13, 1871, to Izambard, and May 15 to Demeny, Rimbaud outlines his theory of the Visionary.

The origins of this theory of illuminism, of degradation in order to obtain elevation, of objectivity as the reward of total experience, are perhaps traceable; what is staggering, though, is to think that these ideas of perverting all the senses, of finding a method that will yield visions of the Unknown, of being "the one who will create God," occur in the mind of a pedantic country schoolboy. At what other age would anyone think so seriously of turning an abstraction into reality, of putting such a program into practice? And now all the tenacity, the rigorous purpose, the seriousness, and the strength of a sixteen-year-old boy are devoted to becoming "the great invalid, the great criminal, the great accursed—and the Supreme Scientist!"

EVENING PRAYER

I spend my life sitting, like an angel in a barber's chair,
Holding a beer mug with deep-cut designs,
My neck and gut both bent, while in the air
A weightless veil of pipe smoke hangs.

Like steaming dung within an old dovecote
A thousand Dreams within me softly burn:
From time to time my heart is like some oak
Whose blood runs golden where a branch is torn.

And then, when I have swallowed down my Dreams
In thirty, forty mugs of beer, I turn
To satisfy a need I can't ignore,

And like the Lord of Hyssop and of Myrrh
I piss into the skies, a soaring stream
That consecrates a patch of flowering fern.

THE SITTERS

Black with warts, picked with pox, eyelids all green,
Their knobby fingers curled around their balls,
Skulls smeared with nastinesses, obscene
As the crud that grows on rotten walls;

A kind of epileptic embrace screws
Their skinny skeletons to the black bones
Of their chairs; and there for days and days
Their old feet wriggle on the rickety rungs.

These old men always entangled in their chairs
Watch their skin in the hot sun corrode;
They stare at a window where wet snow glares,
Or shake with the painful shaking of a toad.

And their Chairs take care of them; their asses
Are worn, but the straw seats cup them like a palm,
And the soul of suns gone by still burns
In those strips of straw, those rotting grains.

The Sitters gnaw their knees; green piano players,
Their fingers move in rhythm beneath their chairs;
They hear themselves splashing a sad barcarole,
And their heads go floating off on waves of love.

Oh, don't get up! It's just a little flood . . .
They heave themselves in waves, snarling like wet cats;
—Are they mad! Their shoulderblades unfold
And their pants puff out over their fat butts.

You hear them bumping bald heads against the walls;
They catch you walking down the long dark halls,
And if you look, the buttons on their flies
Watch you like a lot of hungry eyes!

And they have these fast invisible hands
That get you, and their eyes have a poisonous stare;
You feel like a beaten puppy dog, and
You sweat, caught in that awful corridor!

They sit back down, fists drowned in dirty cuffs,
Thinking of those who made them get up.
In agitated lumps, from dawn to dusk,
The goiters quiver in their nervous necks.

A fit of sleep; they pull their eyeshades low;
They fold their arms and dream of fucking chairs;
They dream of having baby chairs that grow
In groups: in quartets, trios, and in pairs.

Flowers of ink spurt commas in showers
That hover above them, over their bent buds,
Like dragonflies that buzz a bed of flowers . . .
And the prickle of straw makes their cocks hard.

SQUATTING

Later, when he feels his stomach upset,
Brother Milotus, with a glance at the skylight
Where the sun, bright as a new-polished pot,
Gives him a headache and dazzles his eyesight,
Beneath the bedclothes moves his priestly gut.

He flaps about beneath his grayish sheets
And then gets up and gropes to find his basin,
Scared as an old man who's swallowed his teeth,
Because he has his thick nightshirt to fasten
Around his gut before he can proceed!

He shivers and squats, with his toes tucked up
Beneath him, shaking in sunshine that smears cracker-
Yellow on windowpanes papered at the top;
The old man's nose—it glows like scarlet lacquer—
Sniffs the sunshine, like some fleshy polyp.

The old man stews by the fire, dribbling lip
Over his stomach; his thighs slip, then settle;
He feels his scorched britches, his dying pipe;

Something that was once a bird burbles a little
In a stomach soft as a heap of tripe.

A tangle of banged-up furniture, deep
In greasy rags, bulging like filthy bellies;
Fantastic stools like clumsy toads are heaped
In corners: sideboards have singers' gullets
Gaping with horrid appetite for sleep.

A sickening heat stifles the narrow room;
The old man's brain is stuffed with scraps from junk heaps.
He hears hairs growing deep in his damp skin,
And sometimes burps, and rather gravely hiccups,
And jolts the shaky stool he squats upon . . .

And at night the brightness of the moon's light,
Dribbling on the curves of his ass, discloses
A dark shadow that falls across a bright
Pink snowdrift, pink as blushing summer roses . . .
An odd nose traces Venus through the night.

POOR PEOPLE IN CHURCH

Bent on wooden benches, in church corners
Warmed by the stink of their breath, their eyes dim
In the altar's glitter, turned to the rafters
Where twenty pious faces howl a hymn;

Sniffing the smell of wax like baking bread,
Happy, humble as dogs with a beaten air,
The Poor raise to God, their savior and lord,
An endless, obstinate, ludicrous prayer.

The women like to sit on the smooth seats
After the six black days God puts them through.
They cradle in ill-fitting, twisted coats
Funny kids who cry, their faces turning blue.

Sloppy breasts hang out: these eaters of soup
—Prayer in their eyes, without a prayer within—
Watch a slovenly parade; a gawky group
Of girls in shapeless hats of unknown origin.

Outside—cold, and hunger, and horny husbands.
It's all right here. Another hour, then nameless pain.
Yet all around them, coughs, moans, whispers:
Little clusters of dewlapped women whine.

Those beggars are there, and the epileptics
We avoided yesterday as we crossed the road;
And, nosing their way through ancient prayerbooks,
The blind men dogs drag through our yards.

They dribble faith, and mouth a stupid, begging love,
Reciting their endless complaint to Jesus—
Who dreams in a yellow glow, far above
Skinny failures and potbellied successes,

Far from the meatlike smells, the moldy clothes,
The dark shuffling farce and its repulsive mime;
—Then the litany flowers with elegant woes
And mysteries flutter toward the sublime,

And from out of the nave where sunlight dies,
With stupid silks, sour smiles, and liver complaints,
Come ladies from the Better Side of Town—Jesus!—
Trailing yellowed fingers in the holy water founts.

VENUS ANADYOMENE

Out of what seems a coffin made of tin
A head protrudes; a woman's, dark with grease—
Out of a bathtub!—slowly; then a fat face
With ill-concealed defects upon the skin.

Then, streaked and gray, a neck; a shoulderblade,
A back—irregular, with indentations—
Then round loins emerge, and slowly rise;
The fat beneath the skin seems made of lead;

The spine is somewhat reddish; then, a smell,
Strangely horrible; we notice above all
Some microscopic blemishes in front . . .

Horribly beautiful! A title: CLARA VENUS;
Then the huge bulk heaves, and with a grunt
She bends and shows the ulcer on her anus.

MY LITTLE LOVELIES

A tearful tincture washes
Cabbage-green skies;
Beneath the dribbling bushes
Your raincoats lie;

Pale white in private moonlight,
Like round-eyed sores,
Flap your scabby kneecaps apart,
My ugly whores!

We loved each other in those days,
Ugly blue whore!
We ate boiled eggs
And weed.

One night you made me a poet,
Ugly blond whore.
Get between my legs,
I'll whip you.

I puked up your greasy hair,
Ugly black whore;
You tried to unstring
My guitar.

Blah! Some of my dried-up spit,
Ugly red whore,
Still stinks in the cracks
Of your breast.

O my little lovelies,
I hate your guts!
Go stick big blisters
On your ugly tits!

Break the cracked bottles and jars
Of my feelings;
Come on! Be my ballerinas
Just for a while!

Your shoulderblades are twisted back,
My masterpieces!
Stick stars in your snatches and shake
Them to bits!

And it was for you hunks of meat
I wrote my rhymes!
My love was sticky self-deceit
And dirty games!

Dumb bunch of burnt-out stars,
—Against the walls!
Go back to God, croak in corners
Like animals!

Shining in private moonlight
Like round-eyed sores,
Flap your scabby kneecaps apart,
My ugly whores!

THE SISTERS OF CHARITY

This youth, his brilliant eye and shining skin,
His perfect body and his twenty years, should go
Unclothed, and some strange Genie in a copper crown
Have loved him, in Persia, by moonlight, long ago.

Impetuous youth, dark virginal delights;
His first intoxication spins in his head
Like newborn seas, the tears of summer nights
That turn forever in their diamond bed.

The youth before the squalor of this world
Feels his heart moved with a profound ire—
Pierced with the deep eternal wound,
His Sister of Charity is all his desire.

But Woman, unbridled heap of organs, soft care,
You are never our Sister of Charity, no,
Not in dark looks, nor the belly's sleeping shade,
Nor small fingers, nor breasts more splendid than snow.

Slumbering blindness with enormous eyes,
All our embrace is but a single question:
For you, breast-bearer, have recourse to us;
We cradle you, delightful grave affection.

Your hate, your set torpors, your weaknesses, your spite,
All the brutalities you suffered long ago,
You return to us, all without evil, O Night,
In an excess of blood that every month will flow.

Woman, carried away, an instant appalls him
With love, the call of life and song of action—
Then the bitter Muse and burning Justice call him,
To dismember him with their august obsession.

Ah! Ceaselessly thirsting after splendors and calms,
Forsaken by the relentless Sisters, he moans
Softly for the knowledge that comes in open arms,
And toward bright nature bears a forehead stained with blood.

But obscure alchemy and the occult sciences
Repulse the wounded youth, dark scholar of his pride;
A savage solitude rolls over him.
Then beautiful still, disdainful of the grave,

Let him believe in vast goals, Voyages and Dreams
Endless and immense, across dark midnights of Truth,
And summon you to soothe his soul and fevered limbs,
O Sister of Charity, O mystery, O Death.

THE LADIES WHO LOOK FOR LICE

When the child's forehead, red and full of pain,
Dreams of ease in the streaming of white veils,
To the side of his bed two lovely sisters come
With delicate fingers and long silvery nails.

They take the child with them to an immense
Window, where blue air bathes a flowery grove,
And through his heavy hair, as the dew descends,
Their terrible, enchanting fingers probe.

He listens to their fearful slow breath vibrate,
Flowering with honey and the hue of roses,
Broken now and then with whispers, saliva
Licked back on their lips, a longing for kisses.

He hears their lashes beat the still, sweet air;
Their soft electric fingers never tire—
Through his gray swoon, a crackling in his hair—
Beneath their royal nails the little lice expire.

Within him then surges the wine of Idleness,
Like the sweet deluding harmonica's sigh;
And the child can feel, beneath their slow caresses,
Rising, falling, an endless desire to cry.

SEVEN-YEAR-OLD POETS

The Mother closed the copybook, and went away
Content, and very proud, and never saw

In the blue eyes, beneath the pimply forehead,
The horror and loathing in her child's soul.

All day he sweat obedience; was very
Bright; still, some black tics, some traits he had
Seemed to foreshadow sour hypocrisies.
In the dark halls, their mildewed paper peeling,
He passed, stuck out his tongue, then pressed two fists
In his crotch, and shut his eyes to see spots.
A door opened: in the evening lamplight
There he was, gasping on the banisters
In a well of light that hung beneath the roof.
Summer especially, stupid, slow, he always tried
To shut himself up in the cool latrine:
There he could think, be calm, and sniff the air.

Washed from the smells of day, the garden, in winter,
Out behind the house, filled with moonlight;
Stretched below a wall, and rolled in dirt,
Squeezing his dazzled eyes to make visions come,
He only heard the scruffy fruit trees grow.
A pity! The friends he had were puny kids,
The ones with runny eyes that streaked their cheeks,
Who hid thin yellow fingers, smeared with mud,
Beneath old cast-off clothes that stank of shit;
They used to talk like gentle idiots.
If she surprised him in these filthy friendships
His mother grew afraid; the child's deep tenderness
Took her astonishment to task. How good . . .
Her wide blue eyes—but they lie.

Seven years old; he made up novels: life
In the desert, Liberty in transports gleaming,
Forests, suns, shores, swamps! Inspiration

In picture magazines: he looked, red-faced,
At Spanish and Italian girls who laughed.
And when, with brown eyes, wild, in calico,
—She was eight—the workers' girl next door
Played rough, jumped right on top of him
In a corner, onto his back, and pulled his hair,
And he was under her, he bit her ass
Because she wore no panties underneath;
Then, beaten by her, hit with fists and heels,
He took the smell of her skin back to his room.

He hated pale December Sunday afternoons:
With plastered hair, on a mahogany couch,
He read the cabbage-colored pages of a Bible;
Dreams oppressed him every night in bed.
He hated God, but loved the men he saw
Returning home in dirty working clothes
Through the wild evening air to the edge of town,
Where criers, rolling drums before the edicts,
Made the crowds around them groan and laugh.
—He dreamed of prairies of love, where shining herds,
Perfumes of life, pubescent stalks of gold
Swirled slowly round, and then rose up and flew.

The darkest things in life could move him most;
When in that empty room, the shutters closed,
High and blue, with its bitter humid smell,
He read his novel—always on his mind—
Full of heavy ocher skies and drowning forests,
Flowers of flesh in starry woods uncurled,
Catastrophe, vertigo, pity and disaster!
—While the noises of the neighborhood swelled
Below—stretched out alone on unbleached
Canvas sheets, a turbulent vision of sails!

FIRST COMMUNIONS

I

They're ugly, those churches in country towns
Where fifteen stupid kids smear up the wall
And listen to an ugly priest as he drones
Away—his shoes and rotting stockings smell—
But through leafy branches the sun shines
In the old colors of the crude stained glass.

The stone always smells of the soil outside.
You see those piles of boulders that retain
The solemn motion of the rutting countryside,
Divide the ripening wheat from yellow lanes,
Support blue plums in trees the sun had dried,
Black knots of mulberries, and sticky vines.

Those barns have stood untouched for centuries;
Their dark interiors are cold and dank.
The walls are hung with grotesque mysteries—
Our Lady, or a martyr's bloody flanks—
Still, stinking stable flies and kitchen flies
Devour old wax spilt on the sun-stained planks.

"The child's first duty of course is to the home,
To family cares and good back-breaking work . . ."
They leave, forgetting that their faces burn
Where the Priest of Christ has given them a smack.
—He lets them out at harvesttime, thus earns
His little house with three shade trees in back.

Their first long pants, a perfect day for pastry,
Napoleon, or *The Drummer Boy,* above
An engraving where the Holy Family

Sticks out their tongues in a surfeit of love—
Joined by two maps in an Age of Industry—
These memories of the Great Day are all they have.

The girls would always go to church, content
To hear themselves called bitches by the boys
After Mass, or after vespers during Lent.
The boys, who'll end up stationed overseas,
Disturb decorum in the cafés they frequent
With shouts, with dirty songs, and brand-new clothes.

Yet the Pastor picked out holy pictures
For youngsters; in his room on Saturday night
He heard the distant dances; the strictures
Of heaven crumble, his toes tap with delight
As he reveled in Night's benedictions—
Night, black pirate on a sea of golden light.

II

Among the catechists the Priest recognized
(Not from the better part of town) one child,
An unknown little girl, with large sad eyes
And sallow skin. Her parents seemed poor, and old.
"On the Great Day, choosing her as His prize,
God will rain His choicest blessings on this child."

III

The day before the Great Day, she fell ill.
Like whispering in the church, dark and high,
She felt a shivering she could not still,
And endless shivering: "I am going to die."

Forgiving her stupid sisters' trespasses,
She lay exhausted, and through her head poured

Streams of angels, Virgins, Jesuses,
And, tranquilly, her soul drank down the Lord.

Adonai! A shower of Latin lines,
Green watery clouds, caress her fevered eyes,
And stained with blood in heavenly designs,
Great white linens fall across the skies!

For her virginity—present and to come—
She bites the ice of your Remission.
Yet more than water lilies, more than sweet desserts,
Your forgiveness is frigid, Queen of Sion!

IV

But Our Lady is only a lady in prayerbooks,
And mystic exaltations sometimes fail.
Then pictures grow dark, and bored looks
Lacquer them; engravings grow dim; prints pale.

And then an immodest desire to peek
Startles shining sky-blue dreams of the Good,
Frantic to undo that celestial coat
Whose linen hides the nakedness of God.

She tries, ah, still she tries, her soul distressed
And her face in a pillow, stifling sobs,
To prolong those streaks of aching tenderness,
And drools . . . and shadows fill the house and yard.

The child can stand no more. She turns upon
Her back and pulls the curtains loose
To feel the freshness of the air pour in
Beneath the sheet, onto her burning breast . . .

V

She woke at midnight: white was the window
Beyond the blue slumber of the moon-soaked shade,
Drenched in visions of white veils on Sunday;
She had dreamed red. Her nose bled,

And to enjoy in God, though weak and chaste,
Her burgeoning love, she thirsted after night,
When the heart, beneath the tender gaze
Of heaven, falls and rises in delight;

Night, Virgin Mother impalpable, who bathes
All childish raptures in soft gray surcease;
Thirsted after night, when a bleeding heart
Releases stifled rebellion in peace.

Thus become both Victim and the child bride,
Candle in hand, beneath her star she flees
To the courtyard where a shirt still hung to dry,
White ghost, and raises black ghosts in the trees.

VI

She passed her holy vigil in the outhouse.
Around her small candle swirled the white air,
Moving a wild vine with a purplish gloss
That twisted through a wall in disrepair.

The skylight lit the courtyard; in the east
The sky plated windows with red-gold streams
Of light; the pavement smelled of watery bleach
Beneath sulfurous walls that dripped dark dreams.

VII

Who will describe these filthy agonies,
And the hate that awaits her, you mad priests
Whose divine labor still warps the world,
When leprosy upon her body feasts?

VIII

When she has knotted up her hysterias
And sees through the dolors of happiness
Her lover dream of white millions of Marys,
The morning after love, then, in sadness:

"Do you know I have destroyed you? Turned your head,
And taken your heart, your life, and your dreams;
I am sick: Oh, lay me down among the Dead
Whose thirst is quenched by dark nocturnal streams!

"For I was young, and Christ has soured my soul.
He filled me to the throat with sick disgust!
You kissed my hair, my hair as thick as wool,
And I lay and let you . . . Ah, you love your lust,

"You Men! You little think the woman most in love,
Ruled by a conscience full of sordid terror,
Is prostituted worse than any slave,
And that all our love for you is error!

"My First Communion is over and past.
I can never have understood your kisses:
For my soul and body embraced by your flesh
Crawled with the rotten kiss of Jesus!"

IX

So the festering soul, the soul disconsolate,
Will feel Your curses stream upon her head.
She will have made her bed in Your unsoiled Hate,
And left true passion for an image of death,

Christ! O Christ, eternal thief of energy!
God crucified, whose pallor feeds on women
Nailed to the ground with shame and with migraine,
Or else thrown down upon their backs, in pain.

"THE SAVIOR BUMPED UPON HIS HEAVY BUTT"

The Savior bumped upon his heavy butt,
A ray of light across his shoulder; I sweat,
Begin to shout: "You want to see the sky turn red?
You hanging there waiting for the roar of floods,
For milk-white stars, and swarms of asteroids?

"Your forehead is spiky from your midnight games,
Savior! Come on in out of the rain! And pray—
For a sheet on your mealy mouth to shut you up!
If some lost traveler bumps into your grave, just say:
Brother, move on, I'm crippled and I can't get up!"

But the Savior kept hanging, open-mouthed with fear,
As lawns turn bluish when the sun has died:
"Listen, will you sell your knees as souvenirs?
Old Abraham! Big Pilgrim! Sniveler of psalms!
Velvet glove! Watering Mount Olivet with tears!

"A bore at home, nothing but trouble in town!
Heart among flowers; pious and oh, so sweet!

Love and blindness! Majesty! Virtuous renown,
Savior! Stupid, hot-eyed as a bitch in heat!
I'm the soul in agony! This passion is mine!

"Stupid! I cry, my tears fall down like rain,
And still I laugh at the hope of your favor!
You know I am accursed! And drunk, and pale, insane,
You name it, anything! But go lie down, Savior,
Go lie down. I do not need your sluggish brain.

"You're it! The Savior! Fulfillment of all our hopes!
And still your calm reason and your saintly schemes
Whistle in the night like whales;
You get yourself hung up, and reel off requiems
On broken organs full of reedy stops!

"Behold the son of God! Coward! And if the cold
Heels of the divine feet trampled on my shoulders,
I'd call you coward still! That fly-specked forehead!
Socrates, Jesus: righteous both! Stupid Saviors!
Respect me, Accursed forever in nights of blood!

"Oh, make him go away, with his tonsils tied
Tightly in a scarf of shame, sweet as sugar
On a rotten tooth, sucking my boredom, satisfied—
Like a bitch who's just been jumped by horny doggies
Licks a piece of entrail dangling from her side.

"Forget your filthy charities, you hypocrite;
I hate the look in your runny rag-doll eyes!
Whining for papa like a snot-nosed kid,
An idiot waiting for music from on high!
Savior, your statuary gut is full of shit!"

I cried all this across the face of earth; night,
Calm and pale, as I raved, filled up the skies.

I looked: but the phantom had vanished from sight,
And carried from my lips these awful ironies.
Come, winds of darkness, visit the Accursed! Let light

Fall still across the azure palings of the sky,
While Order, eternal watchman, slowly sails
Among the whirling spaces of the Universe,
Enormous, eventless motion, and his net trails
In a luminous river of fiery stars.

"WHAT DO WE CARE, MY HEART"

What do we care, my heart, for streams of blood
And fire, a thousand murders, endless screams
Of anger, sobs of hell, order destroyed in a flood
Of fire, as over all the North Wind streams:

Vengeance entire? Nothing! Oh, yes, entire!
Captains of Industry, Princes, perish! This we desire!
Power, Justice, History, fall! Down with the old!
You owe us that. Blood! Blood! And flames of gold!

Dream on of war, of vengeances and terrors,
My soul! Though we writhe in these teeth: Ah! Fall,
Republics of this world! Emperors,
Regiments, Colonies, Nations, all!

Who will stir up whirlwinds of furious fire
If we do not, and those whom we call brothers?
Join us, Romantic friends! Forget all others!
And never will we work, O waves of fire!

Europe, Asia, America, vanish!
Our avenging advance has ravished and sacked
Towns and countryside! We will be punished!
Volcanoes will explode! And Ocean attacked . . .

Oh, friends! Be calm, these are brothers, my heart:
Dark strangers, suppose we begin! Let's go, let's go!
Disaster! I tremble, the old earth,
On me, and yours, ah, more and more! The earth dissolves.

It's nothing; I'm here—I'm still here.

THE STOLEN HEART

My weeping heart on the deck drools spit;
They soil it with cigarette butts,
They spatter it with slop and shit;
My weeping heart on the deck drools spit.
The soldiers drink and laugh at it;
The sound of laughing hurts my guts.
My weeping heart on the deck drools spit;
They soil it with cigarette butts.

Soldiers' cocks are a black burlesque;
They rape my heart with what they say.
In scrawls on the mast, grotesque
Soldiers' cocks are a black burlesque.
Ocean, abracadabrantesque,
Take my heart and wash it away!
Soldiers' cocks are a black burlesque;
They rape my heart with what they say.

When they are done, and all worn out
How will I act, my stolen heart?

All I will hear is a drunken shout
When they are done and all worn out.
I will throw up and then pass out,
I know, with my heart torn apart
When they are done, and all worn out.
How will I act, my stolen heart?

A HEART BENEATH A CASSOCK

(The Confessions of a Seminarian)

O Thimothina Labinette! Today, now that I have put on the sacred vestments, I can recall the passion, now dead and cold beneath my cassock, that last year made my heart pound under my seminarian's cloak! . . .

May 1, 18 . . .

Spring is here. Father————'s potted vine is sprouting; the tree in the courtyard has tiny buds like green droplets all along its branches; yesterday, on my way out of class, I saw against a second-story window something that looked like the Super's mushroom of a nose. J————'s shoes smell a little; and I notice that the students leave the room quite often to go outside to ————; they used to stay cramming at their studies, buried in books, heads down to their bellies, red faces turned to the stove, breathing hot and steamy breath like cows! Now they stay outside a lot, and when they return, joking unpleasantly, they close the openings in their pants very deliberately—I am wrong; very slowly—and with great ceremony, seeming to take an unconscious delight in an operation which has nothing in it but futility. . . .

May 2 . . .

The Super came down from his office yesterday, and with closed eyes, hands behind him, apprehensive and shivering, shuffled his bedroom slippers for two seconds around the courtyard! Now my heart is beating time within my breast, and my breast beats against my grimy desk! Oh, how I detest the times, now, when we students used to be fat sheep sweating in our dirty clothes, falling asleep in the stinking air of the study hall, in the gaslight and the fitful heat of the stove! I stretch out my arms! I breathe, I stretch out my legs. . . . Oh, I feel things in my head . . . such things!

May 4 . . .

Finally, yesterday, I could stand it no longer! Like the angel Gabriel, I have heard wings in my heart. The breath of the Holy Spirit has transfixed my being! I took up my lyre, and sang:

> O Virgin fair!
> Mary undefiled!
> O Mother mild
> Of our sweet Jesus!
> Sanctus Christus!
> Pregnant Virgin,
> Queen without sin,
> Hear our prayer!

Oh! If you could only know the mysterious exaltations that shook my soul as I plucked the petals of this poetic rose! I took up my kithara, and like the Psalmist I lifted my pure and innocent voice into celestial spheres!!! *O altitudo altitudinum!* . . .

May 7 . . .

My poetry, alas! has folded its wings, but I say with Galileo, a victim of outrage and torture: And still it moves! (That is, still they move!) I was imprudent enough to drop the preceding inspired lines; J——— picked them up, J———, most savage of Jansenists, most vicious of the Super's henchmen, and he took it in secret to his master; but the monster, to subject me to universal insult, passed my poem around to all his friends!

Yesterday, the Super sent for me; I entered his room and stood before him, calm and strong within. His last red hair trembled on his forehead like a bolt of nervous lightning. His eyes peered from the fat that surrounded them, but calmly and coldly; his enormous nose moved with its usual quiver; he mumbled an *oremus;* he licked the end of his thumb and turned several pages, then took out a dirty, folded piece of paper . . .

Maaryyyy Undeeefilllled!
OOOO Motherrrr Miiild!

He was eating my poetry! He was spitting on my rose! He was playing the idiot, the bumpkin, in order to soil, to ravish my virginal song! He stuttered and prolonged each syllable with a cackle of concentrated hate and when he came to the fifth line . . . *Pregnant Virgin!* he stopped, contorted his nose, and he . . . exploded: *Pregnant Virgin! Pregnant Virgin!* He kept saying it in such a tone, contracting his protruding abdomen with such a shudder in such an *offensive* tone, that a blush of shame covered my forehead. I fell to my knees, arms stretched to the ceiling, and cried out: "O father . . . !"

"Your lyyyre! Your kithaaara! Young man! Your kithaara! Mysterious exaltations! Shaking your soul! That I would like to have seen! Young man, I find in all of this, in this impious confession, something worldly—a dangerous relaxation of discipline, in fact!" He stopped, and his stomach quivered from top to bottom; then in a solemn tone:

"Young man, do you have the gift of faith?"

"Oh, father, how can you ask such a thing? Are you making fun of me? Yes I believe all the teachings of my mother, the Church!"

"But . . . Pregnant virgin! The Immaculate Conception, young man; this touches the Immaculate Conception, the Virgin Birth. . . ."

"Father! I believe in conception. . . ."

"You do well to do so, young man! It is something. . . ." He fell silent. Then:

"Young J——— has reported to me that he observes a change in your attitude in study hall; you spread your legs apart, every day more noticeably; he states that he has seen you stretched out full length beneath the table, in the manner of a young man who . . . lacks control. . . . These are facts to which you can make no protest. . . . Come here—on your knees—close to me; I want to question you quite calmly; answer me: Do you spread your legs often, in the study hall?"

Then he put his hand on my shoulder, around my neck, and his eyes became quite explicit, and he made me tell him things about leg spreading. . . . Well, all I can say is that it was disgusting, and I know what scenes like that are all about, too. . . .

So they had been spying on me, they had slandered my feelings, misrepresented my modesty—and there was nothing I could say about it, all the reports, the anonymous letters of one student against another, to the Super, since it had all been authorized and directed! And I came to that room, to debase myself at the hands of that dirty old man! Oh, the seminary!

May 10 . . .

Oh! My condisciples are terribly wicked and terribly dirty-minded. In the study hall they know everything, the pagans, all about my verses, and the minute I turn my head I see the face of D———, and hear his asthmatic whisper: "Where's your kithara? Where's your kithara? And your diary?" Then that idiot L——— starts in: "Where's your lyre? Where's your kithara?" Then three or four of them hiss in chorus:

> Mary Undefiled!
> Mother mild!

What a great dope I am—Jesus, I don't mean to kick myself—but at least I don't tell tales, and I don't write anonymous notes, and I keep my divine poetry and my sense of modesty to myself! . . .

May 12 . . .
> Can you not imagine why I die of love?
> A flower says to me: hello! . . . and a bird above.

> Hello! Spring is here! Angel of tenderness!
> Can you not see why I burn with drunkenness?
> O angel that hung above my baby bed,
> Can you not imagine what runs in my head,
> That my lyre trembles as I beat my wings,
> And that my heart sings?

I wrote these verses yesterday, during recreation period; I went into the chapel and hid in one of the confessionals, and there my tender poetry was able to revive and fly, in silence and dreams, to the spheres of love. Then, since they are always coming, day and night, to search my pockets for the least little papers, I stitched these verses to the bottom of my inner garment, the one that touches my skin directly, and in study hall, beneath my clothes, I work my poetry up over my heart, and I hold it tight, and dream. . . .

May 15 . . .

Events have happened so swiftly since last I wrote here, and they are events of such a solemn nature, events which will surely influence my future and my innermost existence in a most awful way!

> Thimothina Labinette, I adore you!
> Thimothina Labinette, I adore you!

I adore you! Let me sing upon my lute, like the divine Psalmist on his psaltery, let me recount how I saw you, and how my heart leaped upon yours to find eternal love!

Thursday was our day off; we can go out for two hours. I went out; in her last letter my mother had written: ". . . go, my son, and spend your free time at the home of Monsieur Césarin Labinette, a close friend of your deceased father, whom you must meet sooner or later before your ordination. . . ."

I introduced myself to Monsieur Labinette, who obliged me greatly by leaving me, without saying a word, in his kitchen; his daughter Thimothina remained alone with me. She took a dish towel and wiped a pot-bellied bowl which she clutched to her heart, and suddenly said to me, after a long silence:

"Well, Leonard?" . . .

Until that moment, confused to find myself alone with this young creature in the deserted kitchen, I had kept my eyes lowered and invoked within my heart the sacred name of Mary; I raised my head, blushing, and confronted with the beauty of my questioner, I could only stammer out a feeble: "Ma'am?"

Thimothina! How beautiful you were! If I were a painter, I would have reproduced your features in canvas and entitled them *The Virgin of the Bowl*! But I am a mere poet, and my tongue can honor you only incompletely. . . .

The great black stove, with its openings where embers flamed like red eyes, emitted from its delicately smoking cookpots a celestial odor of bean and cabbage soup, and before it, breathing the odor of these vegetables with your sweet nose, with your beautiful gray eyes on your fat cat, O Virgin of the Bowl, you wiped your vase! The smooth light strands of your hair stuck modestly to your forehead yellow as the sun; your eyes continued in a bluish furrow to the middle of your cheeks, just like Santa Teresa! Your nose, full of the smell of beans, raised delicate nostrils; a delicate down winding across your lips contributed not a little to give an energetic beauty to your face; and on your chin gleamed a charming brown spot where madly beautiful hairs quivered. Your hair was soberly pinned on the nape of your neck, but a few short strands escaped. . . . I looked in vain for your breasts; you had none; you were contemptuous of such worldly ornaments! Your heart is your breasts! When you turned around to kick your golden cat I saw your protruding shoulderblades poke your dress, and I was transfixed with love at the sight of the graceful wiggle of the two wide arches of your loins. . . .

From that moment, I adored you. I adored not your hair, not your shoulderblades, not the wiggling of your lower posterior—what I love in a woman, in a virgin, is holy modesty; the thing that makes me leap up with love is modesty and piety; *this* is what I adored in you, young shepherdess!

I kept trying to make her notice my passion, for my heart, my heart was betraying me! I answered her questions only with broken words; several times I called her "Ma'am" instead of "Miss," I was so upset! Little by little, I felt myself succumb to the magic sound of her voice. Finally I decided to abandon myself, to forgo everything, and so I forget what question she asked me, I leaned back and twisted in my chair, I put one hand upon my heart, with the other I reached into my pocket for a rosary whose white cross I pulled out, and with one eye on Thimothina and the other raised to heaven, I answered sadly and soulfully, like a stag to a doe:

"Yes! Yes! Miss . . . Thimothina!!!"

Miserere! Miserere! Into the eye turned so softly to the ceiling there suddenly fell a drop of brine from a pickled ham hung above me, and when, shaken and red with embarrassment and passion, I lowered my head, I realized that in my left hand I held not a rosary but a brown sucking nipple that my mother had given me last year to give to Mrs. Whatshername's baby! From the eye that was turned to the ceiling dribbled the bitter brine, but from the one that looked at you trickled a tear, O Thimothina, a tear of love, a tear of bitterness!

Some hour or so later, when Thimothina announced a collation of bacon and eggs and beans, still dazzled by her charms, I answered softly:

"My heart is so full, you understand, that my appetite is ruined!" But I sat down at the table, and oh! I remember it still, her heart answered the appeal of my own; during the short meal, she could not eat:

"Don't you smell something?" she kept repeating; her father didn't understand, but my heart understood; it was the Rose of David, the Rose of Jesus, the Mystical Rose of the scriptures; it was Love!

She got up suddenly, displaying the double flower of her hips, went to a corner of the kitchen, and plunged her arms into a shapeless heap of old boots and shoes and socks, out of which her fat cat jumped, and she dumped all this into an empty closet, then she returned to her place and again investigated the atmosphere with a worried look; suddenly she frowned and exclaimed:

"It still smells!"

"Yes, it does smell," said her father rather stupidly (he couldn't understand, the animal!).

I was well aware that all of this was but the echo within my virgin flesh of the hidden workings of my passion! I adored her, and I lovingly ate the gilded omelet, and my fork kept time with my heart, and my feet shook with pleasure in my shoes! . . .

But the great flood of light came later, the gage of eternal love, a diamond of tenderness on Thimothina's part—the delightful kindness she showed by offering me as I left a pair of clean white socks, with a smile and these words:

"Do you want these for your feet, Leonard?"

May 16 . . .

Thimothina, I adore thee, thee and thy father, thee and thy cat. . . .

$$
\text{Thimothina} \left\{ \begin{array}{l} \text{Vas devotionis,} \\ \text{Rosa mystica,} \\ \text{Turris Davidica,} \quad \text{Ora pro nobis!} \\ \text{Coeli porta,} \\ \text{Stella Maris.} \end{array} \right.
$$

May 17 . . .

What do I care any longer about the noise of the world, and the sounds of the study hall? What have I to do with those who sit beside me, bowed with laziness and boredom? This morning every head, heavy with sleep, is stuck to the desk before it; like the trumpet call of the last judgment a sound of snoring, a slow and muffled snoring, rises over this vast Gethsemane. I alone, stoical and serene, rise straight above these dead bodies like a palm tree in the midst of ruins. Disdaining incongruous odors and noises, I lean my head into my hand, listening to my heart beat with Thimothina—my eyes plunge into the azure of the sky, through the highest panes of the window! . . .

May 18 . . .

Thanks to the Holy Ghost who has inspired these charming verses; I intend to engrave them in my heart; and when heaven again grants me the sight of Thimothina I shall give them to her in exchange for her socks!

I have entitled this "The Breeze":

> This cozy cotton bower conceals
> Zephyr wrapped in sweet perfume;
> In a silk and woolen womb,
> Zephyr sleeps with laughing heels.
>
> When the Zephyr lifts his wing
> In his cotton-down retreat,
> When he flies where robins sing,
> His soft breath smells so sweet!
>
> O quintessential breeze!
> O distillate of love!
> Day's dew as it dries
> Perfumes the sky above!
>
> Jesus! Joseph! Jesus! Mary!
> This odor, like a condor's wing,
> Cradles the devotionary . . .
> It sweetens us and makes us sing!

The ending is too personal and too delicate; I shall preserve it in the tabernacle of my soul. On our next day off I shall read this to my divine, my odoriferous Thimothina. Let us wait in calm and contemplation.

Date uncertain . . .

We still wait!

June 16 . . .

Thy will be done, O Lord; I shall put no obstacle before it! If you wish to turn Thimothina's love from thy servant, you are free to do so, of course; but Lord Jesus, have you never been in love? Has the lance of love never taught you to pity the sufferings of the unhappy? Pray for me!

Oh! I waited so long for two o'clock on the fifteenth of June, our day off; I kept my soul in check by telling it that then it would be free! On the fifteenth I combed what modest hair I have, and with a fragrant pink pommade I plastered it across my forehead, like Thimothina's; I put some pommade on my eyebrows, and carefully brushed my black clothes and overcame rather well some embarrassing defects in my appearance, and then went to ring Monsieur Césarin Labinette's long-desired doorbell. He came after a rather long time, his cap stuck over one ear and a strand of stiff pommaded hair stuck to his face like a scar, one hand in the pocket of his yellow-flowered dressing gown, the other on the door latch. . . . He gave me a short good day, wrinkled his nose as he looked down at my black-laced shoes, and went ahead of me, both hands in his pockets pulling his dressing gown in front of him, the way Father —————— does with his cassock, so that his posterior is outlined before my eyes. . . .

I followed him.

He went through the kitchen, and I followed him into the sitting room. Oh! That sitting room! It is fastened in my mind with the sharp pins of memory! The carpet had brown flowers; on the mantel was an enormous clock of black wood, with columns, and two blue vases of roses; on the walls, a painting of the battle of Inkerman and a pencil drawing by a friend of Césarin's, of a windmill beside a brook that looked like a trail of spit; the type of drawing that everyone does when he starts to draw. Poetry is decidedly preferable! . . .

In the middle of the room, at a table covered with a green cloth, my heart saw only Thimothina, though next to her was one of Césarin's friends, a former sacristan from the parish of ————, and his wife, Madame de Riflandouille. Monsieur Césarin went to sit down again as soon as I had entered the room. I took an upholstered chair (hoping that some part of me would thus rest on a needlepoint made by Thimothina herself), greeted everyone, set my black hat like a rampart on the table before me, and listened.

I did not say a word, but my heart spoke! The gentlemen continued the card game they had begun. I noticed with a good deal of sorrowful astonishment that each one cheated worse than the other. When the game was ended, we all sat in a circle around the empty fireplace. I was in one of the corners, almost hidden by Césarin's enormous friend, whose chair was all that separated me from Thimothina; I was rather pleased, actually, at the small attention that was paid to me, stuck behind the sacristan's chair, for I could let my true feelings show on my face without anyone seeing them. So I went into transports of joy, and let the conversation go on and on between the other three—for Thimothina spoke only rarely; she flashed her seminarian looks of love, not daring to look him in the face, for she kept her shining eyes on my well-polished shoes! I sat behind the sacristan, and let my passion sweep me away.

I began by leaning toward Thimothina, raising my eyes to heaven. She had turned her back. I shifted a little, and let out a sigh, with my chin on my chest; she didn't move. I fiddled with my buttons, I stuck out my lips; she saw nothing. Then, carried away, mad with love, I leaned far out toward her, holding my hands as at the communion rail, emitting a long an soulful "ah . . . !" *Miserere!* While I was making signs, while I was praying, I fell off my chair with a hollow thump; the fat sacristan turned around with a snicker, and Thimothina said to her father:

"Hey, Leonard just fell off his chair!"

Her father laughed. *Miserere!*

The sacristan put me back up on my stuffed chair, red with shame and weak with love, and then made a place in the circle for me. But I lowered my eyes, I wanted to go to sleep! Their society was unwelcome; they could not imagine the love that suffered there in the shadows. I wanted to go to sleep . . . but I realized that the conversation had turned to me. . . .

I opened my eyes feebly. . . .

Césarin and the sacristan were each smoking a thin cigar with the strangest affectations, which made them look awfully ridiculous; the sacristan's wife sat on the edge of her chair with her hollow chest bent forward, spreading out behind her the yellow dress that made her look all puffed out near the neck, and delicately plucked the petals of a rose. A ferocious smile parted her lips and revealed in her gums two teeth, blackened and yellow as the porcelain of an old stove. But you, Thimothina, were beautiful, with your little white collar, your lowered eyes, and your flat hair.

"The young man has a future; the present reflects what will come," said the sacristan, releasing a cloud of gray smoke.

"Oh, Leonard will be a credit to the cloth," his wife said through her nose, and displayed her two teeth.

I blushed the way a well-brought-up young man ought to; then I saw them move their chairs apart, and I realized that they were whispering about me. . . .

Thimothina kept looking at my shoes; the two rotten teeth looked threateningly, the sacristan laughed ironically; I kept my head lowered.

"Lamartine is dead," said Thimothina suddenly.

Thimothina dearest! For your adorer, your poor poet Leonard, you brought Lamartine's name into the conversation; then I raised my head, thinking that only the thought of poetry would reawaken the idea of virginity in these boors; I felt my wings begin to flutter, and I said, beaming at Thimothina:

"Indeed, the author of *Poetic Meditations* bears precious jewels in his crown!"

"The swan of poetry is no more," said the sacristan.

"Yes, but he has at least sung his swan song," I continued enthusiastically.

"Ah!" cried the sacristan's wife, "Leonard is a poet himself! Last year his mother showed me some of the efforts of his muse. . . ."

I acted with boldness:

"Ah, Ma'am, I have neither my lyre nor my kithara with me, but. . . ."

"Oh, your kithara! Well, you can bring it another day. . . ."

"And yet I have this, if it would please the honorable . . ."—I pulled a piece of paper from my pocket—"I would like to read you a few verses . . . they are dedicated to Miss Thimothina."

"Yes, yes, young man. Of course! Recite them, by all means! Do stand there at the other end of the room. . . ."

I stepped back. . . . Thimothina kept looking at my shoes . . . the sacristan's wife arranged herself like a Madonna; the two men leaned toward one another . . . I blushed, cleared my throat, and recited, crooning softly:

> This cozy cotton bower conceals
> Zephyr wrapped in sweet perfume;
> In a silk and woolen womb,
> Zephyr sleeps with laughing heels. . . .

The entire assembly exploded with laughter: the men leaned toward one another and whispered vulgar puns, but the most horrible thing was the look of the sacristan's wife, who sat with her eyes rolled up to heaven, playing the mystic, smiling with her disgusting teeth! And Thimothina . . . Thimothina was dying of laughter! I was cut to the core—Thimothina was holding her sides!

" 'Zephyr sleeps with laughing heels . . .'; that's quite delicate, quite delicate," said Césarin with a snort.

I began to notice something, then . . . but the outburst of laughter lasted only a moment; everyone became serious again, though they broke down from time to time. . . .

"Continue, young man, continue, that's quite good."

> When the Zephyr lifts his wing
> In his cotton-down retreat,
> When he flies where robins sing,
> His soft breath smells so sweet! . . .

This time a howl of laughter shook my audience; Thimothina was looking at my shoes; I was terribly hot, my feet burned at her look, I was drowning in sweat; yet I kept saying to myself: The socks I have been wearing for a month are a gift of her love, the looks that cover my feet bear witness to her love; she adores me!

And then a certain indescribable little odor seemed to arise from my shoes. . . . Oh! Then I understood the terrible laughter of the entire group! I realized that fallen into such evil company, Thimothina Labinette, my Thimothina, could never give free rein to her emotion! And I understood, then, that I too would be forced to devour the sad love that had flowered in my heart on a May afternoon in the Labinettes' kitchen, before the wiggling posterior of the Virgin of the Bowl!

Four o'clock, the end of our free day, sounded on the sitting-room clock; in despair, consumed with love and mad with sorrow, I snatched my hat and fled, overturning a chair, and went along the hallway muttering: I adore Thimothina, but I shall bury myself forever in the seminary . . .

The tails of my suit fluttered behind me in the wind, like evil black birds! . . .

June 30 . . .

From this day on, I leave my sorrow in the hands of my divine muse; a martyr to love at the age of eighteen, I remember in my affliction another martyr to the sex that is our happiness and our joy, and so, no longer possessing the one I have, I shall love religion! May Christ and Mary gather me to their bosom; I shall follow them. I am not worthy to undo the shoelaces of Jesus; but, oh, my agony! Oh, my torment! Even I, at the age of eighteen years, and seven months, bear a cross and a crown of thorns! But in my hand, instead of a reed, I bear a kithara! There lies the balm for my wound!

One year later, August 1 . . .

Today, I have put on the sacred vestments; I shall serve God; I shall have a parish and a simple servant in a rich village. I have the gift of faith, I will earn my eternal reward, and without being spendthrift, I shall live like a dutiful servant of the Lord with my housekeeper. Our Holy Mother the Church will comfort me in her bosom: Blessed be the Church! Blessed be God!

. . . As for that cruelly precious passion that I keep locked in my heart, I will learn how to endure it with constancy: without exactly reviving it, I shall be able sometimes to call it to mind; such things are sweet! (I was born, really, for love and religion!)

Perhaps some day, returned to this same town, I will have the happiness of hearing Thimothina's confession. . . . And despite all, I guard a precious memory of her: for a year, I have not taken off the socks she gave me. . . .

O sweet Jesus! I will keep those socks on my feet until I reach the holy gates of Paradise!

RIMBAUD TO GEORGES IZAMBARD

Charleville
May 13, 1871

To Georges Izambard
27 rue de l'Abbaye-des-Champs
Douai (Nord)

DEAR SIR!

There you are, a teacher again. One must pay one's debt to Society, you told me; you are a Member of the Teaching Profession: you're rolling in the right rut. I'm following your principle too: I am getting myself cynically *kept*. I dig up old idiots from school: the stupidest, dirtiest, nastiest things I can think of I dish up for them; I get paid in beers and bottles. *Stat mater dolorosa, dum pendet filius.* I'm paying my debt to Society. Precisely. And I'm right. You're right too, for today. Basically, you see in your principle only a kind of subjective poetry; your obstinacy in getting back to the University trough—sorry—proves it. But you'll always wind up satisfied without having done anything, since you don't want to do anything. Which is not to mention the fact that your subjective poetry will always be horribly wishy-washy. One day, I hope—many others hope the same thing—I will see objective poetry in your principle, and see it more sincerely than you! I will be a worker: That's what holds me back when a wild fury drives me toward the battle in Paris, where so many workers are still dying while I am writing to you! Work, now? Never, never. I'm on strike.

Right now, I'm depraving myself as much as I can. Why? I want to be a poet, and I am working at making myself a *visionary:* you won't understand at all, and I'm not even sure I can explain it to you. The problem is to attain the unknown by disorganizing *all the senses.* The suffering is immense, but you have to be strong, and to have been born a poet. And I have realized that I am a poet. It's not my doing at all. It's wrong to say: I think. Better to say: I am thought. Pardon the pun.

I is an *other*. So what if a piece of wood discovers it's a violin, and the hell with those who can't realize, who quibble over something they know nothing at all about!

You are no *teacher* for me. I give you the following: is it satire, as you would say? Is it poetry? It's fantasy, anyway. But I beg you, don't underline in pencil, nor too much in thought:

THE STOLEN HEART . . .
[see page 97]

That does not mean nothing.

Write me an answer care of M. Deverrière, for A.R.

Very, Very best,

ARTH. RIMBAUD

RIMBAUD TO PAUL DEMENY

Charleville
May 15, 1871

I've decided to give you an hour's worth of modern literature. I begin at once with a contemporary psalm:

PARISIAN WAR CRY . . .
[see page 63]

Here is some prose on the future of poetry:

All ancient poetry culminated in the poetry of the Greeks. Harmonious life. From Greece to the Romantic movement—the Middle Ages—there are writers and versifiers. From Ennius to Theroldus, from Theroldus to Casimir Delavigne, everything is rhymed prose, a game, the stupidity and glory of endless idiotic generations. Racine alone is pure, strong, and great. But had his rhymes been twisted, his hemistichs messed up, the Divine Dumbhead would be as unknown today as the latest-come author of the *Origins*. . . . After Racine, the game gets moldy. It's been going on for two hundred years!

No joke, and no paradox. My reason inspires me with more certainty on the subject than a young radical has fits. Anyway, *newcomers* can swear at their ancestors: it's their house and they've got all the time in the world.

Romanticism has never been fairly judged. Who's to judge it? The Critics!! The Romantics? They illustrate perfectly the fact that the song is very rarely the work of the singer—that is, his thought, sung and understood.

For *I* is an *other*. If brass wakes as a bugle, it is not its fault at all. That is quite clear to me: I am a spectator at the flowering of my thought: I watch it, I listen to it: I draw a bow across a string: a symphony stirs in the depths, or surges onto the stage.

If those old idiots hadn't discovered only the false meaning of EGO, we wouldn't have to sweep away the millions of skeletons that have for ages and ages piled up the products of their one-eyed intelligence, and acclaimed themselves their authors!

In Greece, as I said, words and music gave a rhythm to Action. Afterward music and rhymes became toys, pastimes. Studying this past has a certain charm for the curious: some people delight in reworking these antiquities: that's their business. The universal intelligence has always cast off its ideas naturally; men would pick up some of these fruits of the mind: they were acted upon, they inspired books: and so it went; man didn't develop himself, not yet awake, or not yet aware of the great dream. Pen pushers, these writers: the author, the creator, the poet; that man has never existed!

The first task of the man who wants to be a poet is to study his own awareness of himself, in its entirety; he seeks out his soul, he inspects it, he tests it, he learns it. As soon as he knows it, he must cultivate it! That seems simple: every brain experiences a certain natural development; hundreds of *egoists* call themselves authors; there are many more who attribute their intellectual progress to themselves!—But the problem is to make the soul into a monster, like the comprachicos,* you know? Think of a man grafting warts onto his face and growing them there.

I say you have to be a visionary, make yourself a visionary.

A Poet makes himself a visionary through a long, boundless, and systematized *disorganization of all the senses*. All forms of love, of suffering, of madness; he searches himself, he exhausts within himself all poisons, and preserves their quintessences. Unspeakable torment, where he will need the greatest faith, a superhuman strength, where he becomes among all men the great invalid, the great criminal, the great accursed—and the Supreme Scientist! For he attains the *unknown!* Because he has cultivated his soul, already rich, more than anyone! He attains the unknown, and if, demented, he finally loses the understanding of his visions, he will at least have seen them! So what if he is destroyed in his ecstatic flight through things unheard of, unnameable: other horrible workers will come; they will begin at the horizons where the first one has fallen!

—Back in six minutes—

I interrupt my discourse with another psalm: be kind enough to lend a willing ear, and everybody will be delighted. Bow in hand, I begin:

MY LITTLE LOVELIES . . .
[see page 82]

There. And please note that if I were not afraid of making you spend more than 60 centimes on postage due—poor starving me who hasn't had a single centime in the last seven months!—I would send you also my "Amant de Paris," one hundred hexameters, and my "Mort de Paris," two hundred hexameters!

*The "comprachicos" (in Victor Hugo's *L'Homme qui rit*, published in 1869) were kidnapers of children. They deformed them into freaks in order to exhibit them. (tr. note)

Here we go again:

The poet, therefore, is truly the thief of fire.

He is responsible for humanity, for *animals* even; he will have to make sure his visions can be smelled, fondled, listened to; if what he brings back from *beyond* has form, he gives it form; if it has none, he gives it none. A language must be found; besides, all speech being idea, a time of universal language will come! Only an academic—deader than a fossil—could compile a dictionary, in no matter what language. Weaklings who begin to *think* about the first letter of the alphabet would quickly go mad!

This language will be of the soul, for the soul, and will include everything: perfumes, sounds, colors, thought grappling with thought. The poet would make precise the quantity of the unknown arising in his time in the universal soul: he would provide more than the formula of his thought, the record *of his path to Progress!* Enormity becoming norm, absorbed into everything, he would truly become a *multiplier of progress!*

That future will be materialistic, as you see. Always full of *Number* and *Harmony,* these poems will be made to last. Essentially, it will again be Greek Poetry, in a way.

This eternal art will be functional, since poets are citizens. Poetry will no longer give rhythm to action; it *will be in advance.*

And there will be poets like this! When the eternal slavery of Women is destroyed, when she lives for herself and through herself, when man—up till now abominable—will have set her free, she will be a poet as well! Woman will discover the unknown! Will her world of ideas differ from ours? She will discover strange things, unfathomable, repulsive, delightful; we will accept and understand them.

While we wait, let us ask the *poet* for *something new*—ideas and forms. All the bright boys will soon think they've answered us: but that's not it!

The first Romantics were *visionaries* without completely realizing it: the cultivation of their souls began accidentally: abandoned loco-motives, still running down the tracks—Lamartine is sometimes a visionary, but strangled by old forms. Hugo, *too thick-headed,* has had many visions in his latest volumes: *Les Misérables* is a real poem. I have *Les Châtiments* at hand; *Stella* gives some measure of Hugo's *vision.* Too much Belmontet and Lamennais, too many Jehovahs and columns, old worn-out enormities.

Musset is fourteen times abominable for this present generation of pain, obsessed by visions—whom his angelic laziness has insulted! Oh, those insipid *contes* and *proverbes*! His *Nuits*! His *Rolla, Namouna,* and *La Coupe*! It's all so French, that is, hateful to the highest degree; French, not Parisian! Another work of that same genius that inspired Rabelais, Voltaire, Jean de la Fontaine, commentaries by M. Taine!

Vernal, Musset's mind! Charming, his love! Here it is, painted on enamel, real solid poetry! French poetry will be enjoyed for a long time—but only in France. Any grocery boy can reel off a *Rolla,* every seminarian has five hundred rhymes in a secret notebook. At the age of fifteen these flights of passion give young boys hard-ons; at sixteen they recite them with *feeling;* at eighteen, at seventeen even, every schoolboy who can write a *Rolla* writes a *Rolla*! It probably still kills some of them. Musset couldn't do anything worthwhile; there were visions behind those lace window curtains; he closed his eyes. French, stuffed, dragged from café to schoolroom, the beautiful corpse is a corpse—and from now on let's not even try to wake it up by yelling at it!

The second generation of Romantics are real visionaries: Théophile Gautier, Leconte de Lisle, Théodore de Banville. But to examine the invisible and hear the unheard is something else again from reviving the spirit of dead things, so Baudelaire is the first visionary, the king of poets, *a real God.* And still he lived in too artistic a milieu; and his highly praised form is silly. The inventions of the unknown demand new forms.

Stuck with the old forms: among the idiots, A. Renaud—wrote his *Rolla;* L. Grandet—wrote his *Rolla;* the Gauls and the Mussets: G. Lefenestre, Coran, Cl. Popelin, Soulary, L. Salles; the schoolboys: Marc, Aicard, Theuriet; the dead and the imbeciles: Autran, Barbier,

L. Pichat, Lemoyne, the Deschamps, and the Des Essarts; the journalists: L. Cladel, Robert Luzarches, X. de Ricard; the fantasists:
C. Mendès; the bohemians; the women; the talents, Léon Dierx and
Sully-Prudhomme, Coppée. The new school, called Parnassian, has
two visionaries, Albert Mérat and Paul Verlaine, a real poet. There.

So I am working at making myself a visionary. And let us close with
a pious hymn:

SQUATTING . . .
[see page 79]

You'd be a bastard not to answer; quick, for in a week I'll be in
Paris—maybe.
Goodbye,
A. RIMBAUD

RIMBAUD TO PAUL DEMENY

Charleville
June 10, 1871

To Paul Demeny
Paris

FOR M. P. DEMENY

SEVEN-YEAR-OLD POETS . . .
[see page 86]

POOR PEOPLE IN CHURCH . . .
[see page 80]

Here—don't get mad—is an idea for funny drawings: it's an antith-
esis to those perennial pretty illustrations of cuddly cupids, fluttering
hearts in flames, green flowers, sticky birds, and Leucadian landscapes,
etc. These triolets as well, by the way, are on their way out:

> "With perennial drawings
> and sugary verse."

Here—don't get mad—

THE STOLEN HEART . . .
[see page 97]

That's what I've been doing.

I have three requests to make.

Burn, *I am serious,* and I know you will respect my wishes like those
of the dead, burn *all the poems I was silly* enough to give you while I
was in Douai; please send me, if you can and if you want to, a copy of
your *Glaneuses,* which I would like to reread and which I cannot buy,
since my mother has not deigned to give me a centime in the last six
months—"such a pity!" Finally, please do write me, anything whatsoever, in answer to this and my preceding letter.

I wish you a good day, which is no mean accomplishment.

Write to: M. Deverrière, 95 sous les Allées, for

A. RIMBAUD

RIMBAUD TO PAUL DEMENY

Charleville [*Ardennes*]
August [*28*], *1871*

To Paul Demeny
15 Place Saint-Jacques
Douai

Sir,

You want me to plead my case again; all right. Here is the complete dossier. I am trying to find calm words, but my experience in that art is not very great. Anyway, here goes.

The situation of the accused. I left ordinary life a year ago for you know what. Continually shut up in this unspeakable Ardennes countryside, in no man's company, involved in an infamous, inept, obstinate, mysterious task, answering all questions, all vulgar and nasty remarks, with silence, showing myself all dignity in my extralegal position, I finally provoke an atrocious resolution in a mother as inflexible as seventy-three steel-helmeted armies of occupation.

She wants to force me to get a job—forever, in Charleville (Ardennes!). A job by such and such a day, said she, or out. I refused such a life—without giving my reasons; that would have been cowardice. Until today, I have been able to avoid a final settlement. And she has finally come to this: she constantly desires my immediate departure, my flight! Penniless, inexperienced, I'd end up in reform school. And that would be the end of me!

There is the gag of degradation they've stuffed in my mouth. It's very simple.

I'm not asking for anything, I'm asking for information. I want to be free to work, but in Paris which I love. For example: I am on foot, and nothing else; I arrive in the big city without any material resources: but you told me once if you want to get a job for fifteen centimes a day, go here, do such-and-such, live like so-and-so. I go there, I do such-and-such, I live like so-and-so. I ask you to suggest unimaginative occupations, because thinking requires large amounts of time. All this material nonsense becomes rather endearing when it frees the poet. I go to Paris; I must definitely think of money! Don't you find that sincere? It seems so strange to me that I feel I have to assure you I'm in earnest!

The above is what occurs to me: it was the only idea that seemed reasonable: I give it to you in other terms. I act in good faith, I do what I can, I speak as comprehensibly as anyone in pain. Why scold a child who knows nothing of zoology and wants a bird with five wings? You would only make him want birds with six tails or three beaks! Lend him the encyclopedia: that will undelude him.

So, not knowing what you might write in return, I cut short my explanation and once more entrust myself to your experience, and to your kindness which I blessed when I got your letter, and I invite you to consider my ideas—please. . . .

Would it bore you too much to look at some samples of my work?

A. RIMBAUD

RIMBAUD TO THÉODORE DE BANVILLE

DEAR SIR AND CHER MAÎTRE,

Do you remember having received from the provinces, in June of 1870, a hundred or so hexameters on mythology entitled "Credo in Unam"? You were kind enough to answer!

The same idiot now sends you the following verses, signed Alcide Bava.—Sorry.

I'm eighteen. I will always love the poems of Banville.

Last year I was only seventeen!

Am I making any progress?

ALCIDE BAVA
A.R.

My address:

M. Charles Bretagne

Avenue de Mezières, Charleville,

for A. Rimbaud

To Théodore de Banville

REMARKS TO A POET ON THE SUBJECT OF FLOWERS

I

Forever thus, in azure darkness,
Beyond the trembling topaz sea,
Your evenings will detail the function
Of Lilies, enema bags of ecstasy!

Plants are industrious today:
Without thought of profit nothing grows;
Yet Lilies still, with blue dismay,
Will droop in your religious Prose!

The royal fleur-de-lis still flies
In patriotic sonnets!
In Courts of Love, the Minstrel's prize:
Carnation, lily, amaranth!

Lilies! There are none anymore!
Yet in your verses, like the sleeves
That soft adulteresses wore,
Those pale flowers still wave!

My dear! Whenever you take a bath
Your shirt with sticky yellow spots

In the armpits swells in the air
Over obscene forget-me-nots!

Love lets through your customs sheds
Only Lilacs—Oh, garden swings!
And sweet wild violets in the woods—
Sugar drops of spit on insect wings!

II

You Poets fill your Roses with hot air!
You blow up Roses like balloons!
Roses red in tangles everywhere,
Inflated with your eight-foot lines!

BANVILLE's Roses make a snowy haze,
Blood-spattered, madly spinning;
They strike the foreigner's wild gaze
With a total lack of meaning!

In the fields and forests of your verse
—Oh, you peaceful photographers!—
The flora is about as diverse
As bottle corks and stoppers.

Always this French vegetation abounds,
Grouchy, coughing, silly and sick,
Where the bellies of basset hounds
Wallow through the growing dark;

Always, awful drawings of Sunflowers
Or purple Lotuses, pink plants
On holy cards, pretty posies
For little First Communicants!

The Ode on Asokas is as bad as
The Stained-Glass-Window stanza;
And bright butterflies and cicadas
Leave droppings all over The Pansy.

Old vegetation, worn-out themes!
What vegetable mistakes!
Fake flowers from stuffy living rooms!
Designed for beetles, not for snakes,

Those weepy vegetable baby dolls
That Grandville draws for children's books,
That suck their silly colors in
From vizored planets' wicked looks!

Oh, your drooling flutes
Dribble a mess of glucoses!
A bunch of fried eggs in old hats,
Those Lilies, Lilacs, Lotuses, and Roses!

III

O White Hunter, bootless in a
Panicky Pasture, it
Might really help to recall
Your botany a bit.

I'm sure you'd only change your tune:
Instead of crickets, Spanish fly;
The gold of Rio, not the Rhine;
Florida, finally, not Norway—

But my dear, it is no longer Art—
Believe me, times and styles are stricter—

To hang from your Eucalyptus tree
Your hexameter-boa-constrictor,

Really! As if Mahoganies
Were only, even in our Guianas,
Swings for swarms of monkeys
Or dizzy tangles of lianas!

In brief: is any flower, weed
Or lily, alive or dead,
Worth a sea gull turd?
Worth a candle flame?

And I meant what I said!
You there, sitting in a stuffy
Bamboo hut with brown
Chintz curtains drawn,

You still pick cute bouquets
From some extravagant
Field! Poet! Your reasons
Are ridiculous—and arrogant!

IV

Listen, flowers darken the fields
In springtime: let them go to seed!
Cotton acres, tobacco yields—
These are all the harvests we need!

Listen, pale-face Phoebus tans,
Talk about Pedro Velásquez,
Havana, and how much he earns.
Fill up the sea of Sorrento

With the dung of a thousand swans;
In your new stanzas advertise
Great mango groves, those tangled swarms
Of hydras drifting with the tides!

Plunge your verses in the bloody wood
And seek strange sugars, saps, and gums—
Return and tell us what we should
Accept as subjects for our Poems!

Tell us of those Southern mountains
Whose snowy peaks at times turn blond—
Are those microscopic lichens,
Or egg-laying insects in swarms?

Hunter, find us perfumed plants,
Delicate alizarins
Whose flowers Nature turns to pants—
Bright red trousers for Marines!

Find the dead Forest, in whose mold
The monstrous mouthlike flower grows
That smears an ointment, thick and gold,
In the dark fur of Buffaloes!

Find the mad meadows where blue streams
Wash trembling down from silvery stems,
And flowers full of Eggs in flames
Are lapped in bubbling perfumes!

Find us Thistles full of down
At which ten mules with eyes
Of fire will balk and run!
Find us flowers that could be chairs!

Or find us, deep within some mine,
Those famous flowers, almost stones,
Whose hard, bright ovaries hang
In throats tonsillated with gems!

Provide, Joker—we depend on you;
Get a gilt dish to serve it in—
Syrupy lilies in a stew
That eats away our spoons of tin!

V

Some will say that no man hath
A greater Love than Love Divine—
But Ernest Renan and Murr the Cat
Forget the Thyrses stained with wine!

You! Wake us to be witnesses
When hysterical perfumes explode;
Carry us off to whitenesses
Whiter than the Mother of God . . .

Trader! Settler! Trapper! Medium!
Your pink and white Rhymes bubble
Like shining streams of sodium,
Like rubber dribbling from a tree!

In your black poems, Juggler!
Refractions: red, green, white,
Unfold strange flowers
And electric butterflies!

Look! This is the Infernal Age!
Miles of telegraph poles reveal

The splendor of your shoulderblades—
A lyre that sings a song of steel.

We need, instead of epigrams,
A rhymed treatise on potato blight!
And for the composition of Poems
Of Power and Mystery and Light

You hope to see read in small towns
In either hemisphere,
Subscribe to *The Marvels of Science*!
. . . It's cheaper ordered by the year.

FIFTH SEASON

The Visionary

"I turned silences and nights into words. What was unutterable, I wrote down. I made the whirling world stand still."

A SEASON IN HELL

Now he was a poet. A Visionary. *Vates sum.* A circle of friends in Charleville—the adoring and rather gullible Delahaye; Deverrière, editor of a local paper; and August Bretagne, "old priest," a mystic, musician, versifier, occultist, and tax collector by daylight—sent him off to write to their friend the poet, Paul Verlaine. Arthur admired him already. He wrote, and sent poems. It worked. Verlaine said to come to Paris. Rimbaud came in September 1871 with a present in his pocket, a long poem called "The Drunken Boat."

Verlaine lived with his wife's family, the respectable Mautés. They appreciated art, of course, but a peasant poet was more than they could stomach: muddy shoes, dirty clothes, smelly pipe, coarse language. Out he went after a few days, and into the thick of Parisian literary bohemia; to Montparnasse and Montmartre, the two little mountains, where the poets chipped in to pay the rent in attic rooms for Verlaine's country prodigy.

But not for long. Rimbaud terrorized the whole of Parnassus, an urchin muddying the sacred spring. His soft mouth had stiffened now into a hard scowl, and the word continually in that mouth was "shit." The Parnassians were taken aback by the insults and the jeers, the surliness and sarcasm with which this dirty boy defended himself. Even more by the wicked parodies in their clubroom album, *L'Album Zutique,* parodies of Verlaine and the more popular contemporary poets; the one who came in for the most abuse was François Coppée, whose chatty comfortable rhymes were the delight of the enlightened bourgeois of the day. And even more by what was happening to Verlaine. He had fallen in love with this long-haired kid from the country. He left his newborn son and the wife he called the Mouse Princess, and went off to live with Rimbaud in cobwebby rented rooms on the Left Bank. The systematic disorganization of all the senses had begun.

They drank all night—glass after glass of absinthe. Absumphe, they called it. "The most delicate, the most precarious adornment, to be drunk on the magic of that herb from the glaciers, absumphe! But only to lie down afterward in shit!"

He began to smoke dope. Hashish.

"What did you see?"

"Nothing. White moons, and black moons following them."

Rimbaud's hard-boned country head could stand the punishment; Verlaine's mother-coddled constitution could not. They slept all day. They stayed up all night. They scandalized Paris. They made the newspapers. "Among the well-known writers to be seen in the opening night audience was the poet Paul Verlaine, arm in arm with a most charming young person, a certain Miss Rimbaud."

Little monster. . . . Dirty little. . . . The epithets were endless. Rimbaud replied in kind. Drunk at an after-dinner poetry reading, he punctuated the reader's pauses with "shit." The photographer Carjat tried to throw him out; Rimbaud attacked him with a sword-cane.

In March 1872, while Verlaine tried to repair his marriage and meditated "*luvly vinginces*" on his irate father-in-law, Rimbaud went back to the country, to Charleville. But he was wild now to return to Paris. In May he did so, and the affair with Verlaine went on. Drinking, and more dope. And writing a lot, mostly at night. In July they went to Belgium, then in September to London. But the dream was growing cold. Verlaine was not the nourishing mother either. Rimbaud's poems now seemed cut loose from the real world. He followed models still, Verlaine this time, but the visions never came. Everything he wrote, the songlike poems that Verlaine delighted in, the prose poems, were ending now in dissolution, as the golden vision crumbled. He went back to the country, to his mother's farm at Roche, in April 1873; Verlaine went back to Paris to try once more to make it up with his wife, who wanted to divorce him. In May the two poets were back in London again, in a room in a Mrs. Smith's boardinghouse. Writing, but with no more money. And the scenes got worse.

"It was my turn to go buy the groceries. I come back with a herring in one hand and a bottle of oil in the other. And I was carrying them the way I should, right? Anyway, perfectly normally. I get back to the house and I see Rimbaud watching me from the open window. He starts to snicker. There was no reason for it, right? Anyway, I go upstairs and go in. 'You look like a real asshole with your herring in one hand and your bottle of oil in the other,' he says to me. So I yell right back at him, because I most certainly did not look like an asshole with my herring and my bottle of oil, what the hell. . . ."

In July Verlaine left Rimbaud and went to Brussels, ". . . to blow my brains out." Rimbaud hadn't a cent; he followed him. A day of drinking in Brussels, a hotel room, Verlaine pulled a pistol. "Here's what you get, for wanting to leave!" The whine of a bullet, a hospital, the police. Verlaine was sent to prison for two years. Rimbaud had the scratch on his hand bandaged, and went home to his mother's, to finish writing a book he called *A Season in Hell*.

THE DRUNKEN BOAT

I drifted on a river I could not control,
No longer guided by the bargemen's ropes.
They were captured by howling Indians
Who nailed them naked to colored stakes.

I cared no more for other boats or cargoes:
English cotton, Flemish wheat, all were gone.
When my bargemen could no longer haul me
I forgot about everything and drifted on.

Through the wild splash and surging of the tides
Last winter, deaf as a child's dark night,
I ran and ran! And the drifting Peninsulas
Have never known such conquering delight.

Lighter than cork, I revolved upon waves
That roll the dead forever in the deep,
Ten days, beyond the blinking eyes of land!
Lulled by storms, I drifted seaward from sleep.

Sweeter than children find the taste of sour fruit,
Green water filled my cockle shell of pine.
Anchor and rudder went drifting away,
Washed in vomit and stained with blue wine.

Now I drift through the Poem of the Sea;
This gruel of stars mirrors the milky sky,
Devours green azures; ecstatic flotsam,
Drowned men, pale and thoughtful, sometimes drift by.

Staining the sudden blueness, the slow sounds,
Deliriums that streak the glowing sky,

Stronger than drink and the songs we sing,
It is boiling, bitter, red; it is love!

I watched the lightning tear the sky apart,
Watched waterspouts, and streaming undertow,
And Dawn like Dove-People rising on wings—
I've seen what men have only dreamed they saw!

I saw the sun with mystic horrors darken
And shimmer through a violet haze;
With a shiver of shutters the waves fell
Like actors in ancient, forgotten plays!

I dreamed of green nights and glittering snow,
Slow kisses rising in the eyes of the Sea,
Unknown liquids flowing, the blue and yellow
Stirring of phosphorescent melody!

For months I watched the surge of the sea,
Hysterical herds attacking the reefs;
I never thought he bright feet of Mary
Could muzzle up the heavy-breathing waves!

I have jostled—you know?—unbelievable Floridas
And seen among the flowers the wild eyes
Of panthers in the skins of men! Rainbows
Bridling blind flocks beneath the horizons!

In stinking swamps I have seen great hulks:
A Leviathan that rotted in the reeds!
Water crumbling in the midst of calm
And distances that shatter into foam.

Glaciers, silver suns, waves of pearl, fiery skies,
Giant serpents stranded where lice consume

Them, falling in the depths of dark gulfs
From twisted trees, bathed in black perfume!

I wanted to show children these fishes shining
In the blue wave, the golden fish that sing—
A froth of flowers cradled my wandering
And delicate winds tossed me on their wings.

Sometimes, a martyr of poles and latitudes,
The sea rocked me softly in sighing air,
And brought me shadow-flowers with yellow stems—
I remained like a woman, kneeling . . .

Almost an island, I balanced on my boat's sides
Rapacious blond-eyed birds, their dung, their screams.
I drifted on. Through fragile tangled lines
Drowned men, still staring up, sank down to sleep.

Now I, a little lost boat, in swirling debris,
Tossed by the storm into the birdless upper air
—All the Hansa Merchants and Monitors
Could not fish up my body drunk with the sea;

Free and soaring, trailing a violet haze,
Shot through the sky, a reddening wall
Wet with the jam of poets' inspiration,
Lichens of sun, and snots of bright blue sky;

Lost branch spinning in a herd of hippocamps,
Covered over with electric animals,
An everlasting July battering
The glittering sky and its fiery funnels;

Shaking at the sound of monsters roaring,
Rutting Behemoths in thick whirlpools,

Eternal weaver of unmoving blues,
I thought of Europe and its ancient walls!

I have seen archipelagos in the stars,
Feverish skies where I was free to roam!
Are these bottomless nights your exiled nests,
Swarm of golden birds, O Strength to come?

True, I've cried too much; I am heartsick at dawn.
The moon is bitter and the sun is sour . . .
Love burns me; I am swollen and slow.
Let my keel break! Oh, let me sink in the sea!

If I long for a shore in Europe,
It's a small pond, dark, cold, remote,
The odor of evening, and a child full of sorrow
Who stoops to launch a crumpled paper boat.

Washed in your languors, Sea, I cannot trace
The wake of tankers foaming through the cold,
Nor assault the pride of pennants and flags,
Nor endure the slave ship's stinking hold.

VOWELS

Black A, white E, red I, green U, blue O—vowels,
Some day I will open your silent pregnancies:
A, black belt, hairy with bursting flies,
Bumbling and buzzing over stinking cruelties,

Pits of night; E, candor of sand and pavilions,
High glacial spears, white kings, trembling Queen Anne's lace;

I, bloody spittle, laughter dribbling from a face
In wild denial or in anger, vermilions;

U, . . . divine movement of viridian seas,
Peace of pastures animal-strewn, peace of calm lines
Drawn on foreheads worn with heavy alchemies;

O, supreme Trumpet, harsh with strange stridencies,
Silences traced in angels and astral designs:
O . . . OMEGA . . . the violet light of His Eyes!

"THE SUN HAS WEPT ROSE"

The sun has wept rose in the shell of your ears,
The world has rolled white from your back, your thighs;
The sea has stained rust the crimson of your breasts,
And Man has bled black at your sovereign side.

RIMBAUD'S CONTRIBUTIONS TO THE
ALBUM ZUTIQUE

DRUNKS

Mad
Quean,
Sad.
Been

Had;
Mean
Lad.
Scene.

She
Falls,
Bawls:

"My
Thigh!"
Whee!

YOUNG GLUTTON

Two sick
Young fruits.
Drastic
Pursuits.

Big thick
Black boots,
Paul's trick
Just suits.

"Don't kick,
Just lick."
Disputes.

"Some prick."
"Come quick!"
He shoots.

THE OLD GUARD

Long live the emperor's peasants!
Long live the peasants' emperor!
Hip hooray and Forward March!
Hooray for the great eighteenth of March!
For blessèd is the *Fruit* of thy womb, Eugénie!

PARIS

Al. Godillot, Gambier,
Galopeau, Wolf-Pleyel,
—O Kitchen sinks!—Menier,
—O Christs!—Leperdriel!

Kinck, Jacob, Bonbonnel!
Veuillot, Tropmann, Augier!
Gill, Mendès, Manuel,
Guido Gonin!—Away

With Graces! L'Hérissé!
Elegant shoes to shine!
Displays of bread and wine!

Blind men! But who's to say?
Policeman, Merchant, Brother!
Let's all love one another!

SEALED LIPS; SEEN IN ROME

In Papal Rome, in the Sistine,
Drying in a reliquary
Carved with a pious Christian scene,
Is a nest of noses legendary:

Noses of monks from Theban cells,
Of canons of the Holy Grail,
Where the livid light of night smells
Of an old liturgical wail.

Into their mystic dehydration
Every morning, early enough,
Drops an antique irritation:
A large pinch of schismatic snuff.

Léon Dierx (A.R.)

FÊTE GALANTE

Scapin from habit
Pets the rabbit
In his lap;
But Columbine
(Who fucks just fine)
Tries to tap
The bunny's eye—
And by and by
It sits up.

Paul Verlaine (A.R.)

THE BAD LITTLE ANGEL

Whitewashed doors and roofs of slate
As on a Sunday very late;

The doors are closed, the street is white,
The town is calm, the time is night.

The houses stand, enchanted things
With shutters made of angels' wings.

But in the gutter we can see
A spectacle of misery:

A small black angel getting sick
From eating too much licorice stick.

He takes a shit, then disappears;
But as the empty darkness clears,

Beneath the moon his shit remains
Like dirty blood in dirty drains.

Louis Ratisbonne (A.R.)

LILIES

O Lilies! O Garden swing! O silver Enema bags!
Disdaining viands, raiment, diadems;
Daylight fills you with a sterilized love,
The heavens descend to vaseline your stems!

Armand Silvestre (A.R.)

Mankind put shoes and socks on that growing child, Progress.

Louis-Xavier de Ricard (A.R.)

"ON SUMMER NIGHTS"

On summer nights, before the shining shop windows,
When the sap pulses beneath the tarnished halos
Formed by the grillwork at the feet of fragile elms,
Leaving black gatherings, gay groups or stay-at-homes,
Who light up cheap cigars and pipes and puff away,
Into this narrow, half-stone stall I wend my way.
While overhead hangs a poster—*Ibled*, it states—
I imagine that winter also inundates
Tibet in running water, washing the yellow tide,
And that the winter wind spares nothing left outside.

François Coppée (A.R.)

"TO MY BEDSIDE BOOKS"

To my bedside books, those exquisite editions
Of novels and sermons, my prize acquisitions,
Bored with engravings in half-tone or black and white,
I hope, in my old age, as a source of delight,
To add the great tome of Professor Venetti.
So, when I return from work worn out with petty
Cares, I can revel in plates where the artist paints
Colored illustrations of family complaints . . .
The subject of the work, I am certain, will please:
Venetti—*Study of Venereal Disease*.

François Coppée (A.R.)

"I SAT IN A THIRD-CLASS RAILWAY CAR"

I sat in a third-class railway car; an old priest
By the window took out his pipe—antique, at least—
And leaned against the window an old chin stained puce.
Then this Christian, ignoring insulting abuse,
Turning to me, made a request, forceful, but sad,
For some tobacco—which, as it happened, I had—
He was once, it appeared, chaplain and confessor
To a proscribed nobleman and his successor—
To while away the length of a tunnel—dark vein
Laid open for travelers—by Soissons, near Aisne.

François Coppée (A.R.)

"I'D PROBABLY PREFER"

I'd probably prefer, come spring, an open-air
Café, where stunted trees sprout blossoms everywhere
Along the narrow community fields, in May.
The poor young dogs get yelled at when they try to play
Too close to the Drinkers; they trample down the flowers
In the flower beds. Here, until the hyacinth hours,
On the slate-topped table, carved, in seventeen-seven,
Thin as the inscription beneath some stained-glass heaven,
With a long Latin nickname by a certain monk,
The coughing of black bottles never gets them drunk.

François Coppée (A.R.)

MARTIAL LAW?

The cold conductor on his small platform of tin,
Without a glove to warm his freezing fingers in,
Dangles from his bus as it follows the Left Bank,
And shifts his moneychanger from his swollen flank.
And though its soft shadows are crawling with police,
The honest interior stares at heaven's peace

And at the moon awash in its green misty bower,
In spite of the curfew and the delicate hour
And the bus on its way to the Odéon, where
A soiled reveler yelps in the dark empty square.

François Coppée (A.R.)

RECOLLECTION

The year the dear, dear Prince Imperial was born
I still remember well; tricolored flags adorn
The glittering city, and from palace walls,
From grilles and gratings and the gates of public halls
Hang heavy banners crowned with white and golden N's.
And through the gawking, gaping crowd of citizens
In faded hats, in padded vests with polka dots,
In ancient coats—through this crowd of compatriots—
Across spread-out carpets the Emperor goes
With the Holy Spaniard, quite neat in his black clothes.

François Coppée (A.R.)

"THE BOY WHO PICKED THE BULLETS UP"

The boy who picked the bullets up, Destiny's child,
In whose blood flows the memory of an exiled
Father, now aspires to new stature of his own
And prefers bed curtains to the drapes of the Throne.
His soft features, his exquisite face, were not made
To lead a Nation or to storm a barricade!
His toys are all forgotten, now he only dreams
Of things that are forbidden; from his face he seems
Overcome by an immense desire to grab it—
"Poor young man, I hear he has a certain habit!"

François Coppée (A.R.)

"IT'S ONLY A HUMBLE HANDMADE BRUSH"

It's only a humble handmade brush, too small
For dusting a room or even painting a wall.

Its use is embarrassing—but we must not laugh.
Root left to rot beside some long-forgotten path,
Its silent bristles dry; its handle has turned white,
Like island trees gone dry in summer's heat.
Its tiny cord resembles a frozen curl.
I love this little object's sad, distressing smell,
And would like to wash with it your wide white sides,
O Moon, where the spirit of our dead Sisters hides.

François Coppée (A.R.)

CONFESSIONS OF AN IDIOT OLD MAN

Bless me, Father . . .
                    Young, at our county fairs,
I left the repetitious wheels of chance,
To seek the neighing darkness beyond the tents
Where the cart horses from their steaming loins
Thrust out those blood-choked, glistening tubes
Whose memory terrifies me still; . . .
                              And my mother,
Whose nightdress had a bitter smell,
Frayed at the hem and yellowed as a rotting fruit,
Would get to bed with such strange sounds . . .
. . . This daughter of the soil! . . . her full thigh,
Enormous loins . . . where damp linen caught in cracks
And gave me fevers that I never told . . .

More crude, but calmer, was the shame I felt
When my little sister, coming home from class,
Her muddy boots worn down by sharp ice,
Went out to piss, and watched the delicate urine spurt
Over the rosy lower fold of flesh! . . .
Father, forgive me!
                    . . . I dreamt of my father:
Card games late at night, exciting army-words;
A neighbor visiting—myself sent off to bed, watching . . .

A Father's a frightening thing! Imagining things . . .
Up on his knee: in his lap: my finger
Trembling to touch the front of his pants . . . Oh, God!
To feel the enormous stump, dark and hard,
My father had!
                    While his hard hand stroked me . . .
I cannot talk about the chamber pot, the things
That I caught sight of in the attic,
Almanacs and their red covers, and the rag basket,
The Bible, the toilets, and our maid,
The Holy Virgin and the crucifix . . .
                                        Oh, no one ever
Was so much tormented, so thunderstruck by sin!
And to obtain a pardon . . .
Since these terrors of the flesh have slain my soul,
I confess to God and you my childhood crimes . . .

And now . . . Father, let me address the Lord! . . .
                                                WHY?

WHY this stubborn puberty, this curse of
An insistent gland, too often listened to? Why,
Why this slow darkness creeping from my loins?
These swarming terrors overwhelming all my joy
Like some great black avalanche?
I was always paralyzed before it!
                            . . . to know what?

Contrition?
            Father, put back on
That purple stole.
                Oh, childhood!

                    . . . Let's jack each other off!
                                François Coppée (A.R.)

STUPRA: THREE SCATOLOGICAL SONNETS

"ANIMALS ONCE SPEWED SEMEN"

Animals once spewed semen as they ran,
Their organs streaked with blood and excrement.
Our fathers pouched their members out, and spent
Long hours contriving to display their span.

The medieval woman, saint or whore,
Asked for a gallant with a proud display;
Even Kléber, to look at his pants (they
Lie, perhaps, somewhat), had resource, and more.

Man and the proudest mammals have one source;
Their giant cocks and ours are both the same . . .
And yet a sterile hour now sounds; the horse

And roaring bull have covered up their flame;
No one dares undo his genital force
In those woods where sex was once a children's game . . .

"OUR ASSHOLES ARE DIFFERENT"

Our assholes are different from theirs. I used to watch
Young men let down their pants behind some tree,
And in those happy floods that youth set free
I watched the architecture of our crotch.

Quite firm, in many cases pale, it owes
Its form to muscles, and a wickerwork
Of hairs; for girls, the most enchanting lurk
In a dark crack where tufted satin grows.

The touching and wonderful innocence
Of painted cherubs on a Baroque shrine
Is recalled in that cheek a dimple indents . . .

Oh! If only we were naked now, and free
To watch our protruding parts align;
To whisper—both of us—in ecstasy!

"HIDDEN AND WRINKLED"

Hidden and wrinkled like a budding violet
It breathes, gently worn out, in a tangled vine
(Still damp with love), on the soft incline
Of white buttocks to the rim of the pit.

Thin streams like rivers of milk; innocent
Tears, shed beneath hot breath that drives them down
Across small clots of rich soil, reddish brown,
Where they lose themselves in the dark descent . . . .

My mouth always dribbles with its coupling force;
My soul, jealous of the body's intercourse,
Makes it a tearful, wild necessity.

Ecstatic olive branch, the flute one blows,
The tube where heavenly praline flows,
Promised Land in sticky femininity.

THE WASTELANDS OF LOVE

FOREWORD

These are the writings of a very young *man,* whose life unfolded
nowhere in particular; he had no mother, no country; he cared nothing for the things one cares for, and he fled from every moral law, as
many pitiful young men have already fled. But so tormented was he,
and so afflicted, that he only drew on toward death as toward a terrible
and fatal innocence. Since he did not love women—although full of

passion!—his heart and soul and all his strength were wasted in strange, sad delusions. The dreams that follow (his loves!), that came to him in different beds or in the streets, the way they develop and the way they end, arise perhaps from delicate religious ideas. You may remember the eternal sleep of legendary Mohammedans—honest men and circumcised! Yet these strange sufferings possess a disturbing authority, and force one sincerely to hope that this SOUL, who has lost his way among us, who evidently desires death, may in that final instant find sober consolations—and be worthy of them.

I

This, I am sure, is the same countryside. The same old farmhouse my parents had; above the doors, tapestries with lions and arms, darkened with age. At dinner, a room with candles and wines and old woodwork. The dining-room table was very large. The maids! There were several of them, as many as I had remembered. An old but young friend was there, a priest (and dressed as a priest now); this was in order to be more free. I remember his dark red room and its yellow paper glass-panes, and the sea-stained books he kept hidden away.

I was left to myself in that endless country house: reading in the kitchen, drying the mud on my clothes before the conversation of the guests in the salon, wearied to death by the murmur of the morning's milk, the sound of the last century's night.

I was in a very dark room; what was I doing? One of the maids came near me; she was, I think, a puppy dog; though she was beautiful, and had a maternal nobility I cannot explain; pure, familiar, completely charming! She pinched my arm.

I cannot remember her face very well, nor do I remember her arm, whose skin I rolled between two fingers; nor her mouth, endlessly imitating something, which mine fastened on like a desperate little wave. I pushed her down into a basket of cushions and canvas, in a dark corner. I remember now only her white lace panties.

Then, O despair! The walls changed softly to the shadows of trees—and I sank down into the amorous sadness of night.

II

This time, I saw Woman in the city, and I spoke to her, and she spoke to me.

I was in a bedroom, in darkness. They came to tell me that she was there at my house; and I saw her in my bed, all mine, in darkness! I was very upset and dumb—a great deal because it was my family's house—and anguish seized me. I was dressed in rags; she was a woman of the world, yielding herself to me; she had to go! This nameless anguish. . . . I took her, but let her fall from the bed, almost naked, and in my inutterable weakness, I fell upon her and dragged myself with her across the carpets, in darkness! One after another, the adjoining rooms glowed red with the old familial lamp. It was then that the woman disappeared. I shed more tears than God would have dared to ask.

I went out into the endless city. (O fatigue!) Drowning in the deaf night and in flight from happiness. It was like a winter night, with a fall of snow to smother the world with precision. I cried to friends: "Where is she hiding?" and they gave me false answers. I stood before the windows of the place where she goes every night; I ran through an endless garden. Everywhere I was turned away. At all of this I cried incessantly. I went down at last to a place full of dust, where I sat upon the girders, and in that night wept out all the tears in my body— yet my tears returned, to be wept out again and again.

I understood that she had returned to her everyday life; that mercy would turn in its orbit more slowly than any sun. She never came back, and will never come back, my ADORABLE, who visited me in my room—which I would never have thought possible. This time, believe me, I cried more than all the children in the world.

FRAGMENTS FROM THE BOOK OF JOHN

I

A few people in Samaria had shown their faith in him. He could not find them. Samaria the proud, the parvenu, the egotistical, more rigidly observant of her protestant law than Judea of the Ancient Tablets. Ubiquitous wealth permitted there but little enlightened discussion. Sophistry, that slave and soldier of routine, had already destroyed several prophets there—flattering them first.

A sinister sentence, that he heard from the woman at the well: "You are a prophet—you know what I have done."

Men and women then believed in prophets. Now they put their faith in Chiefs of State.

Just outside of that alien town, unable to menace it materially—if they had taken him as a prophet, since he had shown himself so strangely there, what would he have done?

Jesus could say nothing to Samaria.

II

The light and lovely air of Galilee. . . .

People received him with a curious joy: they had seen him, shaken with holy rage, lashing the moneychangers and livestock sellers from the Temple.

Marvelous reaction of a pale and angry young man, they thought.

He felt his hand between other hands, heavy with rings, and at the mouth of an officer. The officer knelt in the dust; the top of his head was attractive, though half bald.

Wagons wheeled through the narrow streets; movement quite exciting for such a town—it seemed that everything, that evening, should have been more than content.

Jesus withdrew his hand with an involuntary movement of childish, feminine pride.

"The rest of you, if you see no miracles, will not believe."

Jesus had worked no miracles yet. He had, in a pink and green dining room, at a wedding breakfast, spoken rather sharply to the Holy Virgin. . . .

But no one in Capernaum spoke yet of the wine at Cana—not in the marketplace, not on the docks. Among the bourgeois, perhaps.

Jesus said: "Go now, your son is well." So the officer went away, as if he carried some minor prescription, and Jesus went on through the back streets. Goldenrod and burdocks gleamed miraculously between the stones of the street. Finally, far away, he saw the dusty plain, and marigolds and daisies drooping in the sun.

III

Beth-Saida, the pool and its five galleries, was a source of annoyance. It had the atmosphere of a sinister washhouse, always damp and moldy. Beggars squirmed within on steps that paled at the glimmer of storms flickering with the lightnings of hell—they made jokes about their blind blue eyes, and about the white and blue linens that they wrapped around their stumps. It was a regimental laundry, a public bath. The water was always black, and no invalid dreamt of falling into it.

It was here that Jesus took his first serious step: among these horrible cripples. It was a day in February, or March, or April, when the sun at two hours past noon spread out a great sickle-shaped stain of light on the shrouded dark water; from where I stood at a great distance behind the cripples, I would have been able to see all that that ray evoked of flower buds and crystals and verses; in that reflection, like a white angel hovering on its side, an infinity of pale and glimmering light stirred gently.

Then the multitude of sins, persuasive and delicate children of the devil—they made these men more frightening than monsters, to delicate hearts—wanted to rush to the water. The cripples went down to the pool, no longer joking, but anxious. The first ones who bathed came out cured, people said. No. Their sins repulsed them on the steps and forced them to find other corners to beg: for their demon can keep them only in places where alms are sure.

Jesus entered just after the hour of noon. No one was washing, nor leading cattle to drink. The light in the pool was yellow as the last leaves on the vine. The divine master stood by a column: he watched the children of Sin; the Devil stuck out his tongue with their tongues, and laughed, in denial.

The Paralytic arose—who had always lain on his side—and the Damned watched him cross the gallery with a singularly confident step and disappear into the city.

"O SEASONS, O CHÂTEAUS!"

O seasons, O châteaus!
Where is the flawless soul?

O seasons, O châteaus,

I learned the magic of
Felicity. It enchants us all.

Long live Felicity, when
Gaul's cock crows!

Now all desire has gone;
It has made my life its own.

That spell! It caught my heart and soul
And scattered every trial.

What is the meaning of all I say?
It blows my words away!

O seasons, O châteaus!

REMEMBRANCE

I

Water, clear as the salt of children's tears.
Suddenly in sunlight, women's bodies, all white;

Streams of silk, pure lilies, bright banners
Beneath ramparts where an armed Maid appeared.

Diversion of angels; No—the current carries gold
And loads its heavy, black, cool arms with grass,
Sinking beneath its canopy of sky . . . and the arch
And shadows of the hill, like curtains, unfold.

II

Watch! This wet square of stream moves in soft swirls,
In endless glassy gold pavilioning its bed;
Like willow trees where birds hop unhindered
Are the green gauzy dresses of the little girls.

Flowers brighter than coin, warm yellow eyes
That trouble waters—O Wife, your conjugal love!—
The rosy Sun at noon burns sullenly above
This dark mirror, reflected through hazy skies.

III

MADAME in the open field stands too straight
In a swirl of snowy threads, her parasol
Unsheathed; she snaps flower tops to watch them fall . . .
Her children read their red-backed book, and wait,

Wait, in the flowering grass. Alas! HE
Like a thousand bright angels scattering in flight
Scales the mountaintops and fades from sight!
Behind him runs the black, unbending SHE!

IV

Regret for the thick young arms of virgin grass!
Gold of April moonlight in the sacred bed! Joy

Of abandoned boat docks on the riverbank, prey
To the August nights that bred this rottenness!

Now let her weep beneath these walls! The breath
Of towering poplars is the only breeze.
And then this water, sourceless, somber, gray,
And a man who drags the bottom in a motionless barge.

v

Toy for this dull eye of water, I cannot reach
—O motionless boat! Too short, my arms!—
These flowers: the yellow one that bothers me
There, nor the blue, friend to water the color of ash!

From wing-shaken willows a powder drifts;
The roses in the reeds have long since dried.
My boat, still motionless; and its chain pulled
Deep in this edgeless eye of water . . . into what mud?

TEAR

Far from flocks, from birds and country girls,
I knelt down to drink within a leafy screen
Surrounded by tender hazelnut trees
In the warm green mist of afternoon.

What could I drink from this young Oise,
Tongueless trees, flowerless grass, dark skies . . .
What could I draw from the round gourd that grew there?
Some tasteless golden draught to make me sweat.

And a poor sign for an inn would I have made.
Later, toward evening, the sky filled with storms . . .

They became black fields, and lakes, and poles of wood,
Tunnels within the blue night, and waiting rooms.

Water from the woods runs out on virgin sands,
The wind from heaven casts ice thick on the ponds . . .
Now, like one who dives for pretty shells or coin,
Never deny that my thirst has caused me pain!

THE COMEDY OF THIRST

I. FOREFATHERS

We are your Father's Fathers,
      Your Elders!
Glistening with the cold sweat
Of the moon and dripping leaves.
. . . But our dry wines were strong!
Beneath this guileless sun
What is the duty of man? To drink.

I: To die by untamed streams.

We are your Father's Fathers,
      Villagers.
Water murmurs in the reeds:
See where the swirling moat
Circles the sweating château.
Come down with us to the cellars
And you shall have cider and milk.

I: Let us go with the cattle to drink.

We are your Father's Fathers,
      Preservers

Of liquors in cabinets;
Teas! and Coffees! so rare,
Tremble in our stills.
. . . Look at these forms and flowers.
We have come from the graveyard.

I: Ah! If I could empty all the urns . . .

II. THE SPIRIT

Eternal water sprites,
Part the pure waters;
Venus, foam-born,
Dazzle the bright wave.

Wandering Jews of Norway,
Say the snow to me;
Dear age-old exiles,
Tell me the sea.

Forget these pure liquids,
These waterflowers for cups;
No legends, no figures
Can soften my thirst.

Songmaker, see your godchild—
My wild desire to drink,
The headless Hydra in my bowels
That feeds upon my soul.

III. FRIENDS

Come, all Wines go down to the sea,
In inexhaustible waves!

See the foaming Bitter Beer
Pour from mountain caves!

Knowing pilgrims, seek repose
By the emerald pillars of Absinthe . . .

I: Leave these landscapes.
Friends, what is drunkenness?

I would as soon lie dumb
To fester in some pond
Beneath the stinking scum
By a drifting log.

IV. THE POOR MAN DREAMS

I have an evening unspent
When I can drink in peace
In a small quiet place,
And then die content . . .
Since I am patient.

If I forget my pain,
If I can get some gold,
Should I live in the North
Or in the wine-blest South?
. . . Ah, dreaming is vain

Since it's always a loss!
And if I become once more
The wanderer I was,
The doors of the green inn
Can never be opened again.

V. CONCLUSION

The pigeons trembling in the open field,
The wild running things that see the night,
Waterbugs and lap dogs, and the wild
And silly butterfly—alike, all thirst!

Oh, but to vanish like the trackless cloud!
Wrapped in wetness and in dew, to die
Among the violets on the waterside
Daylight leaves in heaps about the wood.

"HEAR HOW IT BELLOWS"

Hear how it bellows
Beneath the acacias
In April, the green
Branch of the vine!

In a cleansing cloud
To Phoebe! See them nod
And turn a head
Like saints of old . . .

Far from shining stones
On capes, from bright roofs,
Dear Ancients desire
This sullen syrup . . .

Never festive, not
Astral, the misty
Breath of this
Nocturnal scene.

Yet still they stay
. . . Germany, Sicily,
In this sad pale
Mist, and justly.

LOVELY THOUGHTS FOR MORNING

At four in the morning, in summertime,
Love's drowsiness still lasts.
Dawn brushes from the shrubbery
    The odor of the night's feast.

Beyond the bright Hesperides,
Within the western workshop of the Sun,
Carpenters in shirtsleeves scramble;
    Work is begun.

And in desolate, moss-grown isles
They carve precious panels
Where the wealth of cities laughs
    Beneath a hollow sky.

For these charming dabblers in the arts
Who labor for a king in Babylon,
Venus! Leave for a moment
    Lovers' haloed hearts.

    O Queen of Shepherds!
Carry the purest eau-de-vie
To these workmen while they rest
And take their bath at noonday, in the sea.

MICHAEL AND CHRISTINE

Damn, Damn! Suppose the sun leaves these shores!
Blow on, bright storm! There's the shadow of the highway.
In the willows, in the old courtyard,
The storm first spatters in the dusty clay.

O flock of lambs, blond soldiers of our idyll,
Flee from these fountains, this spindly thicket!
Now plain and desert, horizon and field
Are still before the reddening storm's toilette.

Black dog, brown shepherd muffled in a cloak,
Flee the towering lightnings of the storm;
Blond flock, scurry through the sulfury dark,
Go and huddle someplace deep and warm.

Yet I, Lord God! See how my soul
Soars into skies frozen with red,
In heavenly clouds that whirl and roll
Above Solognes long as a railroad.

See the thousand wolves, the thousand wild seeds
Borne upon the storm, on this religious afternoon
That loves the weeds and scatters them
Across old Europe where a hundred hordes ride!

Afterward, moonlight! Warriors, over the plain,
Redden their faces in the darkened skies
And gallop their great pale horses away!
The pebbles beneath them spatter like rain!

And we see the yellow wood and the valley of light,
The blue-eyed Bride, the red-faced Gaul, and

The white Pascal Lamb, at their delicate feet,
Michael and Christine—and Christ! The idyll's end.

THE RIVER OF CORDIAL

The River of Cordial rolls ignored
    In empty countryside:
Lulled by the voices of a hundred
    Crows, a celestial tide,
And great pine branches overhead
    That the wild winds ride.

All things roll here: horrors of midnights,
    Campaigns of a lost year,
Dungeons disturbed, and groves of lights;
    Echoing on these shores, still clear,
Dead ecstasies of questing knights—
    Yet how the wind revives us here!

The wanderer who watches these black bands
    Takes courage as he goes;
Forest soldiers that the Lord commands,
    Dear, delightful crows!
Chase the crafty peasant from these lands,
    And the old claw he shows.

THE TRIUMPH OF PATIENCE

BANNERS OF MAY

In the bright branches of the willow trees
The echo of a hunt dissolves,

But elegant songs still beat the air
Among the trembling leaves.
Let our blood laugh in our veins.
This place is a tangle of vines;
The sky has an angel's face.
Air and water are one and the same.
I shall go out. If bright light wounds me
I shall lie down on leaves and die.

To wait, to be bored, is too simple;
All my anguish is empty.
Let high summer dangle me
Behind its fatal glittering car.
O Nature, let me die in you
. . . Less useless, less alone . . .
Not like the Shepherds, who will die
More or less throughout the world.

Let turning seasons do their worst;
To you, Nature, I offer up myself,
My hunger and my everlasting thirst;
To quiet them I ask your help.
Nothing at all can ever deceive me;
We laugh with our parents when we laugh in the sun,
But I will laugh with nothing, with no one;
And I will be free in this misfortune.

A SONG FROM THE HIGHEST TOWER

Idle children
Held in thrall,
Lack of heart
Has cost my life.
Oh, will the day come
When all hearts fall in love?

Leave and go hide,
To myself I cry:
There is no promise
Of a greater joy.
Let nothing prevent
My high retreat.

I have waited so long
That at length I forget,
And leave unto heaven
My fear and regret;
A sick thirst
Darkens my veins.

So the green field
To oblivion falls,
Overgrown, flowering
With incense and weeds
And the cruel noise
Of dirty flies.

Ah! Widowed again and again,
The poor soul
Who has only a picture
Of the Mother of God!
Can one really pray
To the Virgin Mary?

Idle children
Held in thrall,
Lack of heart
Has cost my life.

Oh, will the day come
When all hearts fall in love?

ETERNITY

It is recovered.
What? Eternity.
In the whirling light
Of sun become sea.

Oh my sentinel soul,
Let us desire
The nothing of night
And the day on fire.

From the applause of the World
And the striving of Man
You set yourself free
And fly as you can.

For out of you only,
Soft silken embers,
Duty arises
Nor surfeit remembers.

Then shall all hope fail,
No *orietur*.
Science with patience,
The torment is sure.

It is recovered.
What? Eternity.
In the whirling light
Of sun become sea.

GOLDEN AGE

One of these voices
—Angelically—

Greenly, angrily,
Talks about me.

These thousands of questions
That spread themselves out
Can lead to nothing
But madness and rout;

Remember this tune
So gentle and free:
This flowering wave
Is your own family!

And then the voice sings. Oh
So gently, so free,
And I join the song
For all to see . . .

Remember this tune
So gentle and free:
This flowering wave
Is your own family! . . . etc. . . . .

And then a new voice
—How angelically!—
Greenly, angrily,
Talks about me:

And it sings just then,
A sister of the winds;
In a German accent,
But passionately—

The world is evil;
Does that surprise you?

Live; to the fire
Leave his obscure pain.

O lovely château!
O life full of light!
To what Age do you belong,
Our older brother's
Princely soul? etc. . . .

I have my song too,
Several sisters! Voices
Not to be heard!
Enfold me
In your bashful light . . . etc. . . .

THE NEWLYWEDS AT HOME

The bedroom lies open to the turquoise sky;
No room; nothing but boxes and bins!
The wall without is full of wild flowers
And quivers with goblins' chattering gums!

How like the intrigues of genies is this:
All this expense and these vain disorders!
There is an African fairy who provides
The mulberry and cobwebs in the corners!

Enter severally, disgruntled godmothers
As spots of light upon the wainscoting.
The household departs (but not these others!)
In a lightheaded rush, and nothing gets done . . .

Every husband has a wind (here it blows
All day long) that cheats him unawares . . .
Even wicked fairies from the water
Come to flutter in the alcove's affairs.

The night, the friendly night—oh! the honeymoon
Will snatch away their smile and fill the sky
With a thousand copper coronets!
They will deal with a bad rat by and by.

If a wandering light doesn't happen along
Like a rifle shot just after evensong . . .
Holy white specters of Bethlehem . . . oh!
Enchant instead the sky in their window!

BRUSSELS

July   *Regent's Boulevard*

Flower beds of amaranths up to
The pleasant palace of Jupiter.
You I know spread here your Blue,
Your desert Blue, almost-Sahara Blue!

Roses here and sunlit pines
Play convoluted games with vines,
Cages in a little widow's window . . .
What bands of birds! Oh! ah! oh! ah! oh!

Quiet houses, love calmed long ago!
Kiosk for a Woman Mad with Regret!
Behind the butts of rose trees, low
And shadowy, a balcony for Juliet . . .

. . . Say Juliet, I think of Henriette,
A lovely stop along the railway,
Where in a mountain, at an orchard's end,
A thousand blue devils dance a ballet!

On a green bench in a hurricane cloud
The white girl of Ireland sings to her guitar;
In the Guianan dining room, loud
Sounds of children, where the birdcages are.

Ducal Window makes me think of subtile
Poison slugs and snails, and here below
Asleep in sunshine, boxwood hedge . . . but oh,
It is all too beautiful! Let us be still.

Calm boulevard, empty of life and fire!
Tragedy, Comedy, all in stillness stands;
Infinite imagination here expands,
And I who know you quietly admire.

"DOES SHE DANCE?"

Does she dance? In the first blue hours
Will she wither like the dying flowers . . .
Before this sweep of splendor perfumed
By the flowering breath of the bustling town!

It's all too beautiful! But necessary . . .
For the Fishermaid and the Pirate's song,
And for those masks who linger on
To feast at night upon the pure sea!

THE TRIUMPH OF HUNGER

Hunger, hunger, sister Anne,
Leave me if you can.

I only find within my bones
A taste for eating earth and stones.
Dinn! Dinn! Dinn! Dinn! We eat air,
Rocks and coals and iron ore.

My hunger, turn. Hunger, feed:
    A field of bran.
Gather as you can the bright
    Poison weed.

Eat the rocks a beggar breaks,
Stones of churches' crumbling gates,
Pebbles, children of the flood,
Loaves left lying in the mud.

Hunger, these are bits of black air,
    Cold clouds;
I follow as my stomach bids—
    And despair.

Across the land the leaves appear;
I seek the soft flesh of fruit.
In the heart of the furrow
I look for spring lettuce, and violets.

Hunger, hunger, sister Anne,
Leave me if you can.

SHAME

As long as a knife has not cut
This brain, unfolding
White wrapping, greasy, green,
Its odor always cold,

(He, this thing, should slit
His nose, lips, ears, belly, all!
Disown and leave his legs!
A marvel!)

No; I know that as long as
A knife has not cut his head
Nor a rock crushed his thigh
Nor fire seared his gut,

As long as none has acted, this child,
This bother, this mindless beast,
Will never for an instant rest
From trickery and treason,

And like a Rocky Mountain cat
Will stink in the world's air!
Yet when he dies, O God . . .
Let someone say a prayer.

CHILDHOOD

I

An idol . . .
Black eyes, yellow hair;

Without parents or home,
Nobler than Flemish or Mexican fables;
His empire, in blues and insolent greens,
Spreads over beaches savagely named
in Greek, Celtic, or Slavic
By the shipless waves.

At the edge of the forest, where dream flowers chime,
Brighten and break . . .
An orange-lipped girl, her knees crossed
In the bright flood that rolls from the fields;
Nudity covered, shadowed and clothed
By rainbows, flowers, and the sea.

Ladies tilting on terraces next to the sea.
Children and giants; superb black women in the gray-green moss,
Standing jewels in the shiny rich soil
Of groves and thawing gardens . . .
Young mothers, older sisters, with a look of pilgrimages in their eyes;
Sultanas, princesses, dressed and walking like tyrants,
Foreign little girls, and people sweetly unhappy.

What a bore, all that talk about "dear body" and "dear heart"!

II

There she is, the little girl, dead behind the rose trees.
The young mother, deceased, descends the steps.
Cousin's carriage squeaks on the sand.
Little brother (. . . but he's in India!) is there,
In a field of carnations, before the setting sun.
The old people, already buried, stand upright in a flowery wall.
A swarm of golden leaves surrounds the general's house;
They have gone south.
You follow the red road to come to the empty inn.

The château is for sale; its shutters hang loose.
The priest has probably gone away with the key to the church.
The keepers' lodges all about the park are uninhabited.
The fence of the park is so high
You can see only the rattling treetops beyond.
Besides, there is nothing to see inside.

The meadows lead off to villages empty of cocks,
Empty of anvils.
The floodgates are lifted. O crosses and windmills of the desert!
O islands and millstones . . .

Magic flowers hummed. The slopes cradled him.
Animals of fabulous elegance wandered about.
Clouds gathered on high seas made of an eternity of scalding tears.

III

In the woods there is a bird;
His singing stops you, and you blush.

There is a clock that never strikes.

There is a little swamp, with a nest of pale animals.

There is a cathedral that sinks, and a lake that rises above it.

There is a little ribbon-covered cart, abandoned in the hedge
Or rolling away down the path.

There is a troupe of tiny strolling players all dressed up,
Seen on the road at the edge of the woods.

And when you are hungry or thirsty,
There is always someone to chase you away.

IV

I am a saint on a terrace praying—
Like gentle beasts who graze their way to the sea of Palestine.

I am a scholar in a dark armchair—
Branches and the rain beat at the casement of my library.

I am a highway walker in dwarf woods—
The rush of water in the sluices drown my steps.
My eyes are full of the sad golden wash of the sunset.

I might be an abandoned child,
Left on a causeway running into the sea;
A little lackey on a garden walk, that bumps against the sky.

The paths are bitter,
And broom flowers cover the hills.
The air is still . . .
How far away are the birds and the fountains!
To go on can lead only to the end of the world.

V

Well, then, rent me a tomb, whitewashed and outlined
In cement . . .
                    Far, far underground.

My elbows lean on the table, the lamp glares on newspapers
I am idiot enough to reread; on books without interest . . .

At a great distance above my underground salon, the houses
Entrench themselves; fogs thicken . . . mud is red or black.

                    Cancerous city . . .
                    Night without end!

The sewers are not so high above me. On all sides,
The breadth of the globe.
Perhaps blue depths . . . and wells of fire.
Moons in these dimensions may meet comets; the sea becomes myth.

In my bitter hours, I conjure up spheres of metal and sapphire.
I am Master of Silence.
But why should the appearance of an aperture
Gleam white in the corner of the vault?

TALE

A Prince was annoyed that he had forever devoted himself
Only to the perfection of vulgar generosities.
He foresaw astonishing revolutions in love,
And suspected that his wives were capable of more
Than an agreeable complacency,
Compounded of luxury and air.
He desired to see the Truth, the time of essential desire
And satisfaction.
Whether this would be an aberration of piety or no,
He desired it. And he possessed extensive human power.

All women who had known him were slaughtered.
What destruction in the garden of beauty!
Beneath the ax, they blessed him.
He ordered no new ones brought . . . but women reappeared.
He killed all his followers, after the hunt,
Or his drinking bouts . . .
But everyone followed him.
He amused himself by slaughtering rare animals.
He put the torch to his palaces.
He came down upon the people, and tore them to pieces . . .

The crowd, the golden roofs, the beautiful beasts
Were still there.

Is ecstasy possible in destruction?
Can one grow young in cruelty?
The people made no sound. No one opposed his views.

He was riding one evening proudly alone, and a Genie appeared.
His beauty was ineffable . . . even inexpressible.
In his face and his bearing shone the promise
Of a complex and many-layered love!
Of a happiness unbelievable, almost too much to bear,
The Prince and the Genie were lost in each other—disappearing,
    probably,
Into essential health.
How could they not have died of this?
Together then, they died.

But the Prince expired in his palace, at an ordinary age . . .
The Prince was the Genie.
The Genie was the Prince.

  Our desire lacks the music of the mind.

PARADE

Strange, well-built young men.
Some of them have exploited *your* worlds.
They need nothing, and have little desire to put into play
Their splendid abilities and all that they know of your minds.
What sweet juicy strength!
Their eyes have the animal glaze of the summer night;
Red and black, tricolored,
The shine of steel stuck with stars of gold;

Their faces are warped, pitted, blemished, burned . . .
   The excesses of absolute madness—
   This cruel and tinseled stride!
Some of them are very young . . . (what would they think of
   Chérubin?) . . .
Equipped with frightening voices and several dangerous talents,
They are sent into town to take it from behind,
Tricked out with *disgusting* luxury.
A paradise of violence, of grimace and madness.
No comparison at all with your Fakirs
And your other entertainers on the stage.
Their suits are improvised in the taste of bad dreams;
They play lovesick songs, and tragic plays
Of buccaneers and demigods, wittier and cleverer
Than history or religion ever imagined.
Chinamen, Hottentots, Gypsies, Morons, Hyenas, Molochs,
Ancient insanities, sinister demons,
They distort popular maternal scenes
With bestial positions and caresses.
They play new plays and they sing the songs
Of the spinsters and the knitters in the sun . . .
Marvelous jugglers, with magnetic acting
They transfigure places and people.

Eyes flame, blood sings, bones begin to swell,
Tears start, and networks of scarlet ripple and throb.
Their jibes and their terror endure for a moment
Or can last for months upon end.

     ONLY I HAVE THE KEY TO THIS SAVAGE PARADE!

ANTIQUE

   Graceful son of Pan!
Around your forehead, circled with berries and flowers,

Your eyes, those glittering spheres, revolve.
Stained with the dregs of wine, your cheeks
Become hollow.
Your fangs gleam.
The curve of your breast is a lyre;
Tinklings vibrate in your blond arms.
Your heart beats in those loins
That cradle a double sex.
Wander about through the night,
Softly moving this thigh,
That second thigh . . .
And this leg,
The left . . .

BEING BEAUTEOUS

Against a fall of snow, a Being Beautiful, and very tall.
Whistlings of death and circles of faint music
Make this adored body, swelling and trembling
Like a specter, rise . . .
Black and scarlet gashes burst in the gleaming flesh.
The true colors of life grow dark,
Shimmer and separate
In the scaffolding, around the Vision.

Shiverings mutter and rise,
And the furious taste of these effects is charged
With deadly whistlings and the raucous music
That the world, far behind us, hurls at our mother of beauty . . .
She retreats, she rises up . . .
Oh! Our bones have put on new flesh, for love.

O ash-white face

                O tousled hair

O crystal arms!

On this cannon I mean to destroy myself
        In a swirling of trees and soft air!

FAIRY

For Helen,
The ornamental saps conspired in the virgin dark;
In astral silences the trackless radiance unites.
The passion of summer is left to the tongueless birds,
And our necessary indolence tied
To a rich funeral barge in the eddying calm
Of dead loves and waning perfumes.

      After the moment of the foresters' song,
        The rush of the torrent in wasted woods,
        Cattle bells and echoes in the glen
        And cries from the steppe . . .

For Helen's childhood, hedges shivered, shadows trembled
(And the breast of the beggar, and the legends of Heaven).
Her eyes and her dancing, better far
Than priceless brilliance, cold influence,
Or the pleasures of the certain hour, the unique place.

VIGILS

    I

This is a place of rest and light,
No fever, no longing,
In a bed or a field.

This is a friend, neither ardent nor weak. A friend.

This is my beloved, untormenting, untormented. My beloved.

Air, and a world all unlooked for. Life.
. . . Was it really this?
For the dream grows cold.

II

The lighting comes round to the roof-tree.
From opposite ends of the hall, nondescript
Harmonic elevations rise and meet.
The wall before the watcher
Is a succession of sections of friezes,
Atmospheric strata and geological faults.

A dream, swift and intense, of sentimental groups
Of beings in every character under every appearance.

III

The lamps and the carpets of my vigil
Make the sound of nocturnal waves,
Along the hull and all around the bottom deck.

This sea of my vigil, like Amelia's breasts.

Tapestries hung halfway up, a tangle of emerald lace,
And darting vigil doves . . .

At the back of the black hearth, real suns on seashores:
Ah! Wells of magic; this time, a single sight of dawn.

MYSTIQUE

On the side of the slope, angels revolving
Their dresses of wool, in fields of emerald and steel.

Flames shoot out of meadows, to the top of the hill.
To the left, the face of the ascent is pitted
By all homicides and every battle,
And the sounds of disaster string out on a curve.
Behind the ascent on the right, the orient line of progression.

And while this band in the distance
Is made of the whirling, leaping sounds
Of conch shells and human nights,

The flowery softness of the stars and all the sky
Flows over the side of the slope
Like a basket poured out in our face,
And turns the abyss beneath us a flowering blue.

DAWN

I have kissed the summer dawn.

Before the palaces, nothing moved. The water lay dead.
Battalions of shadows still kept the forest road.

I walked, waking warm and vital breath,
While stones watched, and wings rose soundlessly.

My first adventure, in a path already gleaming
With a clear pale light,
Was a flower who told me its name.

I laughed at the blond *Wasserfall*
That threw its hair across the pines:
On the silvered summit, I came upon the goddess.

Then, one by one, I lifted her veils.
In the long walk, waving my arms.
Across the meadow, where I betrayed her to the cock.
In the heart of town she fled among steeples and domes,
And I hunted her, scrambling like a beggar on marble wharves.

Above the road, near a thicket of laurel,
I caught her in her gathered veils,
And smelled the scent of her immense body.
Dawn and the child fell together at the bottom of the wood.

When I woke, it was noon.

FLOWERS

On a slope of gold,
In ropes of silk, gray gauze, green velvet and crystal disks
Blackening like bronze in the sun, . . .
I watch digitalis unfold
Against a screen of silver filigree, of eyes, of hair.

  Glittering on agate, a shower of gold,
Mahogany pillars supporting an emerald dome,
Bunched streamers of white satin,

      And rubies subtly stemmed
Surround the water-rose.
Like a blue-eyed god in his silhouette of snow,

To marble terraces the sea and sky
Invite a throng of roses, young and strong.

ORDINARY NOCTURNE

One breath tears operatic rents in these partitions,
Destroys the pivots of eroded roofs,
Dispels the limits of the hearth,
Makes casements disappear.

Along the vine I came,
Using a gargoyle as a footrest,
And into this carriage which shows its age
In convex windowpanes, in rounded panels,
In torturous upholstery.

Hearse of my lonely sleep,
Shepherd's cart of my stupidity . . .
The vehicle spins on the grass of an overgrown highway;
In a blemish high on the right window
Revolve pale lunar fictions, breasts and leaves.

A very dark green and a very dark blue blot out the image.
We unhitch and unharness beside a patch of gravel.

—Here we will whistle for storms, for Sodoms and Solymans,
For wild beasts and armies.

(Postilion and dream horses will ride on
        through more dense and suffocating groves,
            to sink me to my eyelids in the silken spring.)

—And drive ourselves off, whipped through splashing water
And spilled drinks, to roll on the barking of bulldogs . . .

One breath dispels the limits of the hearth.

SEASCAPE

Silver and copper the cars—
    Steel and silver the prows—
Beating the foam, and
  Heaving up the briar-bush stumps.

The prairie tides,
    And the deep ruts in the ebbing sea
  Wind in circles away to the east—
To the pillars of forests,
    The pilings of wharves,
In an angle attacked by tornados of light!

WINTER FESTIVAL

Behind the comic-opera huts, the sound of a waterfall.

In the orchards and walks that border the stream,
Girandoles prolong the greens and reds of sunset.

Nymphs out of Horace in Empire coiffures . . .

    Siberian dances . . .

        Chinese ladies out of Boucher.

SCENES

The Old Comedy pursues its conventions and divides
   Its idylls:

      Boulevards of mountebanks' booths.

      A long wooden pier the length of a stony field
Where a savage crowd swirls beneath bare trees.

      Down corridors of black gauze, following the path
Of strollers under lanterns and leaves,

      Bird-actors come crashing down upon a stone pontoon
Propelled by the canopied archipelago of spectators' barges.

      Lyric scenes, to the sound of the flute and the drum,
Bow in spaces set apart on the ceilings
In modern clubrooms or in ancient Oriental halls.

      This magic maneuvers high in an amphitheater
Crowned with bushes—
Or quivers and modulates for Boetians
In the shade of a moving wood, on the slopes of planted fields.

The operetta divides upon a stage

At the intersection of ten panels hung from the balcony
To the footlights.

BOTTOM

The thorns of reality being too sharp for my noble character—
I found myself nevertheless in my lady's bower,

A great gray-blue bird, rising
To the moldings of the ceiling
Trailing a wing in the shadow of evening.
There I was the supporter to a baldachin
That upheld her favorite jewels,
And the exquisite work of her body . . .

A great bear with violet gums, sorrowfully whitening hair,
Crystal eyes shining like sideboard silver.

The world became shadow . . .
A glowing aquarium.

But in the morning—a battlesome morning in June—
I ran like an Ass,
Braying about the wood, brandishing my grievance,
Until the Sabines of the suburbs came,
Came leaping at my breast.

H

The mirror of the movements of Hortense
Images everything monstrous.
Her solitude is erotic mechanics,
Her lassitude the dynamics of love.
Under the guard of her childhood, she has been
For numerous ages and ages
The fiery purge of the race.
Her door is always open to suffering; there,
Human morality dissolves in her passion, or in her acts.

The terrible shudder of hesitant love
On bleeding ground, in a hydrogen glare!

Seek out Hortense.

DEMOCRACY

"Toward that intolerable country
   The banner floats along,
And the rattle of the drum is stifled
   By our rough backcountry shouting . . ."

"In the metropolis we will feed
   The most cynical whoring.
We will destroy all logical revolt."

"On to the languid scented lands!
   Let us implement industrial
And military exploitations."
"Goodbye to all this, and never mind where.
   Conscripts of good intention,
We will have policies unnamable and animal.
   Knowing nothing of science, depraved in our pleasures,
To hell with the world around us rolling . . .

   "This is the real advance!
                     Forward . . .
                              March!"

HISTORIC EVENING

All in some night, let's say, where a simple tourist stands
Rescued from our economic nightmares,

The hand of a master wakes the pastoral harpsichord,
The face of the pond remembers queens and courtesans,
And beneath its glass the game of cards goes on—
Saints and sails, strung against the sunset,
Threads of harmony and half-forgotten iridescence.

He trembles at the passing of hunts and hordes.

Dribblings of comedy on platforms of grass . . .
The hesitations of paupers and cripples on these stupid stages!

Before his captive vision,
Germany schemes its way toward the heavens,
The deserts of Tartary lie, transformed with light,
The heart of the Celestial Empire crawls with ancient revolts;
On stairways and armchairs of rock, a pale flat world,
Africa and Occidents, will rise.

And a ballet of oceans and nights remembered,
Worthless chemistry, impossible melodies.

At every place the stagecoach stops,
The same bourgeois magic!

The youngest physicists understand
That we can no longer submit to an atmosphere so personal,
To this mist of physical remorse,
Whose very diagnosis is a sickness itself.

No! This is the time of the sweat bath, of oceans boiling over,
Of underground explosions, of the planet whirled away,
Of exterminations sure to follow;
Certainties only vaguely indicated in the Bible,
—Or by the Norns—
Which the serious man will be asked to observe.

Though the entire effect will be scarcely one of legend!

VERLAINE TO RIMBAUD

*At the café La Closerie des Lilas
Paris, April 2, 1872*

Friend,

The *Ariette oubliée* is charming, words and music! I had it worked out and sung! Thanks for such a sweet gift!

As for the other things you say you'll send, do it *by mail*, still to Batignolles, rue Lecluse. First find out about the charges, and if you haven't got the money, let me know and I'll send it in stamps or a money order (care of Bretagne). I'll get very busy selling stuff and make some money—send it to you, or keep it till we see each other—whichever you let me know.

And thanks for your beautiful letter! The *little boy* accepts the spanking he deserves, the *toad's friend* takes back everything he said—and never having forgotten your martyrdom, he thinks about it, if possible, with more *fervor* and even more joy, you know he does, Rimb.

You're right: just love me, protect me and trust me. I am very weak, and very much in need of kindness. And just as I won't mess you up any more by carrying on like a little boy, so I won't bother our venerable Priest with all this any more;—and promise him soon soon soon a real letter, with pictures and other good stuff.

You've probably already got my letter on the pink onionskin and prob'ly answered it. I'll go tomorrow to my usual *General Delivery* to pick up your probable letter and answer it. But *when* will we start this *Way of the Cross*, eh?

Gavroche and I spent today moving your things. Your clothes, your pictures and little movables are in safety. Anyway, you're still paid up at rue Campe for another week. I've kept—until you get back—the red crayon drawing of the two dykes, which I intend to put in the black frame the doctor's *Camaieu* is in. So you see, you are taken care of, and wanted. We'll see each other soon—either here or somewhere.

And everything here is yours.

P.V.

still the same address

Shit on Mérat, Chanal, Périn, Guérin! also on Laura! The late Carjat sends his love.

Tell me about Favart, by the way.

Gavroche will write you *ex imo*.

VERLAINE TO RIMBAUD

Paris, April, 1872

Rimbaud,

Thanks for your letter, and *hosannah* for your "prayer," OF COURSE, *We'll see each other again!* When?—Wait a bit! Hard necessity! Stern circumstances! That's all right! And shit on some, shit on others! And like shit on me! And on you!

But send me your "bad" (!!!!) poems, your prayers (!!!!) and just keep sempiternally in touch with me—while waiting for something better, after patching up my marriage. And write to me, right away, care of Bretagne, either from Charleville or from Nancy. M. Auguste Bretagne, 11 rue Mervinelle.

And never believe I've abandoned you!

Remember! Memento!

Your

P.V.

And write me soon! And send me your old poems and your new prayers.

You will, won't you, Rimbaud?

VERLAINE TO RIMBAUD

Paris, May, 1872

My very dear Rimb,

Yours in hand asking for assurance, granted with a thousand thanks, and (I'm mad with joy to be almost sure of it) this time *without fail*. And so until Saturday, at about seven still, isn't it? Anyway, to have leeway, and me to send the money in time.

Meanwhile, any letters about the martyrdom care of my mother; any letters about getting back together, being careful, etc. . . . care of L. Forain, 17 quai d'Anjou, Hotel Lauzun, Paris, Seine (for P. Verlaine).

Tomorrow I hope to write you at last that I got the Job (it's with an insurance company).

Didn't see Gavroche yesterday, tho' supposed to. I'm writing this at the café Cluny (3 o'clock), waiting. We're working up a *luvly vingince* on you know who. As soon as you get back, little as it's likely to amuse you, *tigerish* things will start happening. The gentleman in question hasn't lost any time during your three months in the hills and my six months of shit. You'll see what I mean!

Write me care of Gavroche and let me know what I'm supposed to do, what kind of a life you think we ought to lead, what joy, what agony, little secrets, cynicism are going to be necessary! I, me, all yours, all you—you know it!—write it care of Gavroche.

Care of my mother, your martyrdom letters, without the slightest allusion to getting together again.

One last thing: as soon as you get back, take a firm grip on me right away so there'll be no slipping—and you can do that so well!

Be careful!

Do what you can, at least for a while, to look less of a terror than before: *clean shirt, shoeshine, comb your hair, watch your manners.* All necessary if you get involved in the tigerish affairs. I'll be laundry-woman and shoeshine boy, too . . . (if you want).

(Which projects, by the way, if you get involved, will be very useful to us, because *"a Mr. Big in Madrid"* is *interested*—and *security very good!*

For now, stay well, see you, joy, expect letters, expect You. Dreamed twice this very night: *You, the child-martyrer,—You, all goldez.** Funny, isn't it, Rimb!

Before I seal this, I'll wait for Gavroche. Will he come? Will he stand me up? (Back in a few minutes!)

4 o'clock afternoon

Gavroche came, left for safer ground. He'll write you.

Your old

P.V.

Keep writing me from your hills, I'll write you from my shit.
Why not shit on H. Regnault while you're at it?

RIMBAUD TO ERNEST DELAHAYE

*Parishit
Junphe, '72*

My friend,

Yes, surprising indeed is existence in the Arduan cosmorama. The country, where you are raised on starchy food and mud, drink the local wine and homemade beer; I don't miss it. So you're right to denounce it continually. But this place here—distillation, compromise, all possible narrowness; and suffocating summer: the heat is not especially constant, but when I see that people profit from good weather, and that people are pigs, I hate summer. It destroys me when it appears at all. I'm as thirsty as if I had gangrene: the streams of the Ardennes, the Belgian streams, the caves, these are the things I miss.

---

*English for *doré*; I forgot you know as little of that language as I do.

But there is one watering spot here that I like better. Long live the Absinthe Academy, in spite of nasty remarks from waiters! It is the most delicate, the most precarious adornment, to be drunk on the magic of that herb from the glaciers, absumphe! But only to lie down afterward in shit!

Still the same complaint, I guess. Whatever happens, though, shit on Perrin. And on the bar at the café Universe, whether it faces the square or not. I do not, however, curse the Universe itself. I do hope very strongly that the Ardennes are occupied and more and more unreasonably oppressed. But there's nothing new about that.

What is serious is that you are depressed so often. Perhaps you would do better to walk a lot and read. Better in any case not to shut yourself up in the office or the house. Degradation should go on far away from places like that. I know I have no balm for sale, but I don't think that habit offers any consolation on very bad days.

I work at night now. From midnight to five in the morning. Last month, my room on rue Monsieur-le-Prince opened out on the garden of the Lycée St. Louis. There were enormous trees beneath my narrow window. At three in the morning the candle grew pale; all the birds cried out at once in the trees: and that's that. No more work. I had to look out at the trees, at the sky, held by that indescribable hour, the first hour of morning. I could see the dormitories of the lycée, absolutely still. And already the delightful, echoing, staccato sound of wagons on the boulevards. I used to smoke my pipe and spit onto the roof tiles—my room was in the attic. At five o'clock I'd go down to buy bread. Workmen were on the move, everywhere. That was the time I used to go get drunk in the bars. I would go back to my room to eat, and go to bed at seven in the morning, just as the sun was beginning to make the termites crawl out from under the tiles. Early morning in summer, and evenings in December; those are the times that have always enchanted me here.

But at the moment I have a very nice room, looking out on a bottomless courtyard—but only three meters square. Rue Victor Cousin runs into the Place de la Sorbonne beside the café du Bas-Rhin, and opens onto rue Soufflot at the other end. Here I drink water all night long, I can't watch the morning, I can't sleep, I suffocate. And that's that.

Of course your claims will be honored! Don't forget to shit on the *Renaissance,* that journal of literary and artistic endeavor, if you come cross it. So far I've avoided émigré Charlevillains, the pests. Shit on seasons, and colrage.

Courage.

A.R.
rue Victor Cousin
Hotel de Cluny

RIMBAUD TO ERNEST DELAHAYE

Laitou [*Roche*]
[*Canton d'Attigny*]
May, '73

Dear Friend,

What a shit hole! And what monsters of innacince, these peasants! You have to go more than two leagues to get a drink or two at night. *La mother* has got me into a hell of a hole this time. I don't know how to get out of it—I will though, somehow. I miss that godawful Charlestown, the café Universe, the library, etc. I am working fairly regularly, though; I'm doing some little prose stories; general title: The Pagan Book, or the Nigger Book. It's stupid and innocent. O innocence! innocence, innocence, inno . . . shit!

Verlaine has probably given you the unfortunate job of parleying with Devin, the printer of the *Nóress.* I think this Devin could do Verlaine's book fairly cheaply and perhaps even correctly. (As long as he doesn't use the shitty type he uses for his newspaper. He'd be quite capable of sticking in a couple of ads!)

I haven't anything more to tell you; the contemplostation of nature assorbs me entirely. Nature, O my mother, I am yours!

Very best, hoping to see you soon—I'm doing what I can to make it as soon as possible.

R

I've reopened my letter. Verlaine has evidently proposed a rendez-vol on Sunday the 18th, in Boulion. I can't go. If you do, he will probably give you some prose pieces of mine or his, to return to me.

Mother Rimb. will return to Charlestown sometime in June. That's for sure, and I'll try to spend a little time in that lovely spot.

The sun is killing, and still it freezes mornings. I went to see the Prussmares the day before yesterday at Vouziers, a town of 10,000 about seven kms. from here. That livened me up a bit.

I'm at my wits' end. Not a book, not a bar anywhere near here; nothing goes on in the streets. What a horror the French countryside is. My fate depends on this book, for which a half a dozen stories still have to be thought up. How do you go about thinking up atrocities here? I can't send you any of the stories although I already have three, *it costs too much!* And that's that!

Very best, you'll see it someday.

RIMB.

I'll send you a money order soon to buy and send me Goethe's *Faust*, Pop. Library. It shouldn't cost much to ship. Let me know if there are any translations of Shakespeare among the new books in that series.

If you could even just send me the latest catalog, do.

R.

VERLAINE TO RIMBAUD

Boglione, Sunday the 18th
[*May, 1873*]

Friend,

Thanks for your English lesson; hard but just. You know, I'm *asleep*. It's all sleepwalking, these *thine*, these *ours*, these *theirs*; it's stupidity caused by boredom, by having to use these filthy auxiliary verbs, *to do, to have,* instead of a more expressive analogy. For example, I still defend my *How* at the beginning. The line is:

Mais qu'est-ce qu'ils ont donc à dire que c'est laid?

I still can't find anything except *How!* (which is a kind of astonished exclamation anyway) to get that across. *Laid* seems fairly well rendered by *foul*. Also, how to translate:

Ne ruissellent-ils pas de tendresse et de lait? if not:

Do not stream by fire and milk?

At least that's what it seems to me after ample contrition for carrying on like a fucking fairy godmother (Delatrichine couldn't have thought that one up!).

Arrived here at noon, in the driving rain, on foot. Found no sign of Deléclanche. Am leaving by stagecoach. Had dinner with a Frenchman from Sedan and a tall kid from the Charleville school. Somber feast! However, Badingue is dragging in shit, which is a source of some delight in this bastardly country.

Little brother, I've got lots of things to tell you, but it's already two o'clock and the coach is getting ready to leave. Maybe tomorrow I'll write you about all of my plans, literary and otherwise. You'll be pleased with your old sow. (Screw you, Delamorue!)

For the moment, a big hug and I count on seeing you very soon—I hope this week, as you mention. As soon as you let me know, I'll be there.

Mon frère (*brother,* plainly), I live in hope. Everything goes well. You'll be pleased.

Soon, won't it be? Write soon. Send *Explanade*. You'll have your prose pieces soon.

I remain your *old cunt, open* . . . *or opened,* I'm not sure of my irregular verbs in English yet.

P.V.

Got a letter from Lepelletier (business); he's taking care of ROMANCES—Claye and Lechevallier. Tomorrow I'll send him the manuss.

And tighten them up all over again.

P.V.

Excuse this stupid and *rott lett*. A little drunk. Besides, the penpoint is broken and my pipe is stopped up.

VERLAINE TO RIMBAUD

at sea [*July 3, 1873*]

Friend,

I don't know if you'll still be in London when you get this. But I have to tell you that you must, *thoroughly* understand, *finally*, that I absolutely had to leave, that this life of violence, full of scenes with no motive but your imagination, no longer means a fucking thing to me!

Only, as I used to love you immensely (Honni soit qui mal y pense!) I also want to make you understand that, if three days from now I'm not *right* with my wife, in every respect, I'm going to blow my brains out. Three days in a hotel and a *rivolvita* costs a lot: that's why I was stingy this afternoon. You should have pardoned me.

If, as is only too probable, I have to pull off this last asshole stunt, I will at least do it like a brave asshole. My last thought, friend, will be for you, for you who called me a stone this afternoon, and I didn't want to argue with you, because *I have to die*. FINALLY!

Don't you want me to kiss you when I'm dying?

Your poor
P. VERLAINE

We won't see each other again, in any case. If my wife does come, I'll send you my address, and I hope that you'll write. In the meantime, for the next thee days, *no more, no less,* General Delivery, Brussels, in my name. Give Barrère back his three books.

RIMBAUD TO VERLAINE

London
Friday afternoon
[*July 4, 1873*]

Come back, come back, my dear, my only friend, come back. I swear to you I'll be good. If I was mad at you, it was a joke I carried too far, and I'm sorry for it, more than I can say. Come back, we'll forget the whole thing. It's awful that you should have taken that joke seriously. I haven't stopped crying for two days. Come back. Be brave, dear friend; nothing is lost. All you have to do is make the trip again. We'll live here again very bravely and very patiently. Oh! I beg you, it's for your own good, really. Come back, you'll find all your things here. I hope you realize now that there was nothing serious in our discussion. What a horrible moment! And that time when I waved at you to get off the boat, why didn't you? We've lived together for two years, and this is what it's come to! What are you going to do? If you won't come back here, do you want me to come meet you where you are?

Yes, I'm the one who was wrong. Oh!

Oh! You won't forget me, tell me you won't.

No, you can't forget me.

I have you always with me.

Tell me, answer your friend, aren't we ever going to live together again?

Be brave. Write me an answer right away.

I can't stay here anymore.

Don't listen to anything except your heart.

Quick, tell me if I should come to meet you.

Yours for the rest of my life.

RIMBAUD

Answer right away; I can't stay here beyond Monday evening. I haven't got a penny left; I can't even mail this. I've left your books and manuscripts with Vermesch.

If I can't see you again, I'll join the navy or the army.

Oh, come back, I keep crying all the time. Tell me to come to meet you, I'll come. Tell me; send me a telegram. I must leave Monday night. Where are you going? What are you going to do?

RIMBAUD TO VERLAINE

London
July 5, 1873

Dear friend,

I have your letter dated "at sea." You're wrong, this time. Very wrong. First of all, not a thing positive in your letter. Your wife won't come, or will come in three months, or maybe three years, how should I know? As for shooting yourself, I know you. You'll go around waiting for your wife and for death, wandering all over the place getting in people's way. My God! Haven't you realized yet that all this anger was as phony on one side as on the other? But you're the one who would be wrong in the end, because you keep on persisting in your phony feelings, even after I called you back. Do you think life would be any more fun with other people than with me? *Think it over!*—of course not!

I'm the only one you can be free with. And since I promise to be nice in the future, since I'm sorry for my part in these misunderstandings, since my mind, frankly, is quite clear, and since I am extremely fond of you, then if you won't come back, or if you don't want me to join you, you are committing a crime, and *you will be sorry for it for* MANY YEARS *because you will lose all your liberty, and get troubles that may be worse* than any you've gone through so far. After that, remember what you were before you met me.

In any case, I'm not going home to my mother's. I'm going to Paris. I'll try to leave here by Monday evening. You will have forced me to sell all your clothes, there's nothing else I can do. They aren't sold yet; they won't come to pick them up until Monday morning. If you want to write me in Paris, send in care of L. Forain, 289 rue St. Jacques (for A. Rimbaud). He'll know my address.

I promise you, if your wife comes back I won't compromise you by writing. I'll never write again.

The only honest words are: come back. I want to be with you, I love you. If you listen to this, you will show courage and a sincere mind.

If you don't, then I feel sorry for you.

But I love you, and we will see each other again.

RIMBAUD

8 Great Coll. etc., until Monday evening—or Tuesday noon, if you send for me.

VERLAINE TO MATUSZEWICZ

Brussels, Gen'l Delivery
[July 5, 1873]

My dear friend,

Difficulties, as painful as they were unexpected, have forced me to leave London rather hurriedly. I had to leave Rimbaud a little in the lurch, though it cost me a good deal of suffering frankly (and I don't care what people say), at the same time leaving my books and clothing to have cleaned before going back to France. My wife having refused to come even after a suicide threat by me, I'm going to wait for her until tomorrow noon, but SHE WON'T COME, and I'm beginning to find it a bit stupid to kill myself just like that and I think I'd rather—because I'm so miserable, believe me!—I'd rather join up in the Spanish Republican Volunteers. I'm going tomorrow for that reason to the Spanish Embassy here, and I hope to be gone before long. Would you be kind enough to go *right away* to 8 Gt. College St., Camdentown, to pick up the clothes and the books that Rimbaud won't have wanted—also a rather large stack of manuscripts, notebooks, etc. . . . that he has probably left behind. I beg of you, *especially for the manuscripts,* go right away, immediately, I will be the most grateful bastard in the world—go, I implore you, *as soon as you get this*—and write me by return mail if you can. Tell the landlady (whom I've let know already) that she will receive from me—I'm mailing it tomorrow—a money order for 7 shillings, the price of the 2nd week that I forgot to pay in advance.

And let me know what Rimbaud is doing.

Did he come to see you after I left? Write me about it. I'm vitally concerned (being a real whore, joking aside, eh?) Oh, Christ, it's no longer a joking matter!

So I wait for your answer by return mail, and I'll send you in advance whatever it costs to send the clothes and the manuscripts, as well as my address at that time, since I'm going to get a room for a few days; here starting tomorrow.

Grateful in advance, your friend always,

P. VERLAINE

RIMBAUD TO VERLAINE

[*London,*
July 7, 1873]
Monday noon

My dear friend,

I saw the letter you sent to Mrs. Smith. It's unfortunately too late.

You want to come back to London! You don't know how everyone here would greet you! And the faces Andrieu and the others would make if they saw me with you again! Nevertheless I'll be very courageous. Tell me your idea very honestly. Do you want to come back to

London because of me? And when? Did my letter persuade you? But there's nothing left here in the room. Everything is sold except an overcoat. I got two pounds ten. But the washing is still at the laundry, and I kept a bunch of things for myself: five vests, all the shirts, socks, collars, gloves, and all the shoes. All your books and manuss. are in safe hands. In other words, the only things sold are your pants, black and gray, an overcoat and a vest, the suitcase and a hatbox.

But why don't you write *to me*?

Look, baby, I'm going to stay another week. And you will come, won't you? Tell me the truth. That will show real courage. I hope it's true. Depend on me, I'll behave beautifully.

It's up to you. I'm waiting.

RIMB.

VERLAINE: TELEGRAM TO RIMBAUD

BRUSSELS 8 JULY 1873 8:38 A.M.

VOLUNTEER SPAIN. COME HERE, HOTEL LIEGOIS, LAUNDRY, MANU-SCRIPTS, IF POSSIBLE

VERLAINE

RIMBAUD 8 GT. COLLEGE STREET, LONDON

RIMBAUD: STATEMENT TO THE BRUSSELS POLICE

July 10, 1873 (around 8 P.M.)

For the past year, I have been living in London with M. Verlaine. We wrote for the newspapers and gave lessons in French. His company had become impossible, and I had expressed a desire to return to Paris.

A week ago he left me to come to Brussels, and sent me a telegram to come join him here. I got here two days ago, and went to stay with him and his mother, at no. 1 rue des Brasseurs. I still expressed a desire to return to Paris. He kept telling me:

"All right, leave, and you'll see what will happen!"

This morning he went to buy a revolver next to the Galeries Saint-Hubert, which he showed me when he returned, around noon. We then went together to the Maison des Brasseurs, Grand'Place, where we continued to discuss my departure. When we had returned to where we were staying, around two o'clock, he locked the door and sat down in front of it; then, cocking his revolver, he fired twice and said:

"There! I'll teach you to talk about leaving!"

These shots were fired from a distance of three meters; the first wounded me in the left wrist, the second missed me. His mother was present and gave me first aid. I then went to the Saint-Jean Hospital, where the wound was treated. I was accompanied by Verlaine and his mother. When the treatment was finished, all three of us went back to the hotel. Verlaine still kept telling me not to leave him, to stay with him; but I wouldn't agree and I left around seven o'clock in the evening accompanied by Verlaine and his mother. When we were somewhere near the Place Rouppe, Verlaine went a few paces ahead of me, then he turned back toward me; I saw him put his hand in his pocket to get his revolver; I turned around and ran back the way I had come. I met a policeman and told him what had happened to me and he told Verlaine to come with him to the police station.

If Verlaine had let me go, I would not have brought a complaint against him for shooting me.

A. RIMBAUD

VERLAINE: STATEMENT TO THE BRUSSELS POLICE

July 10, 1873

I arrived in Brussels a week ago, desperately unhappy. I have known Rimbaud for more than a year. I lived with him in London, which I left a week ago to come here to Brussels, in order to be near my affairs, since I am in process of divorce from my wife, who lives in Paris, and who claims that I have immoral relations with Rimbaud.

I wrote to my wife that if she did not come back to me in three days I would blow out my brains; and this is the reason I bought the revolver this morning, next to the Galeries Saint-Hubert, with the case and a box of bullets, for the sum of 23 francs.

After I had arrived in Brussels, I received a letter from Rimbaud who asked me if he could come here to join me. I sent him a telegram saying that I would wait for him, and he arrived two days ago. Today, seeing I was unhappy, he wanted to leave me. I gave in to a moment of madness and shot at him. He did not file a complaint at this time. I went with him and my mother to Saint-Jean Hospital to have his wound treated and we all came back together. Rimbaud wanted to leave no matter what. My mother gave him twenty francs for his trip; and we were on our way to the train station with him when he claimed that I wanted to kill him.

P. Verlaine

VERLAINE: INTERROGATION BY THE COURT

July 11, 1873

Q: Have you ever been convicted of a crime?

A: No. I cannot say exactly what happened yesterday during the day. I had written to my wife, who lives in Paris, to come back to me, and she didn't answer. Also, a friend whom I am very close to joined me here in Brussels two days ago and wanted to leave me to go back to France. All of this drove me to desperation; I bought a revolver in order to kill myself. Returning to my room, I got into a discussion with this friend: in spite of my entreaties, he intended to leave me; in my upset condition I took a shot at him and wounded him in the hand. I then dropped the revolver, and the second shot went off accidentally. I immediately regretted very bitterly what I had done; my mother and I took Rimbaud to the hospital to be treated; the wound was only superficial. In spite of my insisting, he persisted in his decision to return to France. Last evening we went with him to the railway station. On the way I renewed my entreaties; I even stepped in front of him, as if to stop him from continuing, and I threatened to kill myself; he may have thought that I was threatening him, but that was not what I had in mind.

Q: What is the reason for your presence in Brussels?

A: I was hoping that my wife would come to join me here, as she had previously done since we have been separated.

Q: I do not understand how the departure of a friend could drive you to desperation. Does there not exist between you and Rimbaud a relationship other than that of friends?

A: No; that is a calumny which was made up by my wife and her family to harm me; I was accused of that in the testimony presented to the court by my wife in support of her suit for divorce.

I hereby certify that the above statements are correct to the best of my knowledge.

Signed:

P. VERLAINE

RIMBAUD: TESTIMONY BEFORE THE COURT

July 12, 1873

I met Verlaine, about two years ago, in Paris. Last year, after a difference of opinion with his wife and her family, he suggested that I go abroad with him; we would have to earn our living in some way or other, since I have no personal income, and Verlaine has only the income from his writing and some money that his mother gives him. We came together to Brussels during the month of July last year; we stayed here for about two months; seeing that we could find no work here we went to London. We lived there together until very recently, occupying the same lodgings and sharing everything in common.

As the result of a discussion that we had at the beginning of last week, a discussion that began when I reproached him for his laziness and the way he treated certain acquaintances of ours, Verlaine left me unexpectedly, without even telling me where he was going. I supposed, however, that he was going to Brussels, or that he would pass through there, since he took the boat for Antwerp. I then received a letter from him dated "at sea" which I will give you, in which he announced that he was going to ask his wife to come back to him, and that if she didn't reply to his request in three days, he was going to kill himself; he told me also to write to him care of General Delivery at Brussels. I then wrote him two letters in which I asked him to return to London or to agree to let me come to join him in Brussels. That was when he sent me a telegram to come here, to Brussels. I wanted us to get back together again, because we had no reason for splitting up.

So I left London; I arrived in Brussels on Tuesday morning, and met Verlaine. His mother was with him. He had no definite plans; he did not want to stay in Brussels because he was afraid there would be no work for him here; as far as I was concerned, I did not want to return to London, as he kept suggesting to me, because our departure must have produced a very disagreeable impression in the minds of our friends, and I made up my mind to go back to Paris. At one minute Verlaine would express a desire to go back with me, as he said, to go take care of his wife and his in-laws as they deserved; the next minute he would refuse to accompany me, because Paris had too many sad memories for him. He was in a state of extreme hysteria. However, he kept insisting very strongly that I stay with him: one minute he was in despair, the next in a fury. There was no sense in his thoughts. Wednesday evening he drank to excess and became intoxicated. Thursday morning he went out at six o'clock and didn't come back until almost noon; he was once again in a state of intoxication, and showed me a pistol he had bought, and when I asked him what he intended to do with it, he answered jokingly: "It's for you, for me, for everybody!" He was terribly keyed up.

While we were together in our room, he went out several times to have a drink; he still wanted to prevent me from carrying out my plan to go back to Paris. I remained determined to go. I even asked his mother for money for the trip. Then, at a certain point, he locked the door that led onto the landing, and sat down on a chair against that door. I was standing with my back up against the opposite wall. He said to me then: "This is for you, since you're leaving!" or something like that; he pointed his pistol at me and fired a shot that hit me in the left wrist; the first shot was immediately followed by a second, but this time the weapon was no longer pointed at me, but lowered toward the floor.

Verlaine immediately expressed the most profound despair at what he had done; he rushed into the adjoining room, the one occupied by his mother, and threw himself on the bed. He was acting like a madman: he pushed the pistol into my hands and wanted me to shoot him in the temple. His attitude was one of profound sorrow over what had happened.

Around five o'clock in the evening, his mother and he took me to be treated. When we got back to the hotel, Verlaine and his mother suggested that I stay with them to recuperate, or go back to the hospital until the wound was healed. The wound seemed very slight to me, and I announced my decision to go to France that very evening, to Charleville, to my mother's. This news drove Verlaine again to desperation. His mother gave me twenty francs for the trip, and they went out with me to take me to the station.

Verlaine was like crazy. He did everything he could to hold me back; also, he had his hand constantly in the pocket of his suit where his pistol was. When we got to the Place Rouppe, he went several paces ahead of us, and then turned around to face me. His posture made me afraid that he might get violent again. I turned around and ran away. That was when I begged the policeman to arrest him.

The bullet that struck my hand hasn't yet been extracted; the doctor here told me that it could be done only after two or three days.

Q: On what did you live in London?

A: Mostly on the money that Mme. Verlaine sent to her son. We also had French lessons that we gave together, but these lessons didn't bring in much, a dozen francs a week, toward the end.

Q: Are you aware of the reasons for the difference of opinion between Verlaine and his wife?

A: Verlaine did not want his wife to go on living at her father's.

Q: Did she not list as a reason as well your intimacy with Verlaine?

A: Yes, she even accused us of immoral practices; but I will not take the trouble to deny such a calumny.

I hereby certify the above statements to be true to the best of my knowledge.

Signed:

A. RIMBAUD

VERLAINE: FURTHER INTERROGATION BY THE COURT

July 18, 1873

I cannot tell you more than I did in my first interrogation about my motive for shooting Rimbaud. I was at that moment in a complete state of intoxication and could no longer reason. It is true that on the advice of my friend Mourot I had for a moment renounced my plan of suicide; I had decided to enlist as a volunteer in the Spanish army; but as my attempt to do so at the Spanish embassy had led to nothing, my thoughts turned again to suicide. It was in this state of mind that I bought my revolver on Thursday during the morning. I loaded the weapon in a bar on the rue des Chartreux; I had gone to this street to visit a friend.

I do not remember having had with Rimbaud an angry discussion which could have caused the act of which I am accused. My mother, whom I have seen since my arrest, told me that I had thought of going to Paris to try to make a last attempt at reconciliation with my wife, and that I was desirous of not having Rimbaud come with me; but I personally have no recollection of that. Anyway, during the days which preceded the shooting, my ideas were confused and completely lacking in logic.

If I sent for Rimbaud by telegram, it was not to go back to living with him again; at the moment I sent the telegram, I intended to enlist in the Spanish army; it was rather to say goodbye to him.

I remember that on Thursday evening, I attempted to keep Rimbaud in Brussels; but in so doing I was moved by feelings of sorrow and the desire to prove to him by my attitude that there had been nothing intentional in the act I had committed. I felt further that his wound should be completely cured before going back to France.

I hereby certify that the above statements are true to the best of my knowledge.

Signed:

P. VERLAINE

RIMBAUD: FURTHER TESTIMONY BEFORE THE COURT

July 18, 1873

I adhere to the statements that I made recently, that is, that before firing his revolver at me, Verlaine had made all kinds if entreaties for me to stay with him. It is true that at one moment he showed a desire to go to Paris to attempt a reconciliation with his wife, and that he wanted to stop me from coming with him; but he constantly kept changing his mind, he couldn't decide on a single plan. Thus I can find no serious motive for his shooting me. Anyway, his mind was completely confused; he was in a state of intoxication, he had been drinking in the morning, as he generally does, by the way, when he is left to himself.

The revolver bullet was extracted from my hand yesterday; the doctor said that in three or four days the wound will have healed.

I intend to return to France, to my mother's who lives in Charleville.

I hereby certify that the above statements are true to the best of my knowledge.

Signed:

A. RIMBAUD

RIMBAUD: ACT OF RENUNCIATION

Saturday, July 19, 1873

I, Arthur Rimbaud, 19 years of age, writer, residing at Charleville (Ardennes, France), do hereby declare, and certify as the truth, that on Thursday past, the 10th, around two o'clock, at the moment when M. Paul Verlaine, in his mother's room, fired a revolver at me and wounded me superficially in the left wrist, M. Verlaine was in such a state of intoxication that he was unaware of his actions;

that I am thoroughly convinced that when he purchased the weapon, M. Verlaine had no hostile intentions toward me, and that there was no criminal premeditation in the fact that he had locked the door of the room;

that the cause of M. Verlaine's intoxication was simply the thought of his difficulties with Mme. Verlaine, his wife.

I declare furthermore that I desist of my own free will from any criminal, civil, or correctional proceedings, and I renounce as of today all profit in any action that may or might be brought by the public Ministry against M. Verlaine in the present case.

A. RIMBAUD

BY ORDER OF THE COURT

Brussels
August 8, 1873

M. Paul Verlaine is hereby sentenced to two hundred francs fine and two years at hard labor on a charge of assault and battery.

SIXTH SEASON

The Damned Soul

"A hard night! Dried blood smokes
on my face, and nothing lies behind
me but that repulsive little tree! The battle
for the soul is as brutal as the battles
of men; but the sight of justice is
the pleasure of God alone."

A SEASON IN HELL

Here is *A Season in Hell*, the book that Rimbaud wrote that summer of 1873 in the country. He had it published in the fall, but no one read it. He couldn't afford to pay the printer, and it stayed in the cellar of the print shop for twenty-eight years. A few author's copies Rimbaud sent to Verlaine, to other friends.

Some of *A Season in Hell* was written before the scenes in Brussels, some of it after. Rimbaud wrote to Delahaye in May 1873, from his mother's farm: "I am working fairly regularly, though; I'm doing some little prose stories; general title: The Pagan Book, or the Nigger Book. It's stupid and innocent. . . . My fate depends upon this book, for which a half a dozen stories still have to be thought up. How do you go about thinking up atrocities here? I can't send you any of the stories although I already have three, *it costs too much!*" The atrocities were to come later that summer, in London and Brussels.

A Season in Hell has literary precedents: It is a set of philosophical meditations, a confessional handbook, a mystical vision of the Soul. But it wakes new vibrations in its style: a nervous, compacted, often vernacular use of poetic language in prose. It is, as Rimbaud said, "absolutely modern."

The two main preoccupations of the work seem reasonably to reflect the interruption in the writing caused by the two months with Verlaine in London and Brussels. Earlier parts, his Pagan, Nigger Book, attempt to relate bourgeois capitalism, bourgeois science, and the bourgeois Christianity of the nineteenth century to some fundamental innocence to be found in past history and past time, and in the non-Western world of the East, or Africa; to come to terms with personal salvation in historical terms. Onto this is projected all the trauma of his break with Verlaine—a break that was physical, moral, and artistic, clearly and brutally defined. The effect of the amalgamation of these two subjects into a single work reinforces the idea of a struggle to deal with a past—to reject a style of living, a way of writing, a kind of experience, and to accept a new, more difficult, but more honest way of ordering existence. The opening and closing metaphor of *A Season in Hell* is battle, and victory. In the profoundest sense, we are reading the notes of an addict's withdrawal and his attempted cure.

An addiction to Verlaine, to alcohol, to the life of an "artist" and to "artistic" poetry, to mystical flights, to occultism—to all consideration of "the mind's disorder as a sacred thing." And underlying all, a rejection of the pose of revolt, of the pretensions of the rebel. "I am sent back to the soil, to seek some obligation. . . ." The rest of his life was to be a search for that obligation.

A Season in Hell

"ONCE, IF MY MEMORY SERVES ME WELL"

Once, if my memory serves me well, my life was a banquet where every heart revealed itself, where every wine flowed.

One evening I took Beauty in my arms—and I thought her bitter—and I insulted her.

I steeled myself against justice.

I fled. O witches, O misery, O hate, my treasure was left in your care . . .

I have withered within me all human hope. With the silent leap of a sullen beast, I have downed and strangled every joy.

I have called for executioners; I want to perish chewing on their gun butts. I have called for plagues, to suffocate in sand and blood. Unhappiness has been my god. I have lain down in the mud, and dried myself off in the crime-infested air. I have played the fool to the point of madness.

And springtime brought me the frightful laugh of an idiot.

Now recently, when I found myself ready to *croak!* I thought to seek the key to the banquet of old, where I might find an appetite again.

That key is Charity. (This idea proves I was dreaming!)

"You will stay a hyena, etc. . . . ," shouts the demon who once crowned me with such pretty poppies. "Seek death with all your desires, and all selfishness, and all the Seven Deadly Sins."

Ah, I've taken too much of that: still, dear Satan, don't look so annoyed, I beg you! And while waiting for a few belated cowardices, since you value in a writer all lack of descriptive or didactic flair, I pass you these few foul pages from the diary of a Damned Soul.

BAD BLOOD

From my ancestors the Gauls I have pale blue eyes, a narrow brain, and awkwardness in competition. I think my clothes are as barbaric as theirs. But I don't butter my hair.

The Gauls were the most stupid hide-flayers and hay-burners of their time.

From them I inherit: idolatry, and love of sacrilege—oh, all sorts of vice; anger, lechery—terrific stuff, lechery—lying, above all, and laziness.

I have a horror of all trades and crafts. Bosses and workers, all of them peasants, and common. The hand that holds the pen is as good as the one that holds the plow. (What a century for hands!) I'll never learn to use my hands. And then, domesticity goes too far. The propriety of beggary shames me. Criminals are as disgusting as men without balls; I'm intact, and I don't care.

But who has made my tongue so treacherous, that until now it has counseled and kept me in idleness? I have not used even my body to get along. Out-idling the sleepy toad, I have lived everywhere. There's not one family in Europe that I don't know. Families, I mean, like mine, who owe their existence to the Declaration of the Rights of Man. I have known each family's eldest son!

If only I had a link to some point in the history of France!
But instead, nothing.

I am well aware that I have always been of an inferior race. I cannot understand revolt. My race has never risen, except to plunder: to devour like wolves a beast they did not kill.

I remember the history of France, the Eldest Daughter of the Church. I would have gone, a village serf, crusading to the Holy Land; my head is full of roads in the Swabian plains, of the sight of Byzantium, of the ramparts of Jerusalem; the cult of Mary, the pitiful thought of Christ crucified, turns in my head with a thousand profane enchantments—I sit like a leper among broken pots and nettles, at the

foot of a wall eaten away by the sun. —And later, a wandering merce-
nary, I would have bivouacked under German nighttimes.

Ah! one thing more: I dance the Sabbath in a scarlet clearing, with
old women and children.

I don't remember much beyond this land, and Christianity. I will
see myself forever in its past. But always alone, without a family; what
language, in fact, did I used to speak? I never see myself in the councils
of Christ; nor in the councils of the Lords, Christ's representatives.
What was I in the century past? I only find myself today. The vaga-
bonds, the hazy wars are gone. The inferior race has swept over all—
the People (as they put it), Reason; Nation and Science.

Ah, Science! Everything is taken from the past. For the body and
the soul—the last sacrament—we have Medicine and Philosophy,
household remedies and folk songs rearranged. And royal entertain-
ments, and games that kings forbid. Geography, Cosmography,
Mechanics, Chemistry! . . .

Science, the new nobility! Progress! The world moves! . . . And why
shouldn't it?

We have visions of numbers. We are moving toward the *Spirit*. What
I say is oracular and absolutely right. I understand . . . and since I
cannot express myself except in pagan terms, I would rather keep
quiet.

Pagan blood returns! The Spirit is at hand . . . why does Christ not
help me, and grant my soul nobility and freedom? Ah, but the Gospel
belongs to the past! The Gospel. The Gospel . . .

I wait gluttonously for God. I have been of inferior race for ever
and ever.

And now I am on the beaches of Brittany. . . . Let cities light their
lamps in the evening; my daytime is done, I am leaving Europe. The
air of the sea will burn my lungs; lost climates will turn my skin to
leather. To swim, to pulverize grass, to hunt, above all to smoke; to
drink strong drinks, as strong as molten ore, as did those dear ancestors around their fires.

I will come back with limbs of iron, with dark skin, and angry eyes:
in this mask, they will think I belong to a strong race. I will have gold;

I will be brutal and indolent. Women nurse these ferocious invalids come back from the tropics. I will become involved in politics. Saved.

Now I am accursed, I detest my native land. The best thing is a drunken sleep, stretched out on some strip of shore.

But no one leaves. Let us set out once more on our native roads, burdened with my vice—that vice that since the age of reason has driven roots of suffering into my side—that towers to heaven, beats me, hurls me down, drags me on.

Ultimate innocence, final timidity. All's said. Carry no more my loathing and treacheries before the world.

Come on! Marching, burdens, the desert, boredom and anger.

Hire myself to whom? What beast adore? What sacred images destroy? What hearts shall I break? What lie maintain? Through what blood wade?

Better to keep away from justice. A hard life, outright stupor—with a dried-out fist to lift the coffin lid, lie down, and suffocate. No old age this way—no danger: terror is very un-French.

—Ah! I am so forsaken I will offer at any shrine impulses toward perfection.

Oh, my self-denial, my marvelous Charity, my Selfless Love! And still here below!

De profundis, Domine . . . what an ass I am!

When I was still a little child, I admired the hardened convict on whom the prison door will always close; I used to visit the bars and the rented rooms his presence had consecrated; I saw *with his eyes* the blue sky and the flower-filled work of the fields; I followed his fatal scent through city streets. He had more strength than the saints, more sense than any explorer—and he, he alone! was witness to his glory and his rightness.

Along the open road on winter nights, homeless, cold, and hungry, one voice gripped my frozen heart: "Weakness or strength: you exist, that is strength. . . . You don't know where you are going or why you are going; go in everywhere, answer everyone. No one will kill you, any more than if you were a corpse." In the morning my eyes were so vacant and my face so dead that the people I met *may not even have seen me.*

In cities, mud went suddenly red and black, like a mirror when a lamp in the next room moves, like treasure in the forest! Good luck, I cried, and I saw a sea of flames and smoke rise to heaven, and left and right all wealth exploded like a billion thunderbolts.

But orgies and the companionship of women were impossible for me. Not even a friend. I saw myself before an angry mob, facing a firing squad, weeping out sorrows they could not understand, and pardoning—like Joan of Arc!—"Priests, professors and doctors, you are mistaken in delivering me into the hands of the law. I have never been one of you; I have never been a Christian; I belong to the race that sang on the scaffold; I do not understand your laws; I have no moral sense; I am a brute: you are making a mistake. . . ."

Yes, my eyes are closed to your light. I am an animal, a nigger. But I can be saved. You are fake niggers; maniacs, savages, misers, all of you. Businessman, you're a nigger; judge, you're a nigger; general, you're a nigger; emperor, old scratch-head, you're a nigger: you've drunk a liquor no one taxes, from Satan's still. This nation is inspired by fever and cancer. Invalids and old men are so respectable that they ask to be boiled. The best thing is to quit this continent where madness prowls, out to supply hostages for these wretches. I will enter the true kingdom of the sons of Ham.

Do I understand nature? Do I understand myself? *No more words.* I shroud dead men in my stomach. . . . Shouts, drums, dance, dance, dance! I can't even imagine the hour when the white men land, and I will fall into nothingness.

Thirst and hunger, shouts, dance, dance, dance, dance!

The white men are landing! Cannons! Now we must be baptized, get dressed, and go to work.

My heart has been stabbed by grace. Ah! I hadn't thought this would happen.

But I haven't done anything wrong. My days will be easy, and I will be spared repentance. I will not have had the torments of the soul half-dead to the Good, where austere light rises again like funeral candles. The fate of a first-born son, a premature coffin covered with shining tears. No doubt, perversion is stupid, vice is stupid; rottenness must always be cast away. But the clock must learn to strike more than hours of pure pain! Am I to be carried away like a child, to play in paradise, forgetting all this misery?

Quick! Are there any other lives? Sleep for the rich is impossible. Wealth has always lived openly. Divine love alone confers the keys of knowledge. I see that nature is only a show of kindness. Farewell chimeras, ideals and errors.

The reasonable song of angels rises from the rescue ship: it is divine love. Two loves! I may die of earthly love, die of devotion. I have left behind creatures whose grief will grow at my going. You choose me from among the castaways; aren't those who remain my friends?

Save them!

I am reborn in reason. The world is good. I will bless life. I will love my brothers. There are no longer childhood promises. Nor the hope of escaping old age and death. God is my strength, and I praise God.

Boredom is no longer my love. Rage, perversion, madness, whose every impulse and disaster I know—my burden is set down entire. Let us appraise with clear heads the extent of my innocence. I am no longer able to ask for the consolation of a beating. I don't imagine I'm off on a honeymoon with Jesus Christ for a father-in-law.

I am no prisoner of my own reason. I have said: God. I want freedom, within salvation: how shall I go about it? A taste for frivolity has left me. No further need for divine love or for devotion to duty. I do not regret the age of emotion and feeling. To each his own reason, contempt, Charity: I keep my place at the top of the angelic ladder of good sense.

As for settled happiness, domestic or not . . . no, I can't. I am too dissipated, too weak. Work makes life blossom, an old idea, not mine; my life doesn't weigh enough, it drifts off and floats far beyond action, that third pole of the world.

What an old maid I'm turning into, to lack the courage to love death!

If only God would grant me that celestial calm, ethereal calm, and prayer—like the saints of old. —The Saints! They were strong! Anchorites, artists of a kind we no longer need. . . .

Does this farce have no end? My innocence is enough to make me cry. Life is the farce we all must play.

Stop it! This is your punishment. . . . *Forward march!*

Ah! my lungs burn, my temples roar! Night rolls in my eyes, beneath this sun! My heart . . . my arms and legs. . . .

Where are we going? To battle? I am weak! the others go on ahead . . . tools, weapons . . . give me time!

Fire! Fire at me! Here! or I'll give myself up! —Cowards! —I'll kill myself! I'll throw myself beneath the horses' hooves!

Ah! . . .

—I'll get used to it.

That would be the French way, the path of honor!

NIGHT IN HELL

I have just swallowed a terrific mouthful of poison. —Blessed, blessed, blessed the advice I was given!

—My guts are on fire. The power of the poison twists my arms and legs, cripples me, drives me to the ground. I die of thirst, I suffocate, I cannot cry. This is Hell, eternal torment! See how the flames rise! I burn as I ought to. Go on, Devil!

I once came close to a conversion to the good and to felicity, salvation. How can I describe my vision; the air of Hell is too thick for hymns! There were millions of delightful creatures in smooth spiritual harmony, strength and peace, noble ambitions, I don't know what all.

Noble ambitions!

But I am still alive! Suppose damnation is eternal! A man who wants to mutilate himself is certainly damned, isn't he? I believe I am in Hell, therefore I am. This is the catechism at work. I am the slave of my baptism. You, my parents, have ruined my life, and your own. Poor child! —Hell is powerless against pagans. —I am still alive! Later on, the delights of damnation will become more profound. A crime, quick, and let me fall to nothingness, condemned by human law.

Shut up, will you shut up! Everything here is shame and reproach—Satan saying that the fire is worthless, that my anger is ridiculous and silly. —Ah, stop! . . . those mistakes someone whispered—magic spells, deceptive odors, childish music—and to think that I possess the truth, that I can have a vision of justice: my judgment is sound and firm, I am prime for perfection. . . . Pride. —My scalp begins to tighten. Have mercy! Lord, I'm afraid! Water, I thirst, I thirst! Ah, childhood, grass and rain, the puddle on the paving stones, *Moonlight, when the clock strikes twelve*. . . . The devil is in the clock tower, right now! Mary! Holy Virgin! . . . —Horrible stupidity.

Look there, are those not honorable men, who wish me well? Come on . . . a pillow over my mouth, they cannot hear me, they are only ghosts. Anyway, no one ever thinks of anyone else. Don't let them come closer. I must surely stink of burning flesh. . . .

My hallucinations are endless. This is what I've always gone through: the end of my faith in history, the neglect of my principles. I shall say no more about this; poets and visionaries would be jealous. I am the richest one of all, a thousand times, and I will hoard it like the sea.

O God—the clock of life stopped but a moment ago. I am no longer within the world. —Theology is accurate; hell is certainly *down below*—and heaven is up on high. Ecstasy, nightmare, sleep, in a nest of flames.

How the mind wanders idly in the country . . . Satan, Ferdinand, blows with the wild seed . . . Jesus walks on purple thorns but doesn't bend them . . . Jesus used to walk on troubled waters. In the light of the lantern we saw him there, all white, with long brown hair, standing in the curve of an emerald wave. . . .

I will tear the veils from every mystery—mysteries of religion or of nature, death, birth, the future, the past, cosmogony, and nothingness. I am a master of phantasmagoria.

Listen!

Every talent is mine! —There is no one here, and there is someone:

I wouldn't want to waste my treasure. —Shall I give you Afric chants, belly dancers? Shall I disappear, shall I begin to attempt to discover the *Ring*? Shall I? I will manufacture gold, and medicines.

Put your faith in me, then; faith comforts, it guides and heals. Come unto me all of you—even the little children—let me console you, let me pour out my heart for you—my miraculous heart! —Poor men, poor laborers! I do not ask for prayers; give me only your trust, and I will be happy.

Think of me, now. All this doesn't make me miss the world much. I'm lucky not to suffer more. My life was nothing but sweet stupidities, unfortunately.

Bah! I'll make all the ugly faces I can! We are out of the world, that's sure. Not a single sound. My sense of touch is gone. Ah, my château, my Saxony, my willow woods! Evenings and mornings, nights and days. . . . How tired I am!

I ought to have a special hell for my anger, a hell for my pride—and a hell for sex; a whole symphony of hells!

I am weary, I die. This is the grave and I'm turning into worms, horror of horrors! Satan, you clown, you want to dissolve me with your charms. Well, I want it. I want it! Stab me with a pitchfork, sprinkle me with fire!

Ah! To return to life! To stare at our deformities. And this poison, this eternally accursèd embrace! My weakness, and the world's cruelty! My God, have pity, hide me, I can't control myself at all! I am hidden, and I am not.

And as the Damned soul rises, so does the fire.

FIRST DELIRIUM: THE FOOLISH VIRGIN
THE INFERNAL BRIDEGROOM

Let us hear the confession of an old friend in Hell:

"O Lord, O Celestial Bridegroom, do not turn thy face from the confession of the most pitiful of thy handmaidens. I am lost. I'm drunk. I'm impure. What a life!

"Pardon, Lord in Heaven, pardon! Ah, pardon! All these tears! And all the tears to come later on, I hope!

"Later on, I will meet the Celestial Bridegroom! I was born to be *His* slave. —That other one can beat me now!

"Right now, it's the end of the world! Oh, girls . . . my friends . . . no, not my friends . . . I've never gone through *anything* like this; delirium, torments, anything. . . . It's so silly!

"Oh, I cry, I'm suffering! I really am suffering! And still I've got a right to do whatever I want, now that I am covered with contempt by the most contemptible hearts.

"Well, let me make my confession anyway, though I may have to repeat it twenty times again—*so* dull, and *so* insignificant!

"I am a slave of the Infernal Bridegroom; the one who seduced the foolish virgins. That's exactly the devil he is. He's no phantom, he's no ghost. But I, who have lost my wits, damned and dead to the world—no one will be able to kill me—how can I describe him to you? I can't even talk anymore! I'm all dressed in mourning, I'm crying, I'm afraid. Please, dear Lord, a little fresh air, if you don't mind, please!

"I am a widow—I used to be a widow—oh, yes, I used to be very serious in those days; I wasn't born to become a skeleton! He was a child—or almost. . . . His delicate, mysterious ways enchanted me. I forgot all my duties in order to follow him. What a life we lead! True life is lacking. We are exiles from this world, really—I go where he goes; I *have* to. And lots of times he gets mad at me—at *me,* poor sinner! That Devil! (He really *is* a Devil, you know, and *not a man.*)

"He says: 'I don't love women. Love has to be reinvented, we know that. The only thing women can ultimately imagine is security. Once they get that, love, beauty, everything else goes out the window. All they have left is cold disdain; that's what marriages live on nowadays. Sometimes I see women who ought to be happy, with whom I could have found companionship, already swallowed up by brutes with as much feeling as an old log. . . .'

"I listen to him turn infamy into glory, cruelty into charm. 'I belong to an ancient race: my ancestors were Norsemen: they slashed their own bodies, drank their own blood. I'll slash my body all over, I'll tattoo myself, I want to be as ugly as a Mongol; you'll see, I'll scream in the streets. I want to go really mad with anger. Don't show me jewels; I'll get down on all fours and writhe on the carpet. I want my wealth stained all over with blood. I will *never* do any work. . . .' Several times, at night, his demon seized me, and we rolled about wrestling! —Sometimes at night when he's drunk he hangs around street corners or behind doors, to scare me to death. 'I'll get my throat cut for sure, won't *that* be disgusting.' And, oh, those days when he wants to go around pretending he's a criminal!

"Sometimes he talks, in his backcountry words, full of emotion, about death, and how it makes us repent, and how surely there are miserable people in the world, about exhausting work, and about saying goodbye and how it tears your heart. In the dives where we used to get drunk, he would cry when he looked at the people around us—cattle of the slums. He used to pick up drunks in the dark streets. He had the pity of a brutal mother for little children. He went around with all the sweetness of a little girl on her way to Sunday school. He pretended to know all about everything—business, art, medicine— and I always went along with him; I had to!

"I used to see clearly all the trappings that he hung up in his imagination; costumes, fabrics, furniture. . . . It was I who lent him weapons, and a change of face. I could visualize everything that affected him, exactly as he would have imagined it for himself. Whenever he seemed depressed, I would follow him into strange, complicated adventures, on and on, into good and evil; but I always knew I could never be a part of his world. Beside his dear body, as he slept, I lay awake hour after hour, night after night, trying to imagine why he wanted so much to escape from reality. No man before had ever had such a desire. I was aware—without being afraid of him—that he could become a serious menace to society. Did he, perhaps, have secrets that would *remake life*? No, I told myself, he was only looking for them. But of course, his charity is under a spell, and I am its prisoner. No one else could have the strength—the strength of despair!—to stand it, to stand being cared for and loved by him. Besides, I could never imagine him with anybody else—we all have eyes for our own Dark Angel, never other people's Angels—at least I think so. I lived in his soul as if it were a palace that had been cleared out so that the most unworthy person in it would be you, that's all. Ah, *really*, I used to depend on him terribly. But what did he want with my dull, my cowardly existence? He couldn't improve me, though he never managed to kill me! I get so sad and disappointed; sometimes I say to him 'I understand you.' He just shrugs his shoulders.

"And so my heartaches kept growing and growing, and I saw myself going more and more to pieces (and everyone else would have seen it, too, if I hadn't been so miserable that no one even looked at me anymore!), and still more and more I craved his affection. . . . His kisses and his friendly arms around me were just like heaven—a dark heaven, that I could go into, and where I wanted only to be left— poor, deaf, dumb, and blind. Already, I was getting to depend on it. I used to imagine that we were two happy children free to wander in a Paradise of sadness. We were in absolute harmony. Deeply moved, we labored side by side. But then, after a piercing embrace, he would say: 'How funny it will all seem, all you've gone through, when I'm not here anymore. When you no longer feel my arms around your shoulders, nor my heart beneath you, nor this mouth on your eyes. Because I will have to go away some day, far away. Besides, I've got to help out others too; that's what I'm here for. Although I won't really like it . . . dear heart. . . .' And in that instant I could feel myself, with him gone, dizzy with fear, sinking down into the most horrible blackness—into death. I made him promise that he would never leave me. And he promised, twenty times; promised like a lover. It was as meaningless as my saying to him: 'I understand you.'

"Oh, I've never been jealous of him. He'll never leave me, I'm sure of it. What will he do? He doesn't know a soul; he'll never work; he wants to live like a sleepwalker. Can his kindness and his charity by themselves give him his place in the real world? There are moments when I forget the wretched mess I've fallen into. . . . He will give me strength; we'll travel, we'll go hunting in the desert, we'll sleep on the sidewalks of unknown cities, carefree and happy. Or else some day I'll wake up and his magic power will have changed all laws and morals, but the world will still be the same and leave me my desires and my joys and my lack of concern. Oh, that wonderful world of adventures that we found in children's books—won't you give me that world? I've suffered so much; I deserve a reward. . . . He can't. I don't know what he *really* wants. He says he has hopes and regrets: but they have nothing to do with me. Does he talk to God? Maybe I should talk to God myself. I am in the depths of the abyss, and I have forgotten how to pray.

"Suppose he did explain his sadness to me—would I understand it any better than his jokes and insults? He attacks me, he spends hours making me ashamed of everything in the world that has ever meant anything to me, and then he gets mad if I cry.

". . . 'Do you see that lovely young man going into that beautiful, peaceful house? His name is Duval, Dufour; . . . Armand, Maurice, whatever you please. There is a woman who has spent her life loving that evil creature; she died. I'm sure she's a saint in heaven right now. You are going to kill me the way he killed that woman. That's what's in store for all of us who have unselfish hearts. . . .' Oh, dear! There were days when all men of action seemed to him like the toys of some grotesque raving. He would laugh, horribly, on and on. Then he would go back to acting like a young mother, or an older sister. . . . If he were not such a wild thing, we would be saved! But even his sweetness is mortal. . . . I am his slave. . . .

"Oh, I've lost my mind!

"Some day maybe he'll just disappear miraculously, but I absolutely must be told about it, I mean if he's going to go back up into heaven or someplace, so that I can go and watch for just a minute the Assumption of my darling boy. . . ."

One hell of a household!

SECOND DELIRIUM: THE ALCHEMY OF THE WORD

My turn now. The story of one of my insanities.

For a long time I boasted that I was master of all possible land-scapes—and I thought the great figures of modern painting and poetry were laughable.

What I liked were: absurd paintings, pictures over doorways, stage sets, carnival backdrops, billboards, bright-colored prints, old-fashioned literature, church Latin, erotic books full of misspellings, the kind of novels our grandmothers read, fairy tales, little children's books, old operas, silly old songs, the naïve rhythms of country rimes.

I dreamed of Crusades, voyages of discovery that nobody had heard of, republics without histories, religious wars stamped out, revolutions in morals, movements of races and of continents; I used to believe in every kind of magic.

I invented colors for the vowels! A black, E white, I red, O blue, U green. I made rules for the form and movement of every consonant, and I boasted of inventing, with rhythms from within me, a kind of poetry that all the senses, sooner or later, would recognize. And I alone would be its translator.

I began it as an investigation. I turned silences and nights into words. What was unutterable, I wrote down. I made the whirling world stand still.

> Far from flocks, from birds and country girls,
> What did I drink within that leafy screen
> Surrounded by tender hazelnut trees
> In the warm green mist of afternoon?
>
> What could I drink from this young Oise
> —Tongueless trees, flowerless grass, dark skies—

Drink from these yellow gourds, far from the hut
I loved? Some golden draught that made me sweat.

I would have made a doubtful sign for an inn.
Later, toward evening, the sky filled with clouds . . .
Water from the woods runs out on virgin sands,
And heavenly winds cast ice thick on the ponds;

Then I saw gold, and wept, but could not drink.

At four in the morning, in summertime,
Love's drowsiness still lasts . . .
The bushes blow away the odor
    Of the night's feast.

Beyond the bright Hesperides,
Within the western workshop of the Sun,
Carpenters scramble—in shirtsleeves—
    Work is begun.

And in desolate, moss-grown isles
They raise their precious panels
            Where the city
    Will paint a hollow sky.

For these charming dabblers in the arts
Who labor for a King in Babylon,
Venus! Leave for a moment
    Lovers' haloed hearts . . .

    O Queen of Shepherds!
Carry the purest eau-de-vie
To these workmen while they rest
And take their bath at noonday, in the sea.

The worn-out ideas of old-fashioned poetry played an important part in my alchemy of the word.

I got used to elementary hallucination: I could very precisely see a mosque instead of a factory, a drum corps of angels, horse carts on the highways of the sky, a drawing room at the bottom of a lake; monsters and mysteries. A vaudeville's title filled me with awe.

And so I explained my magical sophistries by turning words into visions!

At last, I began to consider my mind's disorder a sacred thing. I lay about idle, consumed by an oppressive fever: I envied the bliss of animals—caterpillars, who portray the innocence of a second childhood; moles, the slumber of virginity!

My mind turned sour. I said farewell to the world in poems something like ballads:

A SONG FROM THE HIGHEST TOWER

Let it come, let it come,
The season we can love!

I have waited so long
That at length I forget,
And leave unto heaven
My fear and regret;

A sick thirst
Darkens my veins.

Let it come, let it come,
The season we can love!

So the green field
To oblivion falls,
Overgrown, flowering
With incense and weeds.

And the cruel noise
Of dirty flies.

Let it come, let it come,
The season we can love!

I loved the desert, burnt orchards, tired old shops, warm drinks. I dragged myself through stinking alleys, and with my eyes closed I offered myself to the sun, the god of fire.

"General: If on your ruined ramparts one cannon still remains, shell us with clods of dried-up earth. Shatter the mirrors of expensive shops! And the drawing rooms! Make the city swallow its dust! Turn gargoyles to rust. Stuff boudoirs with rubies' fiery powder. . . ."

Oh, the little fly! Drunk at the urinal of a country inn, in love with rotting weeds; a ray of light dissolves him!

I only find within my bones
A taste for eating earth and stones.
When I feed, I feed on air,
Rocks and coals and iron ore.

My hunger, turn. Hunger, feed:
    A field of bran.
Gather as you can the bright
    Poison weed.

Eat the rocks a beggar breaks,
The stones of ancient churches' walls,
Pebbles, children of the flood,
Loaves left lying in the mud.

Beneath a bush the wolf will howl,
Spitting bright feathers

From his feast of fowl:
Like him, I devour myself.

Waiting to be gathered
Fruits and grasses spend their hours;
The spider spinning in the hedge
Eats only flowers.

Let me sleep! Let me boil
On the altars of Solomon;
Let me soak the rusty soil
And flow into Kedron.

Finally, O reason, O happiness, I cleared from the sky the blue which is darkness, and I lived as a golden spark of this light, Nature. In my delight, I made my face look as comic and as wild as I could:

It is recovered.
What? Eternity.
In the whirling light
Of the sun in the sea.

O my eternal soul,
Hold fast to desire
In spite of the night
And the day on fire.

You must set yourself free
From the striving of Man
And the applause of the World!
You must fly as you can . . .

No hope, forever;
No *orietur*.

Science and patience,
The torment is sure.

The fire within you,
Soft silken embers,
Is our whole duty—
But no one remembers.

It is recovered.
What? Eternity.
In the whirling light
Of the sun in the sea.

I became a fabulous opera. I saw that everyone in the world was doomed to happiness. Action isn't life; it's merely a way of ruining a kind of strength, a means of destroying nerves. Morality is water on the brain.

It seemed to me that everyone should have had several *other* lives as well. This gentleman doesn't know what he's doing; he's an angel. That family is a litter of puppy dogs. With some men, I often talked out loud with a moment from one of their other lives—that's how I happened to love a pig.

Not a single one of the brilliant arguments of madness—the madness that gets locked up—did I forget; I could go through them all again, I've got the system down by heart.

It affected my health. Terror loomed ahead. I would fall again and again into a heavy sleep, which lasted several days at a time, and when I woke up, my sorrowful dreams continued. I was ripe for fatal harvest, and my weakness led me down dangerous roads to the edge of the world, to the Cimmerian shore, the haven of whirlwinds and darkness.

I had to travel, to dissipate the enchantments that crowded my brain. On the sea, which I loved as if it were to wash away my impurity, I watched the compassionate cross arise. I had been damned by the rainbow. Felicity was my doom, my gnawing remorse, my worm.

My life would forever be too large to devote to strength and to beauty.

Felicity! The deadly sweetness of its sting would wake me at cock-crow—*ad matutinum,* at the *Christus venit*—in the somberest of cities.

O seasons, O châteaus!
Where is the flawless soul?

I learned the magic of
Felicity. It enchants us all.

To Felicity, sing life and praise
Whenever Gaul's cock crows.

Now all desire has gone—
It has made my life its own.

That spell has caught heart and soul
And scattered every trial.

O seasons, O châteaus!

And, oh, the day it disappears
Will be the day I die.

O seasons, O châteaus!

All that is over. Today, I know how to celebrate beauty.

THE IMPOSSIBLE

Ah! My life as a child, the open road in every weather; I was unnaturally abstinent, more detached than the best of beggars, proud to have no country, no friends—what stupidity that was!—and only now I realize it!

I was right to distrust old men who never lost a chance for a caress, parasites on the health and cleanliness of our women—today when women are so much a race apart from us.

I was right in everything I distrusted . . . because I am running away!

I am running away!

I'll explain.

Even yesterday, I kept sighing: "God! There are enough of us damned down here! I've done time enough already in their ranks. I know them all. We always recognize each other; we disgust each other. Charity is unheard of among us. Still, we're polite; our relations with the world are quite correct." Is that surprising? The world! Businessmen and idiots!—there's no dishonor in being here—but the company of the elect; how would they receive us? For there are surly people, happy people, the false elect, since we must be bold or humble to approach them. These are the real elect. No saintly hypocrites, these!

Since I've got back two cents' worth of reason—how quickly it goes!—I can see that my troubles come from not realizing soon enough that this is the Western World. These Western swamps! Not that light has paled, form worn out, or movement been misguided. . . . All right! Now my mind wants absolutely to take on itself all the cruel developments that mind has undergone since the Orient collapsed. . . . My mind demands it!

. . . And that's the end of my two cents' worth of reason! The mind is in control, it insists that I remain in the West. It will have to be silenced if I expect to end as I always wanted to.

I used to say, to hell with martyrs' palms, all beacons of art, the inventor's pride, the plunderer's frenzy; I expected to return to the Orient and to original, eternal wisdom. But this is evidently a dream of depraved laziness!

And yet I had no intention of trying to escape from modern suffering—I have no high regard for the bastard wisdom of the Koran. But isn't there a very real torment in knowing that since the dawn of that scientific discovery, Christianity, Man has been making a fool of himself, proving what is obvious, puffing with pride as he repeats his proofs . . . and living on that alone? This is a subtle, stupid torment—and this is the source of my spiritual ramblings. Nature may well be bored with it all! Prudhomme was born with Christ.

Isn't it because we cultivate the fog? We swallow fever with our watery vegetables. And drunkenness! And tobacco! And ignorance! And blind faith! Isn't all this a bit far from the thought, the wisdom of the Orient, the original fatherland? Why have a modern world, if such poisons are invented?

Priests and preachers will say: Of course. But you are really referring to Eden. There is nothing for you in the past history of Oriental races. . . . True enough. It was Eden I meant! How can this purity of ancient races affect my dream?

Philosophers will say: The world has no ages; humanity moves from place to place, that's all. You are a Western man, but quite free to live in your Orient, as old a one as you want . . . and to live in it as you like. Don't be a defeatist. Philosophers, you are part and parcel of your Western world!

Careful, mind. Don't rush madly after salvation. Train yourself! Ah, science never goes fast enough for us!

But I see that my mind is asleep.

—If it stays wide awake from this moment on, we would soon reach the truth, which may even now surround us with its weeping angels! . . .

—If it had been wide awake until this moment, I would have never given in to degenerate instincts, long ago! . . .

—If it had always been wide awake, I would be floating in wisdom! . . .

O Purity! Purity!

In this moment of awakening, I had a vision of purity! Through the mind we go to God!

What a crippling misfortune!

LIGHTNING

Human labor! That explosion lights up my abyss from time to time.

"Nothing is vanity; on toward knowledge!" cries the modern Ecclesiastes, which is *Everyone*. And still the bodies of the wicked and the idle fall upon the hearts of all the rest. . . . Ah, quick, quick, quick! there, beyond the night . . . that future reward, that eternal reward . . . will we escape it?

What more can I do? Labor I know, and science is too slow. That praying gallops and that light roars; I'm well aware of it. It's too simple, and the weather's too hot; you can all do without me. I have my duty; but I will be proud, as others have been, to set it aside.

My life is worn out. Well, let's pretend, let's do nothing; oh, pitiful! And we will exist, and amuse ourselves, dreaming of monstrous loves and fantastic worlds, complaining and quarreling with the appearances of the world, acrobat, beggar, artist, bandit—priest! . . . on my hospital bed, the odor of incense came so strongly back to me . . . guardian of the holy aromatics, confessor, martyr. . . .

There I recognize my filthy childhood education. Then what? . . . turn twenty: I'll do my twenty years, if everyone else does.

No! No! Now I rise up against death! Labor seems too easy for pride like mine: To betray me to the world would be too slight a punishment. At the last moment I would attack, to the right, to the left. . . .

Oh! poor dear soul, eternity then might not be lost!

MORNING

Hadn't I *once* a youth that was lovely, heroic, fabulous—something to write down on pages of gold? . . . I was too lucky! Through what crime, by what fault did I deserve my present weakness? You who imagine that animals sob with sorrow, that the sick despair, that the dead have bad dreams, try now to relate my fall and my sleep. I can explain myself no better than the beggar with his endless Aves and Pater Nosters. *I no longer know how to talk!*

And yet, today, I think I have finished this account of my Hell. And it *was* Hell; the old one, whose gates were opened by the Son of Man.

From the same desert, toward the same dark sky, my tired eyes forever open on the silver star, forever; but the three wise men never stir, the Kings of life, the heart, the soul, the mind. When will we go, over mountains and shores, to hail the birth of new labor, new wisdom, the flight of tyrants and demons, the end of superstition, to be the *first* to adore . . . Christmas on earth!

The song of the heavens, the marching of nations! We are slaves; let us not curse life.

FAREWELL

Autumn already! . . . But why regret the everlasting sun, if we are sworn to a search for divine brightness—far from those who die as seasons turn. . . .

Autumn. Our boat, risen out of hanging fog, turns toward poverty's harbor, the monstrous city, its sky stained with fire and mud. Ah! Those stinking rags, bread soaked with rain, drunkenness, and the thousands of loves who nailed me to the cross! Will there never, ever be an end to that ghoulish queen of a million dead souls and bodies *and who will all be judged!* I can see myself again, my skin corroded by dirt and disease, hair and armpits crawling with worms, and worms still larger crawling in my heart, stretched out among ageless, heartless, unknown figures. . . . I could easily have died there. . . . What a horrible memory! I detest poverty.

And I dread winter because it's so *cozy!*

—Sometimes in the sky I see endless sandy shores covered with white rejoicing nations. A great golden ship, above me, flutters many-colored pennants in the morning breeze. I was the creator of every feast, every triumph, every drama. I tried to invent new flowers, new planets, new flesh, new languages. I thought I had acquired supernatural powers. Ha! I have to bury my imagination and my memories! What an end to a splendid career as an artist and storyteller!

I! I called myself a magician, an angel, free from all moral constraint. . . . I am sent back to the soil to seek some obligation, to wrap gnarled reality in my arms! A peasant!

Am I deceived? Would Charity be the sister of death, for me?

Well, I shall ask forgiveness for having lived on lies. And that's that. But not one friendly hand . . . and where can I look for help?

True; the new era is nothing if not harsh.

For I can say that I have gained a victory; the gnashing of teeth, the hissing of hellfire, the stinking sighs subside. All my monstrous memories are fading. My last longings depart—jealousy of beggars, bandits, friends of death, all those that the world passed by—Damned souls, if I were to take vengeance!

One must be absolutely modern.

Never mind hymns of thanksgiving: hold on to a step once taken. A hard night! Dried blood smokes on my face, and nothing lies behind me but that repulsive little tree! The battle for the soul is as brutal as the battles of men; but the sight of justice is the pleasure of God alone.

Yet this is the watch by night. Let us all accept new strength, and real tenderness. And at dawn, armed with glowing patience, we will enter the cities of glory.

Why did I talk about a friendly hand! My great advantage is that I can laugh at old love affairs full of falsehood, and stamp with shame such deceitful couples—I went through women's Hell over there—and I will be able now *to possess the truth within one body and one soul.*

April–August, 1873

SEVENTH SEASON

A Few Belated Cowardices

"Yet this is the watch by night.
Let us all accept new strength, and
real tenderness. And at dawn, armed
with glowing patience, we will enter
the cities of glory."

A SEASON IN HELL

And now what? Where was the child? Where was the poet? If the postures of rebellion or perversion and the creations they made possible could not bring happiness, what was left? What was possible? In the indistinct atmosphere of this complex biography, we are always unsure; here we can only guess what Rimbaud was doing, only conjecture what he was writing. "A philomath, and very proper, rummaging in libraries," said Verlaine later; he was in prison himself at the time, but his description fits; what else Rimbaud was doing we must find in his writing. That he had a new conception of what writing was to do seems clear from the last pages of *A Season in Hell*. It was a new resolution—"one must be absolutely modern"—and a firm one, to set himself a task, "to possess the truth within one body and one soul." But how, and where?

In poems that we imagine written at this period, poems like "Genie," there seems to be a sense of harmony, a metaphysics of glory that transfigures the experience they record. These poems are easily, fittingly seen as transcriptions of the harmonious world of the smoker of dope. Profoundly illuminated, they are scenes that fade as quickly as they burst upon our consciousness.

What poems were written now, what poems were merely recopied, we can only conjecture. But the pathways are familiar. Paris, London, and back to his mother's. Some of the same old acquaintances—"Gavroche" the painter, perhaps. Certainly the poet Germain Nouveau. They went together to England in March 1874. Rimbaud spent his days at the British Museum; he worked his way through the English alphabet, copying out words and idioms: ". . . no one will help me through it—help yourself to anything you like—he helped himself—what a helpless being—hem—hemlock tree—hemp—henroost. . . ." His mother and his rather unwilling sister Vitalie came over to visit him in July of that year. Arthur was looking for work as a teacher, wrote Vitalie in her journal. "No mail for Arthur, no news. I'm sure it's more disagreeable for him than it is for me. Probably. Oh, if only he could find a position! . . . there are lots of jobs! If he had wanted to, he could have gotten something and we could be gone. Had he been willing we might be leaving today. Oh, when I think that such joy might be mine at this very moment . . ."

The Rimbaud family left London on July 31, mother and Vitalie to return to Charleville, Arthur to a position in Reading. But by Christmastime he was back at his mother's.

He went to Germany in February 1875, to Stuttgart, to study German. Verlaine had gotten out of prison by then, and went to visit him in Stuttgart. Rimbaud got him drunk and beat him up. He went that summer to Italy, and possibly to Paris, but by the end of August he was back at his mother's.

He made a half-hearted attempt to blackmail Verlaine in September, and in October wrote a letter to his friend Delahaye to inquire about the requirements for completing a degree in science. The letter contains Rimbaud's last known poem—thirteen lines about soldiers farting. It is a more telling denial of poetry than any grand testament could ever be. His concerns are now with other things, grownup things: making money. He was no longer a child. How then could he still be a poet? Together then they died, the child and the poet, abandoned, passed over, swallowed up in practicalities. And Rimbaud went off, a man half-grown, to wander through the world.

AFTER THE FLOOD

As soon as the thought of the Flood had subsided,
A rabbit stopped in the clover and trembling bell flowers,
And said his prayers to the rainbow, through a spider's web.

Oh! what precious stones lay hidden,
What flowers were already looking down.

In the dirty main street they hung up signs on their shops,
And dragged off boats to the sea, up there, fixed as if engraved.

In Bluebeard's Castle, the blood ran—
In slaughterhouses, in the circuses, where the seal of God
Paled at the windows. Blood flowed, and milk.

The beavers were building; coffee glasses steamed in the little cafés.

In the great house, its windowpanes still streaming,
Children in mourning looked at marvelous picture books.

A door slammed—and on the village square, a child waved his arms,
Making windmills and weathercocks everywhere,
Beneath a drizzling rain.

Madame X set up a piano in the Alps. Masses and first Communions
Were offered at the hundred thousand altars of the cathedral.

Caravans departed. The Hotel Splendide was erected
In a chaos of ice and polar night.

Since then, the Moon has heard the jackals,
Wailing in a desert full of thyme, and wooden-footed eclogues
Clumping in the orchard. Then, within a violet budding grove,
Eucharis told me it was spring.

Rise, pond—Foam, roll
Over the bridge and through the woods;

Black hangings and organ music, lightning and thunder—
Rise up in torrents;
Waters and sadness, rise and raise up the Floods!

For since they have swept on and vanished—

Oh burrowing jewels, oh open flowers . . .

What a bore!
And the Queen, the Witch who lights her fire in an earthen pot,
Will never tell us what she knows,
And we do not.

VAGABONDS

Pitiful brother! What terrible sleepless nights he caused me!

"I was never strongly in control of that undertaking.
I took advantage of his weakness.
Through my fault we would have gone back into exile,
Into slavery."
He credited me with a strange ill luck, a strange innocence—
But for disturbing reasons.

I would answer this satanic doctor with sneers, and end
By leaving through the window. I was creating, beyond a country
Haunted with bands of rare music, the ghosts of future nocturnal
    debauch.

After this vaguely hygienic distraction, I would stretch out
On a pallet of straw. And almost every evening, no sooner asleep,

My poor brother would rise up, with stinking mouth and gouged
    eyes—
As he dreamt himself!—and drag me into the next room, howling
His dreams of idiot sorrow.

I had in all sincerity of mind undertaken to return him
To his primitive state of child of the Sun, and we used to wander,
Nourished on the wine of caverns and the dry bread of travelers,
While I searched continually to find the place and the formula.

LINES

When the world comes down to this one dark wood
Before our four astonished eyes . . .
To a beach for two faithful children . . .
To a house of music, for our clear accord . . .
    I will find you.

Let there be no one here below but one old man,
Beautiful and calm, surrounded with "unimagined luxury" . . .
    I will be at your feet.

Let me penetrate all of your memories . . .
Let me be *that woman* who can bind you hand and foot . . .
    I will strangle you.

When we are very strong—who can hold us back?
And very gay—how can ridicule harm us?
When we are very bad—what can they do to us?
    Dress yourself up,
    And dance,
    And laugh.
I could never throw Love out the window.

My companion, my beggar girl, monstrous child!
How little you care,
About these unhappy women, about the intrigues of misfortune,
About my own extremity.

Beguile us with your impossible voice—
That voice!
The single flatterer of our abject despair.

A lowering morning in July.
A taste of ashes fills the air;
A smell of sweating wood stains the hearth.
Drowned flowers,

The spoils of long walks . . .
A misty rain from canals beyond the fields.

Why not even trinkets and incense?

I have strung ropes from steeple to steeple;
Garlands from window to window;
And golden chains from star to star . . .

And I dance.

Smoke always rises from the distant pond.
What witch will ascend against the white sunset?
What violet streamers will come dropping down?

While the public funds dwindle in feasts of fraternity,
A bell of rosy fire rings in the clouds.

Breathing a sweet smell of India ink,
A powdery blackness drifts slowly over my lateness . . .

I lower the lights, lie down on my bed,
And, rolled into the shadows, I see you—

My darlings, my queens!

DEVOTION

To sister Louise Vanaen de Voringhem: her blue habit flapping
By the North Sea. For picking up castaways.

To sister Leonie Aubois d'Ashby: Boo! the grass of summer,
Buzzing and stinking. For fever in mothers and children.

To Lulu . . . a demon . . . who has kept a taste for churches
From the days of girlfriends and her incomplete education. For men.

To Madame X.

To the adolescent I was. To this holy old man, hermitage
Or mission.

To the spirit of the poor. And to high-ranking clergy.

As well to all worship, in any place of memorial worship
Among any events which it may be necessary to attend,
According to the aspirations of the moment,
Or even our own important vices.

This evening, to Circeto and her tall mirrors, fat as fish,
Painted like the ten months of red night
  (Her heart of amber and smoldering fuze)

For my lonely prayer silent as these regions of night,
Proceeding from exploits more violent than this polar chaos.

At any cost and in every air, even on metaphysical voyages.

But that's all over.

TO A REASON

Your finger strikes the drum, dispersing all its sounds,
And new harmony begins.

Your step is the rise of new men, their setting out.

You turn away your head: New Love!
You turn your head again: New Love!

"Alter our fates, destroy our plagues,
Beginning with Time," sing the children.
They beg of you: "Make out of anything
The stuff of our fortunes and desires."

Come from always, you will go away everywhere.

DRUNKEN MORNING

Oh, *my* Beautiful! Oh, *my* Good!
Hideous fanfare where yet I do not stumble!
    Oh, rack of enchantments!

For the first time, hurrah for the unheard-of work,
For the marvelous body! For the first time!

It began with the laughter of children, and there it will end.

This poison will stay in our veins even when, as the fanfares depart,
We return to our former disharmony.
Oh, now, we who are so worthy of these tortures!
Let us re-create ourselves after that superhuman promise
Made to our souls and our bodies at their creation:
That promise, that madness!
Elegance, silence, violence!
They promised to bury in shadows the tree of good and evil,
To banish tyrannical honesty,
So that we might flourish in our very pure love.

It began with a certain disgust, and it ended—
Since we could not immediately seize upon eternity—
It ended in a scattering of perfumes.

Laughter of children, discretion of slaves, austerity of virgins,
Horror of faces and objects here below,
Be sacred in the memory of the evening past.

It began in utter boorishness, and now it ends
In angels of fire and ice.

Little drunken vigil, blessed!
If only for the mask that you have left us!
Method, we believe in you! We never forget that yesterday
You glorified all of our ages.
We have faith in poison.

We will give our lives completely, every day.

FOR THIS IS THE ASSASSINS' HOUR.

LIVES

I

Oh, the enormous avenues of the holy land . . . the terraces of the
  Temple!
What have they done with the Brahman who taught me the Proverbs?
From then, from far below, I can still see even those old women . . .
I remember hours of silver and sun near rivers,
With the hand of the countryside upon my shoulder,
And I remember our embraces, standing in the scented plain.

A flight of scarlet pigeons thunders about my thoughts . . .

In my exile here, I have a stage where I can play
The sweeping tragedies of all literatures.
I will show you unheard-of riches. I watch the history
Of the treasures you have found. I can see what will follow!
But my wisdom is as much ignored as chaos.
What is my nonbeing, compared with the stupor which awaits you?

II

I am an inventor much more deserving,
Different from all who have preceded me;
A musician, even, who has found something which may be the key to
  love.
At present, gentleman of a bleak countryside beneath a frugal sky,
I attempt to awaken my feelings in the memory of a wandering
  childhood,

Of my apprenticeship, my arrival in wooden shoes . . . of polemics,
Of five or six widowhoods, and of several wild nights where my hard head
Kept me from reaching the exaltation of my companions.
I do not regret my former share of divine gaiety;
The frugal air of this bleak countryside
Fortifies very effectively my atrocious skepticism.
But as this skepticism can no longer be put to work,
And since I am now devoted to a new preoccupation . . .
    I expect to become a very wicked madman.

III

In an attic where I was locked up at the age of twelve,
I found out the world . . . I made illustrations for the Human Comedy.
In a closet I learned my history.
At an evening celebration in a northern town, I met all the women
Of the painters of the past.
In an old alley in Paris, I was taught the classic sciences.
In a magnificent house encircled by the Orient entire,
I brought my life's work to completion, and I passed my illustrious retirement.
I have drunk my own blood. My task has been lifted from me . . .
No longer must I even think of it.
I am actually from beyond the grave . . .
                  and can do nothing for you.

DEPARTURE

Everything seen . . .
    The vision gleams in every air.

Everything had . . .
    The far sound of cities, in the evening,
    In sunlight, and always.

Everything known . . .
    O Tumult! O Visions! These are the stops of life.

Departure in affection, and shining sounds.

ROYALTY

On a brilliant morning, in a city of *lovely* people,
A wonderful man and a wonderful woman
Were shouting out loud, in the middle of town:
    "Oh, my friends . . . I want her to be queen!"
    "*I* want to be a queen!"
She kept on laughing and trembling,
While he talked to his friends about revelations,
And tribulations at an end.
They laughed and they leaned close to one another.
And, of course, they *were* royal . . .
All morning long, when scarlet draperies hung upon all the houses,
And even in the afternoon,
When they appeared at the edge of the gardens of palms.

WORKERS

A warm morning in February.
The inopportune South came to revive our memories
Of being ridiculous paupers, of our young poverty.

Henrika had a cotton skirt with brown and white checks,
Probably worn in the century past,
A little hat with ribbons and a kerchief made of silk.
It looked sadder than mourning clothes.

We went for a walk in the suburbs.
The sky was heavy, and that wind from the South
Sharpened the sour smells that rose from trampled gardens,
And fields half dead.

This did not depress my wife so much as me.

In a puddle still standing from the previous month's flood,
On a rather high path, she pointed out some tiny little fish.

The city, with its smoke and the sounds of its trades
Crept behind us, far along the roads . . .
   Oh, other world, sky-blessed land of shade!
The South made me remember the terrible times of my childhood,
My summer despairs, the horrible amount of strength and knowledge
That fate always kept far from me.
   No! We will spend no summers in this grasping land,
   Where we will forever be nothing but orphans betrothed.

This hardened arm will drag along no more "sweet memories."

BRIDGES

Crystal gray skies.

An odd pattern of bridges, some straight, some round,
Others cutting in or going off at angles on the others;
These images repeat themselves in the lighted curves of the canal,

But all so long and light that the banks, covered with domes,
Seem to lower and shrink.
Some of these bridges are still covered with masonry.
Others hold up masts, signals, fragile parapets.
Minor chords cross and disappear.
Ropes rise from the banks.
I can make out a red jacket, other costumes, and musical instruments.
Are these popular songs, bits of lordly concerts,
Remnants of public hymns?
The water is gray and blue, wide as an arm of the sea.

A white light falling from the heights of heaven
Obliterates this scene.

CITY

I am a temporary and not at all discontented citizen
Of a metropolis considered modern because all known taste has been
    eluded
In the furnishings and the outsides of the houses,
As well as in the plan of the city.
Here you will find no trace of a single monument to superstition.
Morals and language have been reduced
To their simplest expression, that is all!
These millions of people with no need to know each other
Lay down so equally the path of education, of trade and old age,
That the course of life is probably several times shorter
Than anything a crazy statistic sets up for people on the continent.
And from my window, what original specters roll
Through this thick eternal smoke—
Our Crowded Shade, our Midsummer Night!
Latter-day Erinys fly before this cottage
Which is my country and the depth of my heart,

Because everything here looks like this:
Dry-eyed Death, our diligent daughter and servant,
A hopeless Love and a pretty Crime wailing in the mud of the road.

WHEEL RUTS

On the right the summer morning stirs the leaves,
Waking mists and noises in this corner of the park . . .
The slopes upon the left hide
In their violet shade
A thousand moving ruts in the damp road.

Parade of Enchantments.
This is how it was:
Chariots carrying animals of gilded wood,
Masts and motley tents,
Twenty spotted circus horses at a great gallop,
And children and men, on the most amazing beasts . . .

Twenty studded carriages, with banners and with flowers,
Like faraway fairy tale coaches, full
Of little children, all dressed up
For a suburban pastorale . . .

Even the coffins under their canopies
Flourish their ebony plumes,
And out trot great fat blue black mares.

PROMONTORY

The golden dawn and a shivering evening
Discover our boat lying along the coast

Below this villa and its outbuildings,
A promontory vast as Epirus and the Peloponnesus,
As the great isle of Japan,
As Arabia!
Shrines that glow with the return of processions;
Vast views of modern coastal fortifications;
Dunes patterned with burning flowers and bacchanales;
The great canals of Carthage and embankments
Of a sinister Venice; soft eruptions of Etnas,
Crevasses of flowers and melting glaciers;
Washhouses in a grove of German poplars;
The slopes of unusual gardens
Rise above Japanese trees;
The circular façades of the "Royals" and "Grands"
Of Scarborough or Brooklyn;
Their overhanging railways parallel and plumb
The appointments of this hotel,
Taken from the most elegant and colossal constructions
In the history of Italy, America, and Asia,
Whose windows and terraces, at present full of lights,
Of drinks and heady breezes,
Open in the minds of travelers and noblemen
Who permit, at every hour of the day,
Every tarantella of the seashore,
Every ritornello of the valleys of art,
To deck with miracles
The face of Promontory Palace.

CITIES I

This is what cities are like!

For this people they have raised these Alleghenies
and these Lebanons in dreams!

Chalets of wood, chalets of crystal
move along rails on invisible pulleys.
Ancient craters surrounded by colossi and by coppery palms
bellow melodious fires.
Gabbling parties of lovers echo on canals
strung out behind the chalets.
The rush of pealing bells cries out in gorges.
Corporations of giant singers assemble in robes and halos
brighter than the white light of high peaks.
On platforms in passes, Rolands trumpet defiance.
On catwalks in the pit, from the roofs of country inns
The fires of heaven hang suspended from poles.
Crumbling apotheoses fall in high fields
where seraphic centaurs spin among avalanches.

Beyond the highest cliffs, upon a sea
that labors in the eternal birth of Venus,
swept in swarms by Orpheonic fleets, vibrant
with pearls and strange conches,
the shadow of a deathly brightness
sometimes dims the waves.

From hillsides breathes the soughing sound
of harvests of flowers as large as our weapons, our vessels.
In opaline procession, flashing
Mabs in russet wrappings wind
down into deep ravines.
In a waterfall
high in a towering hoof-trodden thorn thicket,
Diana gives suck to her stags.

Suburban Bacchantes wail; the moon growls and burns.
Venus visits the blacksmiths, the recluses,
in their caves.

The ideas of peoples sound from thickly clustering bell towers.
Unknown music vibrates in towering castles of bone.
All legend evolves, and excitement
rushes through the streets.
A paradise of whirlwinds melts away.
Savages dance, endlessly
dancing the Triumph of Night.
And once I went down into the tumult of Baghdad
in a boulevard, where companies shouted the joys of new labor
into thick air, restlessly moving
but never escaping those phantoms come down
from the heights where we were to have met.
What strong arms, what shining hour
will bring me back this country,
the source of my repose,
moving the least of my movements?

CITIES II

The official acropolis outdoes
The most colossal conceits of modern barbarity.
How can I describe the dull daylight of unchanging gray skies,
The imperial effect of these buildings, the eternally snow-covered
    ground?
Here, with an odd flair for enormity,
Are reconstructed all the wonders of classical architecture.
I visit expositions of paintings
In halls twenty times the size of Hampton Court.
What paintings!
A Norwegian Nebuchadnezzar commanded the staircases of the
    ministries;
The mere subalterns I caught sight of are prouder than Brahmans;
I trembled at the look of the guards before the colossi

And the building officials.
In the arrangement of buildings in squares, courts, and covered
   terraces,
They have done away with hacks and cabs.
The parks are examples of primitive nature
Ordered with marvelous art.

The upper town has strange sections;
An arm of the sea rolls empty, a blanket of blue hailstones,
Between quais covered with candelabra.
A short bridge leads to a postern gate
Directly under the dome of the Holy Chapel.
   This dome is an armature of wrought steel
   Fifteen thousand feet in approximate diameter.

At several points, from the copper causeways, the platforms,
The stairs that wind through the markets, that twist around the pillars,
I thought I could plumb the depth of the city!
This prodigy eternally amazes me:
How far above or below the acropolis is the rest of the city?
For the stranger in our time, recognition is impossible.
The commercial quarter is a circus in a single style,
With galleries in arcade. No shops are seen,
Yet the snow on the pavements is trampled;
Occasional nabobs, rare as Sunday-morning strollers in London,
Approach a diamond carriage. Occasional red velvet divans;
They serve cold drinks
At prices from eight hundred to eight thousand rupees.
I think of looking for theaters on this circus,
But I decide that the shops will contain dark dramas enough—
I believe there exists a police; but the law must be so different,
I cannot imagine what criminals here must be like.

The suburb, elegant as a Paris street,
Bathes in an air made of light—

The democratic element comprises some hundred souls.
Here again, the houses do not stretch out beyond each other;
The suburb disappears oddly into the country—the "County"—
That fills the enduring west with forests
And prodigious plantations
Where savage noblemen hunt down their memoirs
Beneath a light we have created.

METROPOLITAN

From the indigo straits to the oceans of Ossian,
Across orange and rosy sands washed in the wine-dark sky
Boulevards of crystal rise, crisscross—

They swarm instantly with the young families of the poor,
Fed from the fruit-sellers' stands—Nothing too rich.

This is the city!

Fleeing out of the bituminous waste
In rout through sheets of mist rising in terrible bands
To the hovering sky, high, then low, full of the blackest,
Most sinister smoke of a mourning Ocean,
    Roll helmets, wheels, wagons, and horses' flanks—

This is battle!

Lift up your head: this high-arched wooden bridge,
The straggling kitchen gardens of Samaria;
Painted masks beneath a lantern beaten by cold nights,
A stupid water nymph in shrieking garments
Deep in the riverbed.
Gleaming skulls in the garden vines,

And other phantasmagorias—

        This is the country.

Highways edged with iron grilles and walls,
Barely holding back their groves,
The terrible flowers called sisters, called hearts—
Damascus damned and endless—
The holdings of enchanted aristocracies
(High Rhenish, Japanese, Guaranian)
Still fit to resound with the music of the ancients,
—There are inns that will never ever open again;
There are princesses, and (if you are not yet overwhelmed)
The stars to gaze at—

        This is the sky.

The morning when, with Her, you struggled
In the glaring snow; green lips, ice, black banners,
Blue rays of light,
And the dark red perfumes of the polar sun—

        This is your strength.

ANGUISH

Can she make me forgive my constantly defeated ambitions—
Can an easy finale repair ages of misery—
Can a day of success destroy the shame
Of our fatal lack of skill?

    (O palms! Diamond! Love! Strength!
    Beyond all joys and glories!

Everywhere, in every way, demon and god!
The Youth of this being: Myself!)

Can accidents of scientific magic and movements
Of fraternal union be considered a slow return
To time remembered before our fall from grace?

But the Vampire who makes us kind
Expects us to be entertained with what she leaves us,
Or in another way to be much more amusing.

Convulsed with wounds from the dying air and the sea,
Racked by the murderous silence of water and air,
By torments that laugh, their silence a terrible howl.

BARBARIAN

Long after days and seasons pass,
And the living have gone, and the land,

   A Banner of meat that bleeds
Onto the silk of seas and arctic flowers; (they do not exist).

Echoes of heroics, and the old fanfares
That still attack us, head and heart—
Far from the assassins of the past,

   A Banner of meat that bleeds
Onto the silk of seas and arctic flowers; (they do not exist).

Delight!
   Bright fires, raining in squalls of sleet—

Delight!
　Fires in the rain of a diamond wind
Thrown from this terrestrial core, charred forever,
And for us,
O World!
　(Far from old retreats and ancient flames we hear and feel.)

Bright fires and foam. Music, turning in crevices;
The shock of ice against the stars.

O Delight, O music, O world!

　There . . .
Forms; sweating, hair and eyes, drifting . . .
White tears, burning tears . . . O delight!
The voice of Woman in gulfs of fire,
and frozen caves of ice.

　And a Banner . . .

WAR

When I was a child,
my vision was refined in certain skies;
my face is the product of every nuance.
All Phenomena were aroused.
At present, the eternal inflections of the moment
and the infinity of mathematics hunt me over this earth
where I experience all civil successes,
respected by strange childhood and devouring affections.

I envisage a war, of justice or strength,
of a logic beyond all imagining.
　It is as simple as a musical phrase.

MOVEMENT

A winding movement on the slope beside the rapids of the river.
The abyss at the stern,
The swiftness of the incline,
The overwhelming passage of the tide,
With extraordinary lights and chemical wonders
Lead on the travelers
Through the windspouts of the valley
And the whirlpool.

These are the conquerors of the world,
Seeking their personal chemical fortune;
Sport and comfort accompany them;
They bring education for races, for classes, for animals
Within this vessel, rest and vertigo
In diluvian light,
In terrible evenings of study.

For in this conversation in the midst of machines,
Of blood, of flowers, of fire, of jewels,
In busy calculations on this fugitive deck,
Is their stock of studies visible
   —Rolling like a dike beyond
   The hydraulic propulsive road,
   Monstrous, endlessly lighting its way—
Themselves driven into harmonic ecstasy
And the heroism of discovery.

Amid the most amazing accidents,
Two youths stand out alone upon the ark
   —Can one excuse past savagery?—
And sing, upon their watch.

SALE

For sale—
     Whatever the Jews have left unsold,
What nobleness and crime have never tasted,
What damned love cannot know,
What is strange to the infernal probity of the masses,
What time and science need not recognize:

     Voices reconstituted;
A fraternal awakening of all choral and orchestral energies
and their immediate application.
The occasion, the unique moment, to set our senses free!

For sale—
     Priceless Bodies, beyond race or world or sex or line of descent!
Riches in ubiquitous flood!
Unrestricted sales of diamonds!

For sale—
     Anarchy for the masses;
Wild satisfaction for knowing amateurs;
Atrocious death for the faithful and for lovers!

For sale—
     Homesteads and migrations, sports,
Enchantment and perfect comfort, and the noise,
the movement, and the future they entail.

For sale—
     Extravagant uses of calculation, unknown harmonic intervals.
Discoveries and unsuspected terms, immediately available.

Senseless and infinite flight toward invisible splendor,
Toward insensible delight—
The madness of its secrets shocks all known vice!
The mob is aghast at its gaiety!

For sale—
Bodies and voices, immense and unquestionable opulence,
Stuff that will never be sold.

The sellers sell on!
Salesmen may turn in their accounts later . . .

GENIE

He is love and the present because he has opened our house
to winter's foam and to the sounds of summer,
He who purified all that we drink and eat;
He is the charm of passing places,
the incarnate delight of all things that abide.
He is affection and the future, the strength and love
that we, standing surrounded by anger and weariness,
See passing in the storm-filled sky
and in banners of ecstasy.

He is love, perfect and rediscovered measure,
Reason, marvelous and unforeseen,
Eternity: beloved prime mover of the elements, of destinies.
We all know the terror of his yielding, and of ours:
Oh, delight of our well-being, brilliance
of our faculties, selfish affection and passion
for him, who loves us forever . . .

And we remember him, and he goes on his way . . .
And if Adoration departs, then it sounds, his promise sounds:

"Away with these ages and superstitions,
These couplings, these bodies of old!
All our age has submerged."

He will not go away, will not come down again from some heaven.
He will not fulfill the redemption of women's fury
nor the gaiety of men nor the rest of this sin:
For he is and he is loved, and so it is already done.

Oh, his breathing, the turn of his head when he runs:
Terrible speed of perfection in action and form!
Fecundity of spirit and vastness of the universe!

His body! Release so long desired,
The splintering of grace before a new violence!

Oh, the sight, the sight of him!
All ancient genuflections, all sorrows are *lifted* as he passes.

The light of his day!
All moving and sonorous suffering dissolves in more intense music.

In his step there are vaster migrations
than the old invasions were.

Oh, He and we! a pride more benevolent than charities lost.

Oh, world! and the shining song of new sorrows.

He has known us all and has loved us.
Let us discover how, this winter night, to hail him
    from cape to cape, from the unquiet pole to the château,
    from crowded cities to the empty coast,
    from glance to glance, with our strength and our feelings
        exhausted,

To see him, and to send him once again away . . .
And beneath the tides and over high deserts of snow
To follow his image,
his breathing, his body, the light of his day.

YOUTH

I. SUNDAY

All calculations set to one side;
The inevitable Descent from Heaven,
A visitation of memories and a séance of rhythms
Invades the house, my head,
    And the world of the mind.

A horse leaps forward on suburban turf,
Past planted fields and stretches of woods
Misty with carbonic plague.
A wretched theatrical woman, somewhere in the world,
· Sighs after an improbable indulgence.
Desperadoes lie dreaming of storm, and of wounds and debauch.
Along small streams the little children sit,
    Stifling their curses.

Let us turn once more to our studies,
To the noise of insatiable movement
That forms and ferments in the masses.

II. SONNET

Man of average constitution, was the flesh not once
A fruit, hanging in an orchard?
                            O infant hours!

Was the body not a treasure to be unsparing of?
Oh, Loving—either Psyche's peril, or her strength.
 In princes and artists, the earth had fertile watersheds,
But the suite of generations and race
Drives us to crime and to mourning—
The world is our salvation and our danger.
At present, with this labor completed,
You—your calculations,
You—your impatience,
Are reduced to no more than your dancing, your voice,
Indeterminate, unforced,
Yet reason for a double occasion of invention and success;
Quiet fraternal humanity in an imageless universe.
Strength and justice shine through this dancing, this voice,
 That only the present can appreciate.

III. TWENTY YEARS OLD

Exiled the voices of instruction;
Physical ingenuousness staled in bitterness . . .

                                        . . . Adagio.

Ah! The endless egoism of adolescence,
Its studious optimism:
 How the world this summer was full of flowers!
Dying airs, dying shapes . . .
A chorus to appease impotence and absence!
A chorus of glasses of nocturnal melodies . . .

(Of course, our nerves are quickly shot to hell!)

IV

You are playing still at the temptation of Saint Anthony—
The looseness of failing zeal, tics of puerile pride,

Faltering and fright.
But you will undertake this task;
All the possibilities of Harmony and Architecture
Rise up about your seat. Unlooked for,
Creatures of perfection will throng your experience.
Dreaming around you will hover the curiosity
Of forgotten crowds and halting luxuries.
Your memories and your senses will become
The food of your creative impulses.

And what of the world?
What will it become when you leave it?
   Nothing, nothing at all like its present appearance.

RIMBAUD TO ERNEST DELAHAYE

Stuttgart
March 5, 1875

Verlaine showed up here the other day, rosary in hand. . . . Three hours later God was denied and the 98 wounds of Our Divine Savior were bleeding. He stayed for two and a half days, quite reasonable, and at my insistence has gone back to Paris, to go eventually to finish studying "*over on the island.*"

I only have a week of Wagner left, and I regret all that money paying for hate, and all this time shot to hell. On the 15th I will have *ein freundliches Zimmer* someplace, and I work at the language in a frenzy, so much so that I'll be finished in two more months.

Everything here is pretty poor—with one exception: Riesling, vich I trink to you a glass from vere it comz.

Sunshine and freezing weather; it tans your hide. (after the 15th, Genl. Delivery, Stuttgart)

Yours,
RIMB.

RIMBAUD TO ERNEST DELAHAYE

[*Charleville*]
October 14, 1875

Dear Friend,

Got the Postcard and letter from V. a week ago. To make things simpler I told them at the Post Office to send his Gen'l Delivery to my house, that way you can write here if the Gen'l Delivery doesn't work. I have no comment to make about the recent vulgarities of our Loyola, and I have no more energy to devote to all that now. It seems that the 2nd group of the contingent from the class of '74 will be called up for the draft on the third of November coming, or of the month following: scene in the Barracks at night:

"DREAM"

Everyone's hungry in the barracks at night—
That's right!
Blasts, and bursts of wind!
A Genie: I am Gruyère!
Lefebvre: Give me air!
The Genie: I am Brie!
The Soldiers hack at their bread—
That's life! Whee!
The Genie: I am Roquefort!
We will die from it!
"I am Gruyère, and Brie . . . etc."

WALTZ:

We are a pair, Lefebvre and I, etc.

Preoccupations of this kind are absolutely engrossing. Anyway be kind enough to send on any "Loyolas" that may turn up.

Do me a small favor: can you tell me clearly and precisely about the present requirements for a degree in science: classics, math, etc.; tell me how much you have to get in each subject, math, phys, chem, etc., and also the current titles (and how to get them) of the texts used in your school, for example, for the degree, as long as it doesn't change depending on the university; in any case, find out what I've indicated from some professors or from some students that seem to know. I've really got to get the exact facts, since I've got to buy the books soon. Military Inst. and a science degree, you can imagine, will give me two or three enjoyable seasons! And anyway, the hell with "my craft and art." Only be good enough to let me know exactly how I should go about getting started.

Nothing going on here.

I love thinking that the Dogfarts and the Stinkers full of patriotic beans or whatever are giving you the kind of diversion you need. At least it doesn't snow like hell the way it does here.

Yours "to the fullest of my failing strength."

Write

> A. Rimbaud
> 31 rue Saint-Bartlémy
> Charleville,
> obviously

p.s. The "official" corresp. has got to the point that the Post Office gives Loyola's newspapers to a *policeman* to bring over here!

VERLAINE TO RIMBAUD

> *London*
> *Sunday, December 12, 1875*

My dear friend,

I haven't written to you, contrary to my promise (if I remember correctly), because, frankly, I was expecting an acceptable letter at long last from you. No letter, no answer. Today I am breaking my long silence to repeat everything I wrote you about two months ago.

The same as always. Strictly religious, because it is the only *wise* thing to do. All the rest is trickery, evil, and stupidity. The Church has made modern civilization, science, and literature: the Church made France, especially, and France is dying because she has broken with the Church. That is quite clear. The Church makes men as well; she *creates* them. I am surprised that you don't see that, it's quite striking.

I had the time—during those eighteen months in prison—to think this over and over, and I assure you I hold on to it as my only security. And seven months among protestants have confirmed me in my catholicism, in my legitimism and in the courage of resignation.

Resignation for the excellent reason that I feel, that I see I have been *punished,* humiliated, justly, and that the severer the lesson, the greater the grace and the need to respond to it.

I find it impossible that you should imagine this is a pose or a pretext on my part. And as for what you wrote me—I don't remember your words exactly, "modifications of the same sensitivity," "rubbish," etc.—that is nonsense and stupidity worthy of Pelletan and the rest.

And so, the same as always. The same affection (modified) for you. I so much want to see you enlightened, reflecting. It is a source of great sorrow to me to see you in the pathways of stupidity, you who are so intelligent, so *ready* (though that may astonish you!). I appeal to your own disgust of everyone and everything, to your perpetual anger against the world—a just anger, basically, though ignorant of the reason *why.*

As for the question of money, you cannot seriously not realize that I am the soul of *generosity:* it is one of my very rare qualities—or one of my numerous faults, as you will. But considering first of all my need to repair even meagerly as I can the enormous inroads made in my slender income by *our* absurd and shameful life three years ago, and then the thought of my son, and finally my new and unshakable beliefs, you must surely understand that I cannot support you. Where would my money go? On bottles and barkeeps! Piano lessons? What *nonsense!* Can't your mother pay for them, for heaven's sake?

You wrote me, in April, letters that were too explicit in vile, evil intent for me to risk giving you my address—although of course any attempts to harm me would be ridiculous and useless a priori, and in any case, I warn you, they would receive a *legal* reply, with documentary evidence.

But I reject such an odious hypothesis. This is, I am sure, some passing caprice of yours, some unfortunate brainstorm that a little reflection will have dissolved. But prudence is ever the mother of trust, and you won't get my address until I can trust you.

This is why I have asked Delahaye not to give you my address, and requested him to be good enough to forward any letters from you.

But make some gesture, have a heart, what the hell! A little consideration and affection for someone who will always be, and you know it,

Your affectionate,

P.V.

I will elaborate on my plans—quite simple!—and on the advice I desire to see you follow, even leaving religion aside, although that is my great, great, great advice, as soon as you answer me properly, via Delahaye.

P.S. Useless to write me here marked *hold*. I am leaving tomorrow on a great, a distant voyage . . .

EIGHTH SEASON

The Man with the
Wind at His Heels

"I! I called myself a magician,
an angel, free from all moral constraint!
. . . I am sent back to the soil
to seek some obligation, to wrap gnarled
reality in my arms! A peasant!"

A SEASON IN HELL

A t this point we are concerned no longer with poetry, but with biography alone. The writings of Rimbaud from 1875 on, as far as we know, consist only of letters and business documents. Why read them? For the chilling contrast they provide to his poetry. The voice we hear in them is that of Rimbaud the businessman, clearly distinguished from the voice of Rimbaud the poet. Rarely are the two voices so distinct. Poets' letters tend always to be just that—conscious, literary, "artistic" pieces of writing. Only occasionally do we find the vatic voice so clearly distinguished from the mundane one. With Rimbaud the separation is complete.

The logic of it is rigorous—and so, as the events of Rimbaud's life become more and more luxuriant, his letters become more and more banal. His flights from home are now carried out on a grand scale. In the spring of 1876 to Vienna, where he was rolled by a cab driver. In June he enlisted in the Dutch colonial army, and deserted two months later into the jungles of Java. He was picked up by a British ship, and by the beginning of the winter was in France, once more at his mother's. In November of 1878 he heads east again, crossing the Alps on foot, the St. Gotthard Pass in a blizzard, carping at the monks and dogs of the hospice of St. Bernard as he goes. In December he is working on a construction crew in Cyprus, but by June 1879 he is ill with typhoid and returns to his mother's. In 1880 he returns to Cyprus, then proceeds by stages down the Red Sea to Aden—and here documents and his letters home pin him down for us, and describe his next ten years as a trader on the Red Sea coast and in Ethiopia. Here he stayed, a good bourgeois from Charleville, the son of a miserly mother, out to seek his fortune: to explore Africa, to make a lot of money, to become a success, to become rich and famous. And none of it ever happened. The letters and documents are plain, and tell all. He was a poor businessman, a nervous one, an unprofitable mixture of avarice, morality, and gullibility. He was generally in the pay of other men; the record of his major independent venture as a trader is a comedy of errors; he was royally fleeced by Menelik, the shrewd black king of Shoa. And so it went, described in letters that are more and more depressing to read, until we feel a kind of embarrassment at seeing them at all. Could he not simply have disappeared? Or died young?

As it was, he died young enough. It was a miserable end. A cancerous tumor in his leg, an agonizing voyage to Marseilles, the leg cut off, and a final return to his mother's. But the cancer spread, and the pain grew worse; then a feverish desire to go back to the East, to the sun and warm weather. He got as far as Marseilles, and died in the hospital there, on November 10, 1891. He was thirty-seven.

TO HIS FAMILY

Aden
August 25, 1880

Dear friends,

I think I mailed you a letter recently, telling how I unfortunately had to leave Cyprus and how I arrived here after sailing down the Red Sea. Here I am working in the office of a coffee importer. The company agent is a retired general. Business is good, and is going to get better. I don't earn much, it comes to about six francs a day, but if I stay here, and I have to stay, it's so far from everywhere that I'll have to stay a couple of months just to make a few hundred francs so I can leave if I have to, well, if I stay, I think they'll give me a responsible job, maybe an office in another city, and that way I'd be able to make something a little quicker.

Aden is a horrible rock, without a single blade of grass or a drop of fresh water: we drink distilled sea water. The heat is extreme, especially in June and September, which are the dog days here. The constant temperature, night and day, in a very cool and well-ventilated office, is 95 degrees. Everything is very expensive, and so forth. But there's nothing I can do: I'm like a prisoner here, and I will certainly have to stay at least 3 months before getting on my own two feet again, or getting a better job.

How are things at home? Is the harvest finished?

Tell me what's new.

ARTHUR RIMBAUD

CONTRACT WITH THE FIRM OF VIANNAY AND BARDEY, ADEN

Aden
November 10, 1880

Arthur Rimbaud
Aden

DEAR SIR:

I am pleased to confirm in writing the conditions under which you agree to work for the firm of Viannay, Bardey and Co., Lyon and Aden.

You agree to join the staff of the firm as an employee at the branch office in Harar (East Africa), or at any other branch or office on the African or Arabian coast where the requirements and interests of the firm may require your presence.

You will devote your time and effort entirely to the business of the firm and its interests. For their part, the firm of Viannay, Bardey and Co. promise the following:

You will receive one thousand eight hundred rupees per year; that is, one hundred and fifty rupees per month, payable monthly.

You will also receive a share, one percent, of the net profits from the Harar office.

You will receive food and lodging free of charge; maintenance and personal effects will be at your own expense.

The present contract is accepted by both parties for a duration of three years, and we will strive on both sides to fulfill it with probity and diligence.

In case of termination of this contract, it is furthermore agreed that you will not work for any other trading firm with stores or offices on the coast of Africa or Arabia or in the interiors of these regions for a period of time equal to the duration of the present contract, that is for three years from November 1, 1880, to October 31, 1883.

Please acknowledge receipt of this letter signifying acceptance of all the clauses and conditions therein.

> Yours very truly,
> DUBAR
> *General Agent for Africa and Arabia, V.B. and Co.*

TO HIS FAMILY

Harar
December 13, 1880

Dear friends,

I have arrived here after twenty days on horseback across the Somali desert. Harar was colonized by the Egyptians and is governed by them. The garrison has several thousand men. Our office and our warehouses are located here. The commercial products of the country are coffee, ivory, skins, etc. The country is elevated, but not unfertile. The climate is cool and not unhealthful. All kinds of European goods are imported here, by camel. This is, besides, a country of opportunity. We have no regular mail service here. We have to send mail to Aden whenever we are able. So you won't get this for quite a while. I expect that you have received the hundred francs that I had sent to you from the bank in Lyon, and that you have been able to send off the things I asked for. I have no idea though when I'll get them.

I am here in the country of the Gallas. I think I will have to push on farther very soon. Please let me hear from you as often as possible. I hope everything is going well for you and that you are in good health. I will find time to write more soon. Address your letters or packages:

> "M. Dubar, general agent at Aden
> for M. Rimbaud, Harar."

TO HIS FAMILY

Harar
May 25, 1881

Dear friends,

Dear mama, I got your letter of May 5th. I'm glad to know that your health is better and that you can rest for a while. At your age, it would be too bad to have to work. Alas, I have no great attachment to life; if I go on living, it's because I'm too tired to do anything else; but if I am forced to go on wearing myself out like this, living with problems as overwhelming as they are stupid, in these horrible places, I fear I may end my life.

I am still in the same circumstances here, and in three months I may be able to send you 3,000 francs I've saved; but I think I will keep them to start a small business of my own in these parts, as I have no intention of spending my entire life in slavery.

Well, let us hope we will be able to spend a few years of real rest in this life; thank God this life is the only one—and that's sure, since I can't imagine another life with as many troubles as this one!

Very best,
RIMBAUD

TO HIS FAMILY

Harar
Friday, July 22, 1881

Dear friends,

I got a letter from you recently, dated May or June. You are annoyed at the mail being late, that's not fair; it comes more or less regularly, but at long intervals; as for packages, boxes, and books from you, I got everything all at once more than four months ago, and I wrote to tell you so. It's just a long way, that's all; it's the desert to cross twice that doubles the mailing time.

I don't forget you at all, how could I? and if my letters are too short, it's because I am always traveling, and so have always been rushed to make the time when the mail leaves. But I think about you, and I think only about you. What can you expect me to tell you about my work here, which I hate so much, and the country, which I detest, and so forth? Why should I tell you about the plans I've made with extraordinary effort, which have got me only a fever that I still have after two weeks, as bad as the one I had at Roche two years ago? But what can you expect? I can take anything now; I'm afraid of nothing.

I will make an arrangement with the company soon so that my salary will be paid to you in France regularly every three months. I will have them send you what they owe me up to now, and then it will come regularly. What can I do with useless cash in Africa? You must buy some income property immediately with the amount you get, and you must register it in my name with a reputable notary; or you must think of some other convenient arrangement, and deposit it locally with a safe broker or banker. The only two things I want are: (1) that it be taken care of safely, and *in my name*, (2) that it bring in a regular income.

Only I have to be sure I am in no way in trouble with the draft board, so they can't keep me from enjoying it later on in one way or another.

You can take for yourselves whatever you need from the interest of the amounts you take care of for me.

The first amount you will probably get in three months may be as much as 3,000 francs.

This is all quite sensible. I don't need money at the moment, and I can't get any return on it here.

I wish you success in your work. Don't wear yourselves out, it's an insane thing to do! Aren't health and life more precious than all the filth in the world?

Live peacefully,
RIMBAUD

TO HIS FAMILY

Harar
September 2, 1881

Dear friends,

I believe I've written you once since your letter of July 12.

I am still miserable in this part of Africa. The climate is sticky and humid; the work I do is absurd and back-breaking, and living conditions are generally absurd as well. Besides I have had some disagreeable set-tos with the management and the rest, and I have almost decided to pack up and leave soon. I intend to try some projects on my own in the region; and if it doesn't turn out (which I will find out right away) I will leave soon for, I hope, more intelligent work in a better atmosphere. It's also quite possible that I'll even continue working with the company, somewhere else.

You say you've sent me things, boxes, supplies, which I haven't acknowledged. All I've received is a shipment of books according to your list and some shirts. Anyway, my orders and letters have always gone around in circles in this crazy place. Imagine, I ordered two new linen suits from Lyon a year ago November, and haven't got anything yet!

I needed some medicine six months ago; I asked them to send it from Aden, and I haven't got it yet! Everything is always on the way—to hell.

All I want in this world is a good climate and some suitable, interesting work. I've got to find it some day or other! I also hope to hear only good news from you, and that you are in good health. It is my greatest pleasure to hear from you, dear friends; and I wish you more luck and happiness than me.

Goodbye.

RIMBAUD

I've had them tell the company's office in Lyon to mail you in Roche the sum total of my wages in cash from December 1, 1880, to July 31, 1881, which comes to 1,165 rupees (a rupee is worth around 2 francs 12 centimes). Please let me know as soon as you get it, and invest it suitably.

About the draft board, I think I'm still in good standing, and I would be very upset not to be. Find out exactly about it. I will soon have to get a passport at Aden, and I will have to explain my situation.

Say hello to Frédéric.

TO HIS MOTHER

Aden
April 15, 1882

Dear Mother,

I got your letter of March 30 on April 12.

I see with pleasure that you are feeling better, and you must keep in good spirits about your health. There's no use thinking depressing thoughts as long as you're alive.

As for my interests that you talk about, they are not much and that doesn't bother me in the least. What can I lose, when all I have is my own self? I am a capitalist with nothing to fear from his own speculations, nor from other peoples'.

Thank you for the hospitality you extend, my dear friends. That goes without saying for me as well.

Excuse me for not having written for a month. I have been harassed with all kinds of work. I am still with the same company, under the same arrangement; only I work more and spend almost everything, and I have decided not to stay in Aden long. In a month I'll either be back in Harar, or on my way to Zanzibar.

From now on I won't forget to write as often as possible. Good weather and good health.

Yours,

RIMBAUD

TO HIS FAMILY

Aden
September 10, 1882

Dear friends:

I got your July letter with the map; thank you.

Nothing is new with me, everything is still the same. I have only thirteen months left with the Company; I don't know if I'll finish them. The present agent in Aden is leaving in six months; there's a possibility I may replace him. The position pays around 10,000 francs a year. It's much better than being an employee, and at that rate I'd stay here another five or six years.

Anyway, we'll see which way the ball bounces.

I wish you all the best.

Be careful what you say in your letters, I think they're trying to examine my correspondence here.

Yours,

RIMBAUD

TO THE FRENCH VICE-CONSUL

Aden
January 28, 1883

M. de Gaspary
Vice-Consul de France
Aden

DEAR SIR,

Excuse my presenting the following matter for your consideration.

Today, at 11 o'clock in the morning, one Ali Chemmak, a worker at the warehouse where I am employed, became very insolent toward me, and I allowed myself to strike him, without anger.

The warehouse coolies and various arab witnesses then seized me, in order to allow him to strike back, and the said Ali Chemmak hit me in the face, tore my clothes, and finally grabbed a stick and threatened me with it.

Some people present intervened, and Ali left, to go shortly thereafter to lodge a complaint against me at the police station for assault and battery, and brought several witnesses to state that I had threatened to stab him, etc., etc., and other lies designed to prejudice the case in his favor, and to arouse the hatred of the natives against me.

I have been summoned to appear in Police Court in Aden on this matter, and have taken the liberty of advising you as French consul of the threat I have received from the natives, and to request official protection if the outcome of the case should seem to require it. I remain,

Very truly yours,
RIMBAUD
Employed by Mazaran,
Viannay and Bardey and Co.
Aden

TO HIS FAMILY

Harar
May 6, 1883

My dear friends,

I got your letter of March 26 here in Harar on April 30. You say you've sent me two boxes of books. I only got one box in Aden, the one Dubar said he saved me 25 francs on. The other has probably arrived in Aden by now, with the graphometer. I did send you, before I left Aden, a check for 100 francs with another list of books. You must have cashed this check, and have probably bought the books. Anyway, I don't remember the dates exactly. I'll send you another check soon for 200 francs, because I have to order some more photographic plates.

This was an extremely good idea; and, if I want, I could quickly get back the 2,000 francs it all cost me. Everybody here wants to have his picture taken; they're even willing to pay a guinea a photograph. I haven't got everything set up yet, and I still don't know that much about it, but I soon will, and I'll send you some interesting things.

I include two photos of me that I took myself. I'm always better off here than I am in Aden. There's less work, and more air, more greenery, etc. . . .

I renewed my contract for three years here, but I think the company is closing soon, the profits don't cover expenses. Anyway, it's agreed that when I am let go they will give me three months' salary as compensation. At the end of this year, I'll have had three full years in this hole.

Isabelle is very wrong not to get married if someone serious and educated shows up, someone with a future ahead of him. That's the way life is, and being alone is a bad deal in this world. As far as I'm concerned, I'm sorry I never married and had a family. But now I'm condemned to wander, caught up in distant ventures, and every day I lose any desire for the climate, the way of life, and even the language of Europe.

Alas! What are these comings and goings for, these hardships and these adventures among strange races, these languages the head is full of, these nameless difficulties, if I am not someday, some years hence, to be able to get some rest in a place I find more or less agreeable, and to get a family, and have at least one son that I can spend my life bringing up in my own way, and give him the most complete education possible in this day and age, so I can see him become a famous engineer, a man made rich and powerful by science? But who knows how long I'll have to spend in these mountains? And I could vanish among these savages without the news of it ever getting out.

You tell me about politics. If you only knew how little that means to me! More than two years since I've seen a newspaper. All those arguments are incomprehensible to me nowadays. Like the Moslems, I know that what happens happens, and that's all.

The only things that interest me are news of home, and I am always happy to picture the peace of your pastoral labors. It's too bad it's so cold and mournful there in winter! But you're having spring at the moment, and the weather there at this time of year is the same as I have here in Harar at the moment.

These photos show me, one, standing on the terrace of the house, the other, standing in a coffee grove, another, with arms folded, beneath a banana tree. It's all become pale because of the bad water I have to use for rinsing them. But I'll do better work soon. This is only to recall my face, and to give you an idea of the countryside hereabouts.

Goodbye,
RIMBAUD

TO HIS FAMILY

Harar
January 14, 1884

Dear friends,

I only have time to say hello, and tell you that the company is in trouble (because of the repercussions the war is having here), and is in the process of liquidating its office in Harar. I will probably leave here for Aden in a few months. As far as I'm concerned I've got nothing to lose in the company's problems.

I am in good shape, and I wish you health and prosperity for the year 1884.

RIMBAUD

MAZARAN, VIANNAY AND BARDEY TO RIMBAUD

Aden
April 23, 1884

DEAR M. RIMBAUD,

The events that have forced us to liquidate the company require us to deprive ourselves of your excellent services.

We take this opportunity to pay tribute to the work, the intelligence, the probity and devotion that you have always demonstrated in defense of our interests in the different positions you have filled for us over the last four years, in particular as director of our office in Harar.

With thanks, we remain.

Yours very sincerely,
MAZARAN, VIANNAY AND BARDEY

TO HIS FAMILY

Aden
June 19, 1884

Dear friends,

This is to let you know that I have got rehired in Aden for 6 months, from July 1 to December 31, 1884, on the same terms. Business is going to pick up, and for the moment I am staying at the old address, in Aden.

That box of books that didn't reach me last year must have been left at the shipping office in Marseilles, where of course they wouldn't send it on since I didn't have anyone there to sign a shipping order and pay the charges. If it is still at the Marseilles shipping office, get it back and try to send it off to me again, in separate bundles, by mail. I don't understand how it could have got lost.

Very best,
RIMBAUD

TO HIS FAMILY

Aden
July 10, 1884

My dear friends,

Ten days ago I started my new job, for which I am hired until the end of December 1884.

I am grateful to you for your offer. But as long as I can find work and can manage to stand it, I'd better stay here working and making a little money.

I really wanted to send you at least 10,000 francs; but since business is very slow at the moment, I may have to quit my job and go into business for myself in the near future. In any case, it's safe here, so I'll wait a couple of months more.

I hope you have a good harvest and a cooler summer than the one here (113° inside).

RIMBAUD
Bardey & Co., Aden

VITALIE CUIF RIMBAUD TO A. RIMBAUD

Roche
October 10, 1885

Arthur, my son,

Your silence is long, and why such silence? Happy are those who have no children, or happier still those who do not love them: they are unmoved by whatever may happen to them. I ought perhaps not to worry; last year at this time you had already let six months go by without writing us and without answering a single one of my letters, urgent as they were; but this time it is eight long months since we have heard from you. It is useless to speak to you of us, since what happens to us interests you so little. However, it is impossible that you should forget us in this way: what has happened to you? Are you no longer at liberty to act? Or is it that you are so sick you cannot hold pen in hand? or are you no longer at Aden? Have you moved to China? We have truly lost our minds trying to track you down, and I say again: Happy, oh, happy those who have no children, or who do not love them! They at least have no fear of being deceived, since their heart is closed to all that surrounds them.

Why should I exert myself any further? Who knows whether you will ever read this letter? It may perhaps never ever reach you, since I do not know where you are or what you are doing.

Soon you are to be called up for your two weeks of military training; the police may come here once again to try to find you. What shall I say? If at least you had sent me your deferment papers, as you did once before, I could have shown it to the military authorities; but this is the third time already that I have asked you for it without an answer. God's will be done, then! I did what I could.

Yours,
V. Rimbaud

CERTIFICATE OF EMPLOYMENT

I, Alfred Bardey, hereby state that I have employed M. Arthur Rimbaud as agent and buyer from April 30, 1884, through November 1885. I have nothing but praise for his services and his discretion. He is free from any contract with me.

(For P. Bardey)
ALFRED BARDEY
Aden, October 14, 1885

CONTRACT WITH LABATUT

I, Pierre Labatut, trader in Shoa, hereby declare that I will pay to M. Arthur Rimbaud, within a year or less from the present date, the sum of 5,000 Maria-Theresa dollars, for value received, reckoned in Aden on this day, and I agree to pay all the expenses of M. Rimbaud, who is to convey my first caravan to Shoa.

PIERRE LABATUT
Aden, October 4, 1885

TO HIS FAMILY

Aden
October 22, 1885

Dear friends,

When you get this I will probably be in Tadjoura, on the Dankali coast, in the colony of Obock.

I quit my job after a violent argument with those worthless skin-flints who thought they could grind me down forever. I did a great deal for those people, and they thought I was going to stay there for the rest of my life just to please them. They did everything they could to get me to stay, but I told them to go to hell with their benefits and their business and their stinking company and their dirty town! Not mentioning that they were always getting me into trouble and always trying to get me to give up anything profitable. Well, they can go to hell! . . . They gave me an excellent recommendation for the five years.

Several thousand rifles are on their way here from Europe. I am forming a caravan to take them to Menelik, the King of Shoa.

The route to Shoa is very long: two months' trek almost to get to Ankober, the capital, and the country between here and there is horrible deserts. But once there, in Abyssinia, the climate is delightful, the people are Christians and hospitable, and life is very cheap. There are only a few Europeans there, perhaps ten in all, and their occupation is importing guns, which the King pays well for. If I don't run into trouble, I hope to get there, get paid for the trip, and get back with a profit of 25,000 or 30,000 francs in less than a year.

If everything works out, you may see me in France around the fall of 1886, where I will buy new merchandise myself. I hope it will work out. You hope so too for me; I really need it.

If I could in three or four years add about 100,000 francs to what I already have, I would get out of this rotten country with pleasure.

I have sent you my contract by the mail boat before last, to state my case before the military authorities. I hope that from now on everything will be in order. Just the same, you never managed to let me know what kind of service I'm supposed to do; so now, if I go to the consulate for a certificate I am unable to let him know what my situation is, since I don't know myself! It's ridiculous!

Don't write me any more at Bardey's place; those rats would cut off my correspondence. For the next three months, or at least two and a half, after the date of this letter, that is until the end of 1885 (including the two weeks from Marseilles to here), you can write me at the address below:

> Arthur Rimbaud
> Tadjoura
> French colony of Obock.

Good health, a good year, rest and prosperity.
Best wishes,

RIMBAUD

TO HIS FAMILY

Tadjoura
December 3, 1885

My dear friends,

I am here trying to form my caravan for Shoa. It's slow work, as is the custom here; but anyway I hope to leave here by the end of January 1886.

I am fine. Send me the dictionary I asked for, to the address I gave you. From now on, write me always at that address. They will forward it to me.

This Tadjoura was annexed here a year go to the French colony of Obock. It is a small Dankali village with a few mosques and a couple of palm trees. There is a fort, built previously by the Egyptians, and where at the moment six French soldiers are asleep under the orders of a sergeant who commands the post. They have left the place its local sultan and the native administration. The place is a protectorate. The local business is trading in slaves.

This is where the Europeans' caravans leave for Shoa—very few; and there are great difficulties in getting through, since the natives all up and down the coast here are enemies of the Europeans, ever since the

English admiral Hewett made the Emperor John of Tigré sign a treaty abolishing the slave trade, the only local business that made any profit at all. However, under the French protectorate no one tries to interfere with the trade, and things are quieter.

Don't think I've become a slave trader. The stuff we import is rifles (old percussion rifles that were scrapped forty years ago) that cost 7 or 8 francs apiece at secondhand arms dealers in Liège or in France. You can sell them to the King of Shoa, Menelik II, for around forty francs apiece. But there are enormous expenses involved, without mentioning the dangers of the caravan route round trip. The people who live along the route are Dankalis, Bedouin shepherds, fanatical Moslems: they are dangerous. It is true that we have firearms and the Bedouins only have spears: but every caravan is attacked.

Once you pass the Hawash River, you enter the domains of the powerful King Menelik. There they are Christian farmers; the country is elevated, about 3,000 meters above sea level; the climate is excellent; you can live for absolutely nothing; everything made in Europe is in great demand; the people like you. It rains six months out of the year, just like in Harar, which is in the foothills of the great Ethiopian plateau.

I wish you good health and prosperity in the year 1886.

Very best,
A. RIMBAUD

TO HIS FAMILY

Tadjoura
February 28, 1886

My dear friends,
This time it's about two months since I heard from you last.
I'm still here, with the prospect of staying here another three

months. It's very disagreeable; but it will all finally finish, and I'll start out and get there, I hope, without accident.

All my merchandise has been unloaded, and I am waiting for the departure of a big caravan to join them.

I'm beginning to wonder if you have forgotten to arrange to have the dictionary of Amharic sent; nothing has got here yet. Although maybe it's at Aden; but it's six months since I first wrote you about that book, and you see how efficient you are about getting me sent the things I need: six months for a book!

In a month, or six weeks, summer will begin again on this damn coast. I hope I won't have to spend much of it here, and will get away in a few months to the mountains of Abyssinia, which is the Switzerland of Africa, without winters or summers: perpetual springtime and flowers, and life is cheap and easy.

I still plan on getting back here at the end of 1886 or the beginning of 1887.

Very best,
RIMBAUD

TO HIS FAMILY

Tadjoura
July 9, 1886

Dear friends,

I got your letter of May 28 only today. I don't understand the mail service in this damn colony at all. I write regularly.

There has been some trouble here, but no massacres along the coast; one caravan attacked on the road, but that was because it was badly guarded.

My business on the coast still hasn't been fixed, but I plan to be under way in September without fail.

I got the dictionary a while ago.

I am well, as well as can be expected here in summertime, with a temperature of 125°–130° in the shade.

Very best,
A. RIMBAUD

TO HIS FAMILY

Tadjoura
September 15, 1886

My dear friends,

It's been quite a while since I heard from you.

I definitely plan to leave for Shoa by the end of September.

I've been held up here for a long time, because my partner got sick and went back to France and they wrote me he's near dying.

I got an authorization for his merchandise, so I have to go anyway; and I'll be going by myself, since Soleillet (the other caravan I was going to join) is dead too.

My trip will last at least a year.

I'll write you just before I leave. I am very well.

Good health and good weather.

A. RIMBAUD

MENELIK II TO RIMBAUD

Menelik II, King of Shoa, Kaffa, and the lands of the Gallas adjoining.

Salutations to Monsieur Rimbaud. Are you well?

I am, God be praised, in good health, as are all my armies.

The letter you sent has reached us. I thank you for the news.

The interest on the payments on account is too high. I have sent an order to Dejaz Makonnen to pay you. You may receive this amount from him.

If you have news from Europe and from Massawa, send it immediately.

Written in June 1887, in the land of Adea Bagogtu.

TO THE FRENCH VICE-CONSUL

Aden
July 30, 1887

M. de Gaspary
Vice-Consul de France
Aden

DEAR SIR:

Permit me to give you an accounting of the liquidation of the caravan of M. Labatut, deceased, a venture I was associated with by an agreement signed at the Consulate in May 1886.

I learned of Labatut's death only at the end of '86, at the very moment when the first payments had been made and the caravan had set out and could no longer be held up, and thus I could not make new arrangements with the backers of the venture.

In Shoa, negotiations over this caravan were carried out under disastrous circumstances: Menelik confiscated all the merchandise and forced me to sell everything to him at reduced prices, forbidding me to sell it at retail and threatening to send it all back to the coast at my expense! He gave me a total of 14,000 thalers for the entire caravan, keeping out of this 2,500 thalers as payment for the 2d half of the rent for the camels and other caravan expenses paid by the Azzaz, and another sum of 3,000 thalers owed to him by Labatut, he said, although everyone assured me that the King was in fact in Labatut's debt.

Pursued by a band of supposed creditors of Labatut, with whom the King always sided, and unable to get anything out of his debtors, tormented by his Abyssinian family who demanded his inheritance and refused to recognize my power of attorney, I was afraid of being completely ruined and I decided on leaving Shoa, and I was able to get from the King a voucher on the Governor of Harar, Dejazmach Makonnen, for the payment of about 9,000 thalers which was all that was still owing me, after the theft of 3,000 thalers that Menelik got away with and because of the ridiculous prices he was paying me.

Menelik's voucher was not paid at Harar without expense and considerable difficulties, since some of the creditors kept badgering me even there. To conclude, I got back to Aden on July 25, 1887 with 8,000 thalers in bills of exchange and around 600 thalers in cash.

In my agreement with Labatut, I agreed to pay, in addition to the caravan expenses,

1st: in Shoa, 3,000 thalers, by delivering 300 rifles to Ras Govanna, which business the King himself took care of;

2d: in Aden, a debt to M. Suel, which is now taken care of with a reduction agreed upon by all concerned;

3d: a bill of Labatut's owing to M. Audon, in Shoa, a debt which I already paid more than 50 percent of in Shoa and Harar, according to the records I have.

Everything that might have been charged to the expenses of the venture has been taken care of by me. The balance being 2,500 thalers cash in hand, and since Labatut owes me the sum of 5,800 thalers according to the agreement we signed, I get out of the whole thing with a loss of 60 percent of my capital, without counting twenty-one months of incredible hardships spent trying to settle this miserable business.

All the Europeans in Shoa were witnesses to the whole affair, and the documents involved are at your disposition.

I remain

Respectfully yours,
A. RIMBAUD

THE FRENCH CONSUL IN MASSAWA
TO THE VICE-CONSUL IN ADEN

Massawa
August 5, 1887

M. de Gaspary
Vice-Consul de France
Aden

DEAR SIR:

A certain M. Rimbaud, who claims to be a trader in Harar and Aden, arrived here in Massawa yesterday on board the weekly mail boat from Aden.

He is French, tall, thin, gray eyes, small mustache, almost blond, and was brought in by the police.

M. Rimbaud has no passport and no way of proving his identity. The papers he showed me were business documents signed with one Labatut and witnessed by you, which grant him powers of attorney.

I would be much obliged if you could give me some information about this individual, who seems rather suspect.

Rimbaud has on him a bill of exchange for 5,000 thalers payable five days after demand on M. Lucardi, and another bill for 2,500 thalers on an Indian trader in Massawa.

Thanking you for your consideration, I remain

Sincerely yours,
ALEXANDRE MESCINICY
Consulat de France
Massawa

TO HIS FAMILY

Cairo
August 23, 1887

Dear friends,

My trip to Abyssinia is over.

I already explained to you about how, because my partner was dead, I had a lot of trouble in Shoa over his legal obligations. They made me pay his debts twice over, and I had a real hard time saving what I had invested in the business. If my partner hadn't died, I would have made around 30,000 francs; as it is, here I am with the 15,000 I had, after having completely exhausted myself for almost two years. I never have any luck!

I came here because the heat was unbearable this year on the Red Sea: all the time 120° to 130°: and since I was very weak after seven years of hardships like you can't imagine and the most awful privation, I thought that two or three months here would set me up again; but it's just more expenses, since I can't find any kind of work here, and life is like in Europe and quite expensive.

I am being bothered these days by a rheumatism in the small of the back, which is killing me; I've got another in the left thigh which paralyzes me from time to time, a painful stiffness in the left knee, rheumatism (for a long time already) in my right shoulder; my hair is completely gray. I think I am probably in a very bad way.

Think about what someone's health must be, after adventures like the following: crossing the sea in an open boat, going overland by horseback, without the right clothes, without provision, water, etc.

I am exceedingly weary. I have no job at present. I'm afraid of losing what little I have. You know I wear continually a belt containing sixteen thousand and some hundred francs in gold; it weighs around eighteen pounds and keeps giving me dysentery.

Still, I can't come to Europe, for a lot of reasons: first, I'd die in wintertime; then, I'm too used to a wandering and gratuitous existence; finally, I haven't got a job.

So, then, I have to spend the rest of my days wandering in hardship and privations, with only the prospect of a painful death.

I won't stay here long: I haven't got a job and everything costs too much. I'll have to go back toward the Sudan, Abyssinia or Arabia. Maybe I'll go to Zanzibar, from where I can take long trips through Africa, or maybe to China or Japan, who knows?

Well, send me your news. I wish you peace and happiness. All the best,

> Address: Arthur Rimbaud
> Gen'l Delivery
> Cairo, Egypt

FRENCH VICE-CONSUL TO RIMBAUD

> *Aden*
> *November 8, 1887*

M. Rimbaud
Aden

DEAR SIR:

This is to acknowledge receipt of your letter containing the detailed account I had requested of the accounts and various operations dealing with the liquidation of the Labatut Caravan, which you had agreed, under specified conditions, to accompany to Shoa and to dispose of there.

I am aware from the accounts you include with your letter, registered at the Vice-Consulate as no. 552, that this was in fact a disastrous commercial operation for you, and that you did not hesitate to sacrifice your own rights to satisfy the numerous creditors of the deceased Labatut, but I must also state, taking account of the testimony of Europeans who had been in Shoa, and whom you yourself cited as witnesses, that your losses might have been substantially less if, like other traders engaged in dealing with the Abyssinian authorities, you had known how, or been able, to adapt yourself to the particular methods of those places and their rulers.

As for the liquidation account that enumerates various payments by you and for which you received receipts, it would be best if these papers were joined to the said account; for your own records we could provide you with legal copies certified by a notary.

DE GASPARY
Vice-Consul de France

TO HIS FAMILY

Harar
November 10, 1888

Dear friends,

I got your letter of October 1 today. I would have liked very much to come back to France to see you, but it's absolutely impossible for me to leave this corner of Africa for a while yet.

But Mother dear, rest a little and take care of yourself. You've gone through enough trouble. Take care of your health at least and take a rest. . . .

Believe me, my conduct is irreproachable. Whatever I do, it's always the others who take advantage of me.

The life I lead in this place, I've said it often, but I don't say it enough, and I have nothing else to say, the life I lead is difficult, cut shorter by being bored to death, and by endless fatigue. But I don't care! I only want to hear that you are happy and in good health. As far as I'm concerned, I've long been used to life as it is. I work. I travel. I'd like to do something good, something useful. What will the results be? I don't know yet.

Anyway, I'm feeling better since I've moved to the interior, and I'm at least that much ahead.

Write to me more often. Don't forget your son and brother.

RIMBAUD

TO HIS FAMILY

Harar
May 15, 1888

Dear friends,

I'm settled in here once again, for a good while this time.

I'm setting up a French trading post, modeled on the office I ran here a while back, with, however, a few improvements and innovations. I'm involved in some fairly big deals, and make a profit now and again.

Could you give me the name of the biggest cloth manufacturers in Sedan, or in your locality? I'd like to ask for a few small orders of their cloth: I could distribute them in Harar and in Abyssinia.

I am in good shape. I've got a lot to do, and am all by myself. I'm in the cool weather here, and content just to rest, or rather to cool off, after three summers spent on the coast.

Stay well and best wishes,

RIMBAUD

TO HIS FAMILY

Harar
May 18, 1889

Dear Mama, dear Sister,

I've got your letter of April 2. I see with pleasure that everything is going well for you.

I am still very busy in this hellish country. What I earn is out of proportion with the troubles I go through; we lead a pathetic existence among all these niggers.

The only good thing about this place is that it never freezes; it never gets colder than 50° or hotter than 85°. But this is the season when it rains buckets, and, like you, that keeps us from working, that is, from bringing in or sending out caravans.

Anyone who comes here will never make a million—unless he gets it in lice, if he spends too much time with the natives.

You probably read in the newspapers that the Emperor John (some emperor!) is dead, killed by followers of the Mahdi. We here were also indirectly under this emperor. Only we are directly under King Menelik of Shoa, who himself paid tribute to the Emperor John. Our Menelik revolted last year against that monster John, and they were getting ready for a real set-to, when the aforesaid Emperor had the bright idea of going to slap down the Mahdi's people, over near Matama. He stayed there, so the hell with him!

Everything is all quiet here. We are officially a part of Abyssinia, but we are separated from it by the Hawash River.

We are still in touch with Zeila and Aden.

I'm sorry I can't come visit the Exposition this year, but I haven't made anywhere near enough for that, and besides I'm absolutely alone here, and if I left my business would disappear completely. I'll save it for the next one; and at the next one maybe I can exhibit the products of this country, and maybe exhibit myself; I think you must get to look exceedingly baroque after a long stay in a place like this.

I hope to hear from you, and wish you good weather and good times.

RIMBAUD

address: c/o César Tian, trader
Aden

FROM ALFRED ILG,
KING MENELIK'S SWISS ADVISER, TO RIMBAUD

September 16, 1889

I've just been to see the extraordinary stuff you sent me. I'd swear you want me to get everything I own confiscated; it's getting very popular nowadays. Go around waving rosaries, crosses, christs, etc. at the very instant that His Majesty has given Father Joachim a formal order to return to Harar? It's more dangerous than traveling in the desert. At the moment I wouldn't even dare give your stuff away as presents. The Abyssinians would be only too willing to think I was a monk in disguise. You'd do better to use your famous DeCours and Co. pearls for birdshot; you would have made more on them than by dumping them in a bazaar a couple of hundred miles from Harar. I think Brémond's passion for selling junk has turned into an epidemic, and that you're up to your neck in it. Wanting to sell notepaper to people who can't even write, and are totally ignorant of the private use it might be put to—that's really asking too much. It's too bad you don't have a couple of hundred hand-carved shells and a few shoehorns to send me. . . .

ILG

MENELIK II TO RIMBAUD

Menelik II, King of Kings of Ethiopia
Salutations to Monsieur Rimbaud.
I send you my greetings.
The letter you sent me from Harar on the 4th day of the 6th month of the year 1889 has reached me. I have read it thoroughly. Dejaz Makonnen will be returning in haste. He has been instructed to take

care of all business in Harar. It is better that you should come to some agreement with him. If, moreover, he does not speak to me of the matter, I will speak to him of it. If you have lent money in my name to any officials in Harar, you have only to show the documents to the Dejazmach, who will pay you.

In the matter of the prices of M. Savouré's merchandise, we will discuss it with M. Ilg.

September 25, 1889. Written in the city of Antotto.

ILG TO RIMBAUD

October 8, 1889

I must reproach you for one thing where the caravans are concerned. You never give them sufficient provision. Not a single caravan arrives but it is starved and the personnel in a deplorable condition, and everyone complains very bitterly about you. It simply is not worth it, in order to save a few dollars on provisions, to have the personnel and drivers all sick, and worn out for several months. The same thing for the camel loads. In your donkey train with the silk and cretonne, etc., I had to pay six dollars for transport per thousand dollars, since the donkeys you provided would no longer walk. . . . Donkeys can walk for a long time only when they are not overloaded. All the donkeys that arrived from Harar are in such pitiful condition that I have been obliged to turn them all out in my fields to let them heal their sores; not one of them was usable. . . .

ILG TO RIMBAUD

October 26, 1889

We are completely without news here of the Gr-reat Embassy. I await interesting details from you. You can tell stories so well, when you want to; but I hear that big business has completely dissolved the little good humor you had left. Listen, my dear Rimbaud; we only live once; make something pleasant of it, and tell your heirs to go to hell. . . .

ILG

TO HIS FAMILY

Harar
February 25, 1890

Dear Mother and Sister,

I got your letter of January 21, 1890.

Don't be upset that I don't write much; the main reason is simply that I never find anything interesting to say. When you are in places like this, there's more to do than find things to say! Deserts full of stupid niggers, no roads, no mail, no travelers: what do you expect me to write about in a place like this? That I'm bored, that I've got problems, that I'm worn to pieces, that I've had it, but that I can't get myself out of here, etc., etc.! That is all, absolutely all I can say, consequently, and since that's no fun for others either, I do better by saying nothing.

There are massacres, as a matter of fact, and quite a few raids in the locality. Fortunately I haven't been around on those occasions, and I'm not planning to lose my scalp here—that would be dumb! Anyway, I enjoy a certain respect in this region and on the trails, because of my humanity and consideration. I have never wronged anyone. On the contrary, I do a little good whenever I get the chance, and that's the only enjoyment I get.

I do business with that Monsieur Tian who wrote you to tell you that I was all right. Business probably wouldn't be too bad if, as you can read in the papers, the trails weren't closed every other minute by wars and uprisings, which endanger our caravans. This Monsieur Tian is a big trader in the city of Aden, and he never gets out into these parts.

The people in Harar are no more stupid, no more crooked, than white niggers in the so-called civilized countries; they just do things differently, that's all. They are in fact more trustworthy, and in certain cases will show gratitude and loyalty. You just have to treat them like human beings.

Ras Makonnen, whom you probably read about in the newspapers and who was the head of the Abyssinian embassy to Italy that made such a fuss last year, is the Governor of the city of Harar.

Hope to see you soon.

Very best,

RIMBAUD

TO HIS MOTHER

Harar
April 21, 1890

Dear Mother,

I got your letter of February 26.

Unfortunately, I haven't the time to get married, nor to think of getting married. It's absolutely impossible for me to leave business before an indefinite period. When you do business in these hellish places, you never get out of it.

I'm feeling well, but every minute I get another white hair. It's been going on so long I'm afraid I'll soon have a head like a powder puff. It's awful, the way this hairy leather lets us down, but what can you do?

Very best,

RIMBAUD

ILG TO RIMBAUD

About the slaves. I'm sorry, but I can't get involved in that; I've never bought slaves and I don't want to start now. Even on my own, I wouldn't do it. . . .

ILG

TO HIS MOTHER

Harar
November 10, 1890

Dear Mama,

I just got your letter of September 29, 1890.

Speaking of marriage, I have always meant to say that I intend to remain free to travel, to live abroad, even to continue living in Africa. I have got so unused to the climate of Europe that I would have a hard time adjusting to it. I would probably have to spend the winters away, even admitting I might come back to France someday. And then how would I make contacts again, what jobs could I find? That's another question. Anyway, the one thing I cannot stand is a sedentary existence.

I would have to find someone who would follow me in my wanderings.

My savings are taken care of; I can get it when I want it.

Monsieur Tian is a very respected businessman, established in Aden for more than thirty years, and I am his partner in this part of Africa. We have been partners for two years and a half. I also do business on the side for myself alone; and I am free, besides, to liquidate my business whenever I want.

I send caravans down to the coast with local products: gold, musk, ivory, coffee, etc. Whatever I do with M. Tian, half the profits go to me.

For more information, people can write to Monsieur de Gaspary, the French consul in Aden, or to his successor.

No one in Aden can say anything bad about me. On the contrary, I've been well regarded by everyone in this place, for ten years.

Amateurs beware!

For Harar there is no consul, no mail service, no highway: you get there on camelback, and live there among niggers, but at least you are free, and the climate is good.

That's my situation.

Goodbye.

A. RIMBAUD

TO HIS MOTHER

Harar
February 20, 1891

Dear Mama,

I just got your letter of January 5.

I see that everything is going well with you, except the cold which, according to what I read in the papers, is extreme all over Europe.

I'm not very well at the moment. At least, I've got varicose veins in the right leg that are causing me a lot of pain. That's what you get for sweating your life away in such a rotten place! And the varicose veins are complicated by rheumatism. Of course, it doesn't get cold here; but still it's the climate that causes it. Today makes two weeks I haven't slept a wink because of the pain in this damn leg. I'd like to leave, and I think the heat in Aden would do me good, but a lot of people owe me a lot of money and I'd lose it if I left. I ordered a stocking for varicose veins in Aden, but I doubt they'll have one.

So would you do me this favor: buy me a stocking for varicose veins, for a long, skinny leg (I take a size 41 shoe). The stocking has to come up over the knee, because there's a varicose vein above the back of the knee. Varicose vein stockings are made of cotton, or silk woven with elastic that supports the swollen veins. The silk ones are the best and last longer. I don't think they cost too much. Anyway, I'll pay you back.

I've got the leg bandaged while I'm waiting.

Send it well wrapped, by mail, to Monsieur Tian in Aden, and he will get it to me as soon as he can.

You can maybe get these stockings for varicose veins in Vouziers. In any case, your local doctor can order a good one from someplace or other.

This condition was caused by too much time on horseback, and also by a lot of walking. This country is a labyrinth of steep mountains, where you can't even go on horseback. All that with no roads and even without any paths.

The varicose veins aren't dangerous for your health, but they prevent any violent exercise. It's a real problem, because the varicose veins cause sores, if you don't wear a special stocking; and even so the nerves in the legs don't easily put up with the stocking, especially at night. On top of that, I have a rheumatism pain in my damn right knee, which torments me, and hurts only at night! You have to remember that at this time of year, which is winter in this place, it never gets less than 50°. But there are always dry winds, which are very debilitating for whites in general. Even young Europeans, 25 to 30 years old, get rheumatism after two or three years here!

The bad food, unhealthy houses, insufficient clothing, problems of all kinds, boredom, a continual rage against niggers as stupid as they are crooked, all of it affects health and morale very seriously, and in a very short time. One year here is the same as five some place else. You get old very quickly, here, like all the rest of the Sudan.

When you answer, let me know what my situation is with the draft board. Do I still have to serve? Find out about it, and let me know.

RIMBAUD

VITALIE CUIF RIMBAUD TO A. RIMBAUD

Roche
March 27, 1891

Arthur my son,

I'm sending you at the same time as this letter a little package with a jar of ointment to rub on your varicose veins, and two elastic stockings which were made in Paris, which is why I am a few days late, the doctor wanted one of the stockings laced; but we would have had to wait much longer still, so I send them as I was able to get them.

I enclose the doctor's prescription and the directions. Read them very carefully and do exactly what he tells you, most of all you must have rest, and not just a little but in bed, because as he says and as he can tell from your letter your sickness has advanced to a point disturbing for the future. If your stockings are too short you can cut the sole of the foot and pull it up as high as you want. Doctor Poupeau had a brother-in-law, M. Caseneuve, who lived for a long time in Aden, as a naval inspector. If you hear anything nice about the gentleman, do let me know it. That would make the doctor happy. M. Caseneuve died last year somewhere near Madagascar, leaving a large fortune, he died of a fever.

Isabelle is better; but not yet well. We are still in the middle of winter, it's very cold, the wheat is completely lost, there is none left, thus a general despair, what will become of us no one can imagine.

Goodbye, Arthur, and be sure to take good care of yourself and write me as soon as you get my package.

V. RIMBAUD

TO HIS FAMILY

Aden
April 30, 1891

My dear friends,

I've just got your letter and your two stockings; but I got them in rather distressing circumstances.

Seeing that the swelling in my right knee and the pain in the joint kept increasing, without being able to find any remedy or any advice, since Harar is full of niggers and there were no doctors there, I decided to come down to the coast. I had to abandon the business, which wasn't very easy, since I had money out all over the place, but finally I more or less settled everything. For about twenty days I had been in bed in Harar without being able to make the slightest movement, suffering atrocious pain and never sleeping. I hired sixteen native bearers, at 15 dollars a head, from Harar to Zeila; I had a litter made with a canvas top, and it was in that that I just traveled, in twelve days, the 300 kilometers of desert that separate the mountains of Harar from the port of Zeila. It's useless to tell you what I went through on the trip. I couldn't move a step from my litter; my knee kept swelling visibly, and the pain continually increased.

Once I got here, I entered the European hospital. There is one room here for people who pay: I'm in it. The English doctor, as soon as I showed him my knee, said that it was a synovitis tumor that had reached a very dangerous stage, as a result of lack of care and fatigue. At first he talked about cutting the leg off; then he decided to wait a few days to see if the swelling, with medical treatment, would diminish at all. It's been six days now, and no progress, except that since I am resting, the pain has got much less. You know a synovitis is a disease of the fluids in the knee joint: it can be caused by heredity, or by accidents, or by a lot of other things. In my case, it was certainly caused by the exhaustion of trips on foot and on horseback at Harar. Well, in the state I'm in now, I can't expect to be cured before three months from now, and that's if all goes well. And I'm stretched out, my leg bandaged, tied, retied, strapped down, so that I can't move it. I look like a skeleton; I scare people. My back is raw from the bed, I can't get a minute's sleep. The heat here has become very bad. The food in the hospital, which as a matter of fact I pay quite a lot for, is very bad. I don't know what to do. On the other hand, I haven't yet closed my accounts with my partner Monsieur Tian. That won't be finished for another week. I'll get out of all this with around 35,000 francs. I would have had more, but because of my unfortunate departure I lost a few thousand francs. I want to have myself carried to a steamship, and to come and have myself treated in France. The trip would help me pass the time, and in France medical care and medicines are much better, and the air is good. It's quite probable that I'll come. The steamships for France are unfortunately still packed, because everyone is coming home from the colonies at this time of year; and I'm a poor invalid who has to be transported very carefully. Well, anyway, I will take my leave in a week.

Don't be too upset at all this, however. There are better days ahead. But still, it's a sad reward for so much work, so much privation and pain! Alas! What miserable lives we lead, after all!

My heartfelt greetings

RIMBAUD

P.S. As for the stockings, they're of no use. I'll sell them someplace.

TELEGRAM TO HIS FAMILY

MARSEILLES MAY 22, 1891

TODAY, YOU OR ISABELLE, COME TO MARSEILLES BY EXPRESS TRAIN. LEG TO BE AMPUTATED MONDAY MORNING. DANGER OF DEATH. SERIOUS BUSINESS TO SETTLE.

ARTHUR

RIMBAUD: CONCEPTION HOSPITAL

TELEGRAM FROM VITALIE CUIF RIMBAUD TO A. RIMBAUD

I AM COMING. WILL ARRIVE TOMORROW EVENING.
COURAGE AND PATIENCE.

V. RIMBAUD

TO HIS SISTER

Marseilles
June 17, 1891

My dear sister Isabelle,

I got your note with my two letters returned from Harar. In one of those letters they told me they had previously sent back a letter to Roche. Haven't you received anything else?

I still haven't written to anyone, I still haven't got out of bed. The doctor says I'll have another month like this, and even then I won't be able to walk except very slowly. I still have a painful neuralgia in the place where my leg was, I mean in the part that's left. I have no idea how it will all end. Well, I'm resigned to anything, I have no luck!

But what is all this talk about burial for? Don't get so upset, have patience as well, take care of yourself, be brave. Really, I would like to see you, what can be the matter with you? What's wrong? All sicknesses can be cured with time and care. In any case, you have to resign yourself and not despair.

I was very angry when mama left me, I couldn't tell why. But at the moment it's better she should be with you to help you get well. Ask her to excuse me and say hello for me.

Goodbye until we see each other, but who knows when that will be?

RIMBAUD
Conception Hospital
Marseilles

TO HIS SISTER

Marseilles
June 23, 1891

My dear sister,

You haven't written; what's happened! Your letter upset me; you must write me, as long as there are no new troubles to report, because we are too much put upon at once!

I do nothing but cry day and night, I am a dead man, a cripple for the rest of my life. In two weeks I'll be cured, I think; but I'll only be able to walk with crutches. For an artificial leg the doctor says I'll have to wait a long time, at least six months! Until then what shall I do, where can I go? If I come to stay with you the cold would drive me out in three months, and even sooner, because I won't be able to move from here except in six weeks, just enough time to practice using crutches! So I wouldn't get there until the end of July. And then I'd have to leave at the end of September.

I don't know what to do at all. All this is driving me crazy: I never get a minute's sleep.

In the long run our life is a horror, an endless horror! What are we alive for?

Write me how you are.

My best wishes.

RIMBAUD
Conception Hospital
Marseilles

TO HIS SISTER

Marseilles
June 24, 1891

My dear sister,

I got your letter of June 21. I wrote you yesterday. I didn't get anything from you on June 10, neither a letter from you nor a letter from Harar. I only got the two letters of the 14th. I'm very surprised at what must have happened to the letter of the 10th.

What new horror are you talking about? What is this business about the draft? Once I turned 26, didn't I send you, from Aden, a certificate to prove that I was working with a French firm, which means a deferment—and afterward, when I asked mama about it, she always answered that everything was taken care of, that I didn't have anything to worry about. Only four months ago I asked you in one of my letters if there was anything they could do to me, because I wanted to come back to France. And I never got an answer. So I thought you had arranged everything. Now you tell me that I have been reported delinquent, that they are looking for me, etc., etc. Don't go inquiring about it unless you are sure you won't attract attention to me. As far as I'm concerned, there's no danger now, with this business, that I'd come back! Go to jail after what I've already gone through? I'd rather die!

Yes, for a long time now, anyway, I'd rather have died. What can a cripple do in this world? And as of now, reduced to being an expatriate forever! For I'll certainly never come back with all this business—I'll be lucky even if I can get out of here by boat or overland and across the border.

Today I tried to walk with crutches, but I could take only a couple of steps. My leg is cut off very high up, and it's hard for me to keep my balance. I'll never be easy until I can get an artificial leg; but amputation causes neuralgia in what's left of the limb, and it is impossible to put on an artificial leg before the neuralgia has absolutely disappeared, and there are some amputees for whom it lasts four, six, eight, twelve months! They keep telling me that it almost never lasts less than two months. If it lasts me only two months, I'll be lucky! I could spend that much time in the hospital and have the pleasure of leaving with two legs. I don't see what good it would do to leave on crutches. You can't go up or down stairs, it's a terrible business. You run the risk of falling and crippling yourself even worse. I had thought I'd be able to come spend a few months with you, until I got the strength to use the artificial leg, but now I see that's impossible.

Well, I'll get used to my condition. I'll die wherever fate puts me. I hope to be able to go back there where I was, I've got friends there of ten years' duration, they'll have pity on me, I can find work with them, I'll live whatever way I can. I can still live out there, while in France, besides you, I have neither friends nor acquaintances, nor anyone. And if I can't see you, I'll go back out there. In any case, I have to go back there.

If you go to find out about my draft status, never let them know where I am. I'm even afraid they may get my name at the post office. Don't go turning me in.

Best wishes,
RIMBAUD

TO HIS SISTER

Marseilles
June 29, 1891

My dear sister,

I got your letter of June 26. I already got the letter from Harar by itself the day before yesterday. No news about the June 10 letter: it's disappeared, either in Attigny or here in the hospital; but I suppose it was probably in Attigny. From the envelope you sent me I can tell exactly who it was from. It was probably signed Dimitri Righas. (He's a Greek who lives in Harar whom I left in charge of some business.) I'm waiting for news of your inquiries about the draft; but whatever happens, I'm afraid of traps and haven't the slightest desire to come stay with you at the moment, no matter what assurances they may give you.

Besides, I'm completely immobilized and I've forgotten how to walk. My leg is cured, that is, the scar has healed: which happened very quickly, by the way, and makes me think that the amputation might have been avoided. As far as the doctors are concerned I'm cured, and if I want to they'll sign the slip to let me go home tomorrow. But what for? I can't move a step! I spend all day long in the open air, in a deck chair, but I can't move. I exercise with the crutches, but they're no good. Besides, I'm very tall, and my leg is cut off very high up. It's very difficult to keep your balance. I take a couple of steps and stop for fear of falling and crippling myself again!

I'm going to have them make me a wooden leg to start with. They stick the stump into the top padded with cotton, and you walk with a cane. After a little while of getting used to the wooden leg, if the stump has got strong enough, you can order a leg with joints that stays on easily and that you can walk with, more or less. When will I get to that stage? Between now and then maybe something new will happen to me. But the next time, I am ready to rid myself of this miserable existence.

It's not a good idea for you to write me so often that my name is noticed in the post offices at Roche and Attigny. That's where the danger will come from. Here nobody cares about me. Write me as little as possible and only when it is unavoidable. Don't write Arthur, just put Rimbaud by itself. And let me know as soon as possible and as exactly as possible what the military authorities want with me, and in case they're after me, exactly what penalty I'm liable for. Then I'll be on a boat as quick as I can.

I wish you good health and prosperity.

RIMBAUD

TO HIS SISTER

Marseilles
July 2, 1891

My dear sister,

I've got your letters of June 24 and 26, and I just got the one from June 30. The only one that has got lost is the one from June 10, and I have reason to believe that it was intercepted at the Attigny Post

Office. Here nobody seems to be in the least interested in my business. It's a good idea to mail your letters somewhere other than in Roche, so that they don't go by way of the Attigny Post Office. That way you can write me as much as you'd like. About the draft again, I must absolutely find out where I stand: so do what you have to and give me an answer one way or another. I am really afraid of a trap myself, and I'd be very hesitant to return no matter what happened. I don't think you'll ever get a definite answer, and then I'll never be able to come stay with you, because they may come get me while I'm there.

The scar healed quite a while ago, although the neuralgia in the stump is still just as bad, and I am still on my feet; but now my other leg is very weak. It's either because of the long stay in bed or a lack of balance: but I can't walk on crutches for more than a few minutes without the other leg swelling up. I wonder do I have a bone disease, and am I going to lose the other leg? I'm scared to death, and I'm afraid of getting worn out and so I don't use the crutches. I ordered a wooden leg; it only weighs two kilos, it'll be ready in a week. I'll try to walk very gently with that; it'll take me about a month to get used to it little by little, and maybe the doctor, seeing I still have neuralgia, won't let me walk with it yet. About the elastic leg, it's much too heavy for me at the moment, the stump would never be able to stand it. That's only for much later. And besides they get just as much for a wooden leg; it costs about fifty francs. Because of all this I'll still be in the hospital at the end of July. Right now, I'm paying six francs a day and getting about sixty francs' worth of boredom per hour. I never sleep more than two hours a night. It's this insomnia that makes me afraid that I still have some other disease ahead of me. I am terrified when I think of my other leg: it's my only contact with the earth any more! When the abscess in my knee started in Harar, it started just like this, with about two weeks of insomnia. Well, it's probably my fate to become a basket case! Then maybe the draft board would leave me alone!

Let's hope for the best.

I wish you good health, happy times, and best wishes. Goodbye.

RIMBAUD

TO HIS SISTER

My dear sister,

I've gotten your letters of July 4 and 8. I'm glad my draft status is finally settled once and for all. The draft card I must have lost on my travels—when I can get around again, I'll go see if I should get my deferment here or someplace else. But if it's here in Marseilles, I think I'd better have the letter from the draft board with me here. Whatever the case, I think it's better if I have it with me. So send it to me. Nobody can touch me once I have it. I also have the amputation certificate signed by the director of the hospital, since it seems that doctors aren't allowed to sign the papers for their own patients. With both those documents, I'm sure I can get my deferment here.

I'm still on my feet, but I don't feel well. Up till now, I've only learned to walk with crutches, and I still can't go up or down a single step: someone has to get me up or down with an arm around my waist. I had them make me a wooden leg, very light, varnished and padded, very well made (cost 50 francs); I put it on a few days ago and tried to get around still using the crutches, but I got the stump inflamed and I took the damn thing off. I can't possibly use it for two or three weeks, and still with the crutches for at least a month after that, and no more than an hour or two a day. The only advantage is that it gives you three points of support instead of two.

So I'm back to the crutches. What difficulty, what a bother, what disappointment, when I think of all my traveling, and how active I was only five months ago! What happened to my trips across mountains, on horseback, walking, across deserts, rivers, and oceans? And now I'm a *basket case!* And I'm beginning to understand that crutches, wooden legs, and artificial legs are all a bunch of jokes, and all that stuff gets you is to drag yourself around like cripple and never be able to do anything. And just when I had decided to come back to France this summer to get married! Farewell marriage, farewell family, farewell future! My life is over, all I am now is a motionless stump.

I'm still a long way from being able to get around even with the wooden leg, and yet that's the easiest part of it. I figure at least four more months in order just to be able to take a few steps with the wooden leg and nothing but a cane. The most difficult thing is going up or down stairs. Only in six months will I be able to try out an artificial leg, and with great difficulty, and for what? The real problem is that my leg was cut off so high up. First of all the neuralgia after the amputation is more violent and persistent the higher up the limb was cut off. So the ones who get amputated at the knee get used to an artificial device much more quickly. . . . But all of that is nonsense now; so is life itself.

It's no cooler here than it was in Egypt. It's 85° to 95° at noon, and 75° to 85° at night. The temperature in Harar is much pleasanter, especially at night, when it never gets over 50° or 60°.

I can't tell you what I intend to do, I'm still too *down* to be able even to tell myself. I don't feel well, I repeat; I'm really afraid something will happen. The stump of my leg is much more swollen than the other one and full of neuralgia. The doctor, naturally, never comes to see me, because as far as the doctor is concerned once the wound heals he's through with you. He tells you you're cured, and he doesn't pay any attention to you unless you break out in sores, etc., etc., or some other complications develop that he has to get out the knife for. Those people never think of sick people as anything more than something to experiment on, everybody knows that; especially in the hospitals, when they don't get paid. Anyway, they only try to get jobs as hospital doctors in order to build up a reputation and a clientele.

I would definitely like to come to Roche, because it's cool there; but I doubt there are any places there suitable for my acrobatic exercises. Also, I'm afraid that it may turn from cool to cold. But the main reason is that I can't move; I can't, and won't be able to for a long time—and to tell you the truth, I don't feel cured inside and I'm waiting for something terrible to happen. . . . I'd have to be carried to the train, carried out, etc., etc. It's too much trouble, expense, and bother. My room is paid through the end of July; I'll think about it and see what I can do in the meanwhile. Until then I'd like to think that everything will be all right, as you keep trying to make me think—however stupid life may be, man keeps on clinging to it.

Send me the letter from the draft board. There just happens to be a police inspector sick here, and at the same table with me, and he keeps on bothering me with talk about draft boards and military service and is probably getting ready to turn me in.

Excuse me for bothering you. Thanks. I wish you good luck and good health.

Write me.

All the best,
RIMBAUD

TO HIS SISTER

Marseilles
July 15, 1891

Dear Isabelle,

I got your letter of the 13th, and am replying right away. I'm going to see what I can do with the letter from the draft board and the certificate from the hospital. I would certainly like to have the matter settled, but I have no way of doing so myself, since I'm barely able to put a shoe on the foot I have left. Well, I'll make out as best I can. At least, with these two documents I don't run the risk any longer of going to jail; because the army is quite capable of putting a cripple in prison, even if it's only in a hospital. And what about the certificate of return to France, where and how do I get it? There's no one here who can give me any information, and it'll be a long time before I can go find out for myself, with my wooden legs.

I spend all day and night thinking of ways to get around: it's really torture. I want to do this or that, go here and there, see things, live, get out of here: impossible, impossible at least for a long time, if not forever! All I see next to me are those damn crutches; I can't take a step, I don't exist without those sticks. I can't even dress myself without the most painful gymnastics. It's true I've got to where I can almost run on the crutches; but I can't go up or down stairs, and if the ground is uneven the bouncing from shoulder to shoulder wears me out completely. I have an extremely painful neuralgia in my right shoulder and arm, and on top of it the crutch sawing away at my shoulder! I still have neuralgia in my left leg, and with all of this I have to go through these acrobatics all day long just to look like I'm alive.

Here is what I have finally decided was the cause of my getting sick. The climate in Harar is cold from November to March. Usually I never wore much clothing: plain linen pants and a cotton shirt. On top of that I must have walked from 15 to 40 kilometers a day, made insane trips on horseback over the steep mountains around there. I think I must have developed an arthritis in the knee caused by fatigue, the heat, and the cold. In fact it all started with something like a hammer blow (so to speak) under the kneecap, which was repeated very lightly once a minute; a lot of stiffness in the joint and a contraction of the nerve in the thigh. Then the veins all around the knee started to swell, and the swelling made me think it was varicose veins. I kept on walking and working as hard as ever, more than ever, thinking it was just a simple attack from the cold. Then the pain inside the knee got worse. Each step felt like someone was driving a nail in it. I kept on walking, although with great difficulty; especially I kept on horseback riding, although I would dismount practically lame each time. Then the top of the knee swelled up, the kneecap got stiff and heavy, the skin got involved as well. It got painful to move around and the nerves were racked with pain, from my ankle to the small of my back. I could only walk with a heavy limp, and I kept on getting worse. But I still had a lot of work to do, naturally. So I started keeping the leg bandaged from top to bottom, to rub it, bathe it, etc., without any results. Then I lost my appetite. A continual insomnia started. I was getting weaker and got very thin. Around March 15, I decided to go to bed, at least to stay stretched out. I rigged up a bed between my cashbox, my ledgers, and a window when I could keep an eye on my scales at the end of the courtyard, and I paid people more to keep the business going, while I stayed stretched out, or at least the leg. But ever day the swelling made it look like a bowling ball. I observed that the inner surface of the tibia was much larger than on the other leg. The kneecap was becoming immobile, drowning in the secretions produced by the swollen knee, and in a few days I watched in terror as it became hard as bone. At that point the whole leg became stiff, completely stiff in about a week's time; I could go to the bathroom only by dragging myself along. And yet the leg and the top of the thigh kept getting thinner and thinner, and the knee and the skin were still swelling, petrifying, or rather ossifying; and my physical and mental weakness grew. At the end of March I decided to leave. In a few days I had settled all my accounts, at a loss; and since the stiffness and the pain prevented me from getting on a mule or even a camel, I had a litter made with a canvas cover, that 16 men carried to Zeila in about two weeks. The second day of the trip, I had got far ahead of the caravan, and we were caught in an empty spot by a rainstorm where I stayed flat on my back in the rain for 16 hours, without shelter and without being able to move; that did me a great deal of harm. On the trip I was never able to get out of my litter. They set up a tent over me wherever they put me down; and after I dug a hole with my hands near the edge of the litter, I would manage with difficulty to hoist myself over the side so I could relieve myself into that hole, which I then covered over with dirt. In the morning they lifted the tent from over me, then they lifted me up. I got to Zeila, worn out, paralyzed. I only got four hours' rest then; there was a boat leaving for Aden. Dumped on board on my mattress (they had to hoist me on board in my litter), I had to get through three days at sea without anything to eat. At Aden, I was unloaded in the litter. I then spent several days with M. Tian to settle business and then I went to the hospital where the English doctor, after two weeks, told me to go back to Europe.

I am convinced that this pain in the joint, if it had been taken care of right away, would easily have passed and there would have been no complications. I'm the one who spoiled it all by my obstinacy in walking and working too much.

Why don't they teach us medicine in school, at least the little each of us needs in order to avoid such stupid mistakes?

If anyone were to come to me in the condition I was in before all this, to ask my advice, I would say: Have you come to that point already? Never let them cut a part of you off. Let them butcher you, cut you open, tear you to pieces, but never let them cut a part of you off. If you die, that will be better than living with a part of you gone. And that's what a lot of people have done, and if I had to start this all over again, I'd do it too. Better to spend a year in Hell than let them cut part of you off!

Look at me now: I sit. Every once in a while I get up and hop a few steps on my crutches, then I sit down again. I can't hold anything in my hands. When I walk, I can't turn my face from my single foot and the ends of my crutches. My head and shoulders sink, I look like a hunchback. You tremble when you see people and things moving all around you, for fear they'll knock you over and break the leg you have left. People laugh to see you hopping around. You sit back down, your hands are worn out, your shoulder is sawed through, you look like a lunatic. Despair overwhelms you; you stay sitting, absolutely helpless, whimpering and waiting for night, which brings only insomnia and a new day worse than the one before, etc., etc. More in the next installment.

Best wishes,
RIMBAUD

TO HIS SISTER

Marseilles
July 20, 1891

My dear sister,

I write you while suffering from a violent pain in the right shoulder; it almost prevents me from writing, as you can see.

It is all the fault of a condition become arthritic because of poor treatment. But I've had enough of the hospital, in which I am every day liable to catch smallpox, typhus, and all the other diseases it is full of. I'm leaving, since the doctor said I could and that it's better for me not to stay here.

So I'll be out in two or three days and I'll see what I can do about dragging myself up to see you as best I can; for without my wooden leg I can't walk, and even with the crutches I can take only a few steps for the moment, so as not to make my shoulder worse. I'll get off at Voncq station as you said. About the room, I'd prefer to stay upstairs; so don't write me here anymore, I'll be leaving any minute now.

> Goodbye,
> RIMBAUD

DICTATED TO HIS SISTER ISABELLE, THE DAY BEFORE HE DIED

Marseilles
November 9, 1891

One shipment: a single tusk
One shipment: two tusks
One shipment: three tusks
One shipment: four tusks
One shipment: two tusks

To the Director:
DEAR SIR:

I have come to inquire if I have left anything on account with you. I wish today to change over to another transport line, to leave this one whose name I do not even know, but in any case I must get passage from Aphinar. All these transport lines run everywhere, and I am helpless and unhappy and I can find nothing, any dog in the street can tell you that.

Please let me know the cost of passage from Aphinar to Suez. I am completely paralyzed, and so I am anxious to be on board early. Please tell me at what time I must be carried on board. . . .

VITALIE CUIF RIMBAUD TO HER DAUGHTER ISABELLE

Charleville
June 1, 1900
an unlucky day

My daughter,

I feel an interior satisfaction impossible to describe: I feel that I have accomplished the will of God.

The crypt is done, and well done; but still not entirely as I wished. My place is prepared, in the midst of my dear departed; my coffin will be placed between my dear Father and my dear Vitalie on my right, and my poor Arthur on my left. I had them make two little walls out of bricks upon which my coffin will be set, and I had a cross and a branch of blessed yew attached to the wall. I had the gravedigger come, and I showed him clearly where I wanted to be placed. He understood me completely. Everything is arranged.

Before they sealed the entrance stone, referred to as the portal, which is fifty centimeters on each side, just wide enough to let the coffin through, I wanted to see it again, to make sure there was nothing still to be done. The gravediggers let me down very gently into the crypt; some of them held me by the shoulders, the rest by my feet. Everything is fine: it was at that moment that I attached the cross and the yew branch. Getting out of the crypt was more difficult, because it is quite deep; but those men are very clever, and they got me out very nicely, but with great effort.

I have done my duty. My poor Arthur who never asked me for

anything, and who by his hard work, his intelligence, and his good behavior amassed a fortune, and amassed it very honestly; he never cheated anybody; just the opposite, he lost a lot of money, and some of it is still owing to him; and the dear child was very charitable, everybody knows that. You yourself, daughter, know the money you sent back out there for them to give to his servant, according to his instructions.

My dear Vitalie was a hard worker, intelligent and good, everybody who knew her esteemed her, admired her and loved her, at school and everywhere else. My sainted father was a completely honest man, well known to all, and he had given up all the . . . [the rest of the letter is lost].

Index of English Titles

Index of French Titles

Index of First Lines

P.S.

Insights,
Interviews
& More...

Meet Arthur Rimbaud

THOUGH OF HUMBLE ORIGINS, Arthur Rimbaud became one of the greatest, most innovative poets France has ever produced. His relatively short life was marked by incongruity: He wrote all of his poetry before the age of twenty, in a creative burst that lasted less than five years, then never wrote poetry again. After early years marked by public scandal, he faded from view and died virtually forgotten. His small body of work, revived after his death, broke with literary convention and helped usher in the modernist movement, but he himself did nothing to preserve his own poetic legacy.

Jean-Nicolas-Arthur Rimbaud was born October 20, 1854, in Charleville, a small French town near the Belgian border. His father, Frédéric, was an army captain who had been promoted through the ranks. His mother, née Vitalie Cuif, came from a family that had risen from the peasantry to become landowners. Captain Rimbaud fought in the Crimean campaign of 1855–56, then returned to Charleville, but in 1860, shortly after the birth of Arthur's younger sister, he rejoined his garrison and never returned home.

Abandoned with her four children, Madame Rimbaud reared them with a severe code of conduct that prized piety, economy, and conformity. Rimbaud would eventually rebel in spectacular fashion against his mother's narrow notions of respectability. Yet it has been observed that, despite his rebellion, Rimbaud's life was an odd amalgam of each parent's influence: Like his father, he was a lifelong wanderer with no fixed abode, and yet in the second half of his life he would seek financial security like the parsimonious bourgeoisie his mother had raised him to be.

For much of his childhood, Arthur was a tractable child and model student. His teacher and mentor, Georges Izambard, was the first to fully acknowledge and nurture the precocious fifteen-year-old's talent for poetry, introducing Rimbaud to the work of the Parnassian poets, whose art he would emulate and eventually eclipse. When the Charleville school was shut down during the Franco-Prussian War, young Rimbaud's formal education came to an abrupt end. Cut loose, Arthur began his often depraved and always defiant odyssey as a literary vagabond.

Still not yet sixteen, Rimbaud ran away to Paris and was imprisoned upon arrival for not paying his train fare. Izambard secured his release. A week after returning to Charleville, Arthur fled to Belgium with notions of finding work as a journalist. At his mother's insistence, he returned home, promising not to run away again. But just a few months later, with France in turmoil after Napoleon III's surrender to the Prussians, Rimbaud wandered the countryside and finally, in March of 1871, ended up in Paris. The capital was demoralized by defeat and sunk in squalor; Rimbaud joined its destitute citizens, sleeping on park ▶

> " Rimbaud's life was an odd amalgam of each parent's influence: Like his father, he was a lifelong wanderer with no fixed abode, and yet in the second half of his life he would seek financial security like the parsimonious bourgeoisie his mother had raised him to be. "

benches and under bridges, and eating meals out of garbage cans.

Around this time, Rimbaud began to formulate his revolutionary theories of poetry. "A Poet makes himself a visionary through a long, boundless, and systemized *disorganization of all the senses*," he wrote. "All forms of love, of suffering, of madness; he searches himself, he exhausts within himself all poisons, and preserves their quintessences." Rimbaud felt that a poet must reject social conventions, live intensely, and experiment with pleasure in order to write worthwhile poetry. Over the next three years, he put his theory to work, living a rebelliously bohemian life filled with alcohol, drugs, sex, and poetry.

The most notable and scandalous liaison that Rimbaud forged was with the poet Paul-Marie Verlaine. Verlaine was ten years older than Rimbaud and already established as an important poet when the younger man sent him some poems for his criticism. Verlaine was astounded by Rimbaud's talent, and he invited the sixteen-year-old to come stay with him and his wife's family. But Rimbaud, dirty and rude, shocked Verlaine's conservative in-laws, so Verlaine arranged other lodgings for him. Almost immediately after his son was born, Verlaine left his family and moved in with Rimbaud. There is little doubt that the two men became lovers. The relationship would leave an indelible mark on Rimbaud's poetry, and Verlaine

66 Rimbaud felt that a poet must reject social conventions, live intensely and experiment with pleasure in order to write worthwhile poetry. 99

became a great—perhaps the greatest—champion of Rimbaud's work.

Their intimacy was marked by public displays of debauchery and by private turmoil. During a turbulent eighteen-month period, the two men moved numerous times between Belgium, England, and France. Finally, after one of many quarrelsome splits, a distraught Verlaine summoned Rimbaud to Brussels with threats of suicide. Drunk and hysterical, Verlaine fired a gun at Rimbaud, wounding him in the hand. A second threat prompted Rimbaud to hail a passing policeman, and Verlaine was arrested. Despite Rimbaud's withdrawal of the complaint, Verlaine was fined and sentenced to two years in prison.

After Verlaine's imprisonment, Rimbaud returned to Charleville where he apparently wrote much of *Une saison en enfer (A Season in Hell)*, one of his acknowledged masterpieces. He arranged to have the work published in Brussels, but could not pay the printing bill. Except for a few advance author's copies that Rimbaud received and circulated, the bulk of the copies remained in the printer's stockroom until discovered by chance in 1901.

In 1875, Rimbaud and Verlaine met one last time, and it was by all accounts an acrimonious encounter. Rimbaud continued his peripatetic life, traveling to London, Stuttgart, Milan, and Vienna, but always returning to Charleville for short periods of time. At nineteen ▶

years old, he abandoned poetry and completely reinvented himself, joining the Dutch army and sailing for Java. He deserted a month after arrival, and sailed home on a British ship. He found work in Cyprus and North Africa a few years later, and eventually turned up in Abyssinia, now Ethiopia. He lived the rest of his short life as a colonial, dealing in coffee, hides, and armaments. The former profligate regularly sent money home to his mother, who invested it in land.

Rimbaud began to suffer pains in his right knee in February 1891, and he returned to France, arriving in Marseilles in May; a week later, he was diagnosed with cancer and his leg was amputated. However, the cancer had spread, and Rimbaud died on November 10, a month after his thirty-seventh birthday. But for the intervention of Verlaine, who published *Poésies complète d'Arthur Rimbaud* in 1895, Rimbaud's work might have been lost to history.

The savage beauty and lyric intensity of Rimbaud's work greatly influenced subsequent generations of writers. Wallace Stevens, Ezra Pound, Delmore Schwartz, Robert Lowell, Jack Kerouac, and William Burroughs are just a handful of countless writers and poets who owe a literary debt to Rimbaud. The poet's work enjoyed a renaissance in the 1960s, when the counterculture found kinship in his experiments with drugs and sexual freedom. Musician-poets such as Bob Dylan, Jim Morrison, and Patti Smith have all acknowledged their indebtedness to his work.

With so many of the events of Rimbaud's unconventional life shrouded in legend, it is important not to put the life before the work. As F.C. St. Aubyn has suggested, "Readers interested only in his biography must eventually turn to Rimbaud's poetry to discover how this precocious child and provincial bumpkin helped turn Western literature on its ear." ∽

The Secret of Rimbaud

Following is an excerpt from Arthur Symons's literary classic The Symbolist Movement in Literature. *Published in 1899, the book went on to influence many writers, among them T. S. Eliot, who said: "I myself owe Mr. Symons a great debt: but for having read his book I should not, in the year 1908, have read of Laforgue or Rimbaud. . . ."*

THAT STORY OF THE ARABIAN NIGHTS, which is at the same time a true story, the life of Rimbaud, has been told, for the first time, in the extravagant but valuable book of an anarchist of letters, who writes under the name of Paterne Berrichon, and who has since married Rimbaud's sister. *La Vie de Jean-Arthur Rimbaud* is full of curiosity for those who have been mystified by I know not what legends, invented to give wonder to a career, itself more wonderful than any of the inventions. The man who died at Marseilles, at the Hospital of the Conception, on March 10, 1891, at the age of thirty-seven, *négotiant*, as the register of his death describes him, was a writer of genius, an innovator in verse and prose, who had written all his poetry by the age of nineteen, and all his prose by a year or two later. He had given up literature to travel hither and thither, first in Europe, then in Africa; he had been an engineer, a leader of caravans, a merchant of precious merchandise. And this man, who had never written down a line after those astonishing early experiments, was heard, in his last delirium, talking of precisely such visions as those which had haunted his youth, and using, says his sister, "expressions of a singular and penetrating charm" to render these sensations of visionary countries. Here certainly is one of the most curious problems of literature: is it a problem of which we can discover the secret?

Jean-Nicolas-Arthur Rimbaud was born at Charleville, in the Ardennes, October 20, 1854. His father, of whom he saw little, was a captain in the army; his mother, of peasant origin, was severe, rigid and unsympathetic. At school he was an unwilling but brilliant scholar, and by his fifteenth year was well acquainted with Latin literature and intimately with French literature. It was in that year that he began to write poems from the first curiously original: eleven poems dating from that year are to be found in his collected works. When he was sixteen he decided that he had had enough of school, and enough of home. Only Paris existed: he must go to Paris. The first time he went without a ticket; he spent, indeed, fifteen days in Paris, but he spent them in Mazas, from which he was released and restored to his home by his schoolmaster. The second time, a few days later, he sold his watch, which paid for his railway ticket. This time he threw himself on the hospitality of André Gill, a painter and verse-writer, of some little notoriety then, whose address he had happened to come across. The uninvited guest was not welcomed, and after ▶

66 And this man, who had never written down a line after those astonishing early experiments, was heard, in his last delirium, talking of precisely such visions as those which had haunted his youth. 99

The Secret of Rimbaud *(continued)*

some penniless days in Paris he tramped back to Charleville. The third time (he had waited five months, writing poems, and discontented to be only writing poems) he made his way to Paris on foot, in a heat of revolutionary sympathy, to offer himself to the insurgents of the Commune. Again he had to return on foot. Finally, having learnt with difficulty that a man is not taken at his own valuation until he has proved his right to be so accepted, he sent up the manuscript of his poems to Verlaine. The manuscript contained "Le Bateau Ivre," "Les Premières Communions," "Ma Bohème," "Roman," "Les Effarés," and, indeed, all but a few of the poems he ever wrote. Verlaine was overwhelmed with delight, and invited him to Paris. A local admirer lent him the money to get there, and from October 1871 to July 1872, he was Verlaine's guest.

The boy of seventeen, already a perfectly original poet, and beginning to be an equally original prose-writer, astonished the whole Parnasse, Banville, Hugo himself. On Verlaine his influence was more profound. The meeting brought about one of those lamentable and admirable disasters which make and unmake careers. Verlaine has told us in his *Confessions* that, "in the beginning, there was no question of any sort of affection or sympathy between two natures so different as that of the poet of the *Assis* and mine, but simply of an extreme admiration and astonishment before this boy of sixteen, who had

66 On Verlaine his influence was more profound. The meeting brought about one of those lamentable and admirable disasters which make and unmake careers. 99

already written things, as Fénéon
has excellently said, 'perhaps outside
literature.'" This admiration and
astonishment passed gradually into a
more personal feeling, and it was under
the influence of Rimbaud that the long
vagabondage of Verlaine's life began.

The two poets wandered together
through Belgium, England, and again
Belgium, from July 1872 to August 1873,
when there occurred that tragic parting
at Brussels which left Verlaine a prisoner
for eighteen months, and sent Rimbaud
back to his family. He had already
written all the poetry and prose that
he was ever to write, and in 1873 he
printed at Brussels *Une Saison en Enfer*.
It was the only book he himself ever gave
to the press, and no sooner was it printed
than he destroyed the whole edition, with
the exception of a few copies, of which
only Verlaine's copy, I believe, still exists.
Soon began new wanderings, with their
invariable return to the starting-point of
Charleville: a few days in Paris, a year in
England, four months in Stuttgart (where
he was visited by Verlaine), Italy, France
again, Vienna, Java, Holland, Sweden,
Egypt, Cyprus, Abyssinia, and then
nothing but Africa, until the final return
to France. He had been a teacher of
French in England, a seller of key-rings
in the streets of Paris, had unloaded
vessels in the ports, and helped to gather
in the harvest in the country; he had
been a volunteer in the Dutch army,
a military engineer, a trader; and now
physical sciences had begun to attract ▶

his insatiable curiosity, and dreams of the
fabulous East began to resolve themselves
into dreams of a romantic commerce
with the real East. He became a merchant
of coffee, perfumes, ivory, and gold, in
the interior of Africa; then an explorer,
a predecessor, and in his own regions, of
Marchand. After twelve years' wandering
and exposure in Africa he was attacked
by a malady of the knee, which rapidly
became worse. He was transported first
to Aden, then to Marseilles, where, in
May 1891, his leg was amputated. Further
complications set in. He insisted, first,
on being removed to his home, then
on being taken back to Marseilles. His
sufferings were an intolerable torment,
and more cruel to him was the torment
of his desire to live. He died inch by
inch, fighting every inch; and his sister's
quiet narrative of those last months
is agonizing. He died at Marseilles in
November, "prophesying," says his
sister, and repeating, "Allah Kerim!
Allah Kerim!"

The secret of Rimbaud, I think, and
the reason why he was able to do the
unique thing in literature which he
did, and then to disappear quietly and
become a legend in the East, is that his
mind was not the mind of the artist but
of the man of action. He was a dreamer,
but all his dreams were discoveries.
To him it was an identical act of his
temperament to write the sonnet of
the "Vowels" and to trade in ivory and
frankincense with the Arabs. He lived
with all his faculties at every instant of

66 The secret
of Rimbaud, I
think, and the
reason why he
was able to do the
unique thing in
literature which
he did ... is that
his mind was not
the mind of the
artist but of the
man of action. 99

his life, abandoning himself to himself
with a confidence which was at once
his strength and (looking at things less
absolutely) his weakness. To the student
of success, and what is relative in
achievement, he illustrates the danger
of one's over-possession by one's own
genius, just as aptly as the saint in the
cloister does, or the mystic too full of
God to speak intelligibly to the world,
or the spilt wisdom of the drunkard.
The artist who is above all things an
artist cultivates a little choice corner
of himself with elaborate care; he
brings miraculous flowers to growth
there, but the rest of the garden is but
mown grass or tangled bushes. That is
why many excellent writers, very many
painters, and most musicians are so
tedious on any subject but their own.
Is it not tempting, does it not seem a
devotion rather than a superstition, to
worship the golden chalice in which
the wine has been made God, as if the
chalice were the reality, and the Real
Presence the symbol? The artist, who
is only an artist, circumscribes his
intelligence into almost such a fiction,
as he reverences the work of his own
hands. But there are certain natures
(great or small, Shakespeare or Rimbaud,
it makes no difference), to whom the
work is nothing; the act of working,
everything. Rimbaud was a small,
narrow, hard, precipitate nature, which
had the will to live, and nothing but
the will to live; and his verses, and his
follies, and his wanderings, and his ▶

traffickings were but the breathing of different hours in his day.

That is why he is so swift, definite, and quickly exhausted in vision; why he had his few things to say, each an action with consequences. He invents new ways of saying things, not because he is a learned artist, but because he is burning to say them, and he has none of the hesitations of knowledge. He leaps right over or through the conventions that had been standing in everybody's way; he has no time to go round, and no respect for trespass-boards, and so he becomes the *enfant terrible* of literature, playing pranks (as in that sonnet of the "Vowels"), knocking down barriers for the mere amusement of the thing, getting all the possible advantage of his barbarisms in mind and conduct. And so, in life, he is first of all conspicuous as a disorderly liver, a revolter against morals as against prosody, though we may imagine that, in his heart, morals meant as little to him, one way or the other, as prosody. Later on, his revolt seems to be against civilization itself, as he disappears into the deserts of Africa. And it is, if you like, a revolt against civilization, but the revolt is instinctive, a need of the organism; it is not doctrinal, cynical, a conviction, a sentiment.

Always, as he says *rêvant univers fantastiques*, he is conscious of the danger as well as the ecstasy of that divine imitation; for he says: "My life

> 66 He leaps right over or through the conventions that had been standing in everybody's way; he has no time to go round, and no respect for trespass-boards, and so he becomes the *enfant terrible* of literature. 99

will always be too vast to be given up
wholly to force and beauty." *J'attends
Dieu avec gourmandise*, he cries, in a fine
rapture; and then, sadly enough: "I have
created all the feasts, all the triumphs, all
the dramas of the world. I have set myself
to invent new flowers, a new flesh, a
new language. I have fancied that I have
attained supernatural power. Well, I
have now only to put my imagination
and my memories in the grave. What
a fine artist's and story-teller's fame
thrown away!" See how completely he
is conscious, and how completely he is
at the mercy, of that hallucinatory rage
of vision, vision to him being always
force, power, creation, which, on some
of his pages, seems to become sheer
madness, and on others a kind of wild
but absolute insight. He will be silent,
he tells us, as to all that he contains
within his mind, "greedy as the sea,"
for otherwise poets and visionaries
would envy him his fantastic wealth.
And, in that "Nuit d'Enfer," which
does not bear that title in vain, he
exalts himself as a kind of savior;
he is in the circle of pride in Dante's
hell, and he has lost all sense of limit,
really believes himself to be "no one
and some one." Then, in the "Alchimie
du Verbe," he becomes the analyst of
his own hallucinations. "I believe in
all the enchantments," he tells us;
"I invented the color of the vowels;
A, black; E, white; I, red; O, blue;
U, green.[1] I regulated the form and
the movement of every consonant, ▶

and, with instinctive rhythms, I flattered myself that I had invented a poetic language accessible, one day or another, to every shade of meaning. I reserved to myself the right of translation . . . I accustomed myself to simple hallucination: I saw, quite frankly, a mosque in place of a factory, a school of drums kept by the angels, post-chaises on the roads of heaven, a drawing-room at the bottom of a lake; monsters, mysteries; the title of a vaudeville raised up horrors before me. Then I explained my magical sophisms by the hallucination of words! I ended by finding something sacred in the disorder of my mind." Then he makes the great discovery. Action, one sees, this fraudulent and insistent will to live, has been at the root of all these mental and verbal orgies, in which he has been wasting the very substance of his thought. Well, "action," he discovers, "is not life, but a way of spoiling something." Even this is a form of enervation, and must be rejected from the absolute. *Mon devoir m'est remis. Il ne faut plus songer à cela. Je suis réellement d'outre-tombe, et pas de commissions.*

It is for the absolute that he seeks, always; the absolute which the great artist, with his careful wisdom, has renounced seeking. And he is content with nothing less; hence his own contempt for what he has done, after all, so easily; for what has come to him, perhaps through his impatience, but imperfectly. He is a dreamer in whom

66 'I accustomed myself to simple hallucination . . . Then I explained my magical sophisms by the hallucination of words! I ended by finding something sacred in the disorder of my mind.' 99

dream is swift, hard in outline, coming
suddenly and going suddenly, a real
thing, but seen only in passing. Visions
rush past him, he cannot arrest them;
they rush forth from him, he cannot
restrain their haste to be gone, as he
creates them in the mere indiscriminate
idleness of energy. And so this seeker
after the absolute leaves but a broken
medley of fragments, into each of which
he has put a little of his personality,
which he is forever dramatizing, by
multiplying one facet, so to speak,
after another. Very genuinely, he is
now a beaten and wandering ship,
flying in a sort of intoxication before
the wind, over undiscovered seas; now
a starving child outside a baker's window,
in the very ecstasy of hunger; now *la
victime et la petite épouse* of the first
communion; now:

> *Je ne parlerai pas, je ne penserai rien;*
> *Mais l'amour infini me montera*
>   *dans l'âme,*
> *Et j'irai loin, bien loin, comme un*
>   *bohémien,*
> *Par la Nature, heureux comme avec*
>   *une femme!*

He catches at verse, at prose, invents
a sort of *vers libre* before any one else,
not quite knowing what to do with it,
invents a quite new way of writing prose,
which Laforgue will turn to account later
on; and having suggested, with some
impatience, half the things that his own
and the next generation are to busy ▶

themselves with developing, he gives up writing, as an inadequate form, to which he is also inadequate.

What, then, is the actual value of Rimbaud's work, in verse and prose, apart from its relative values of so many kinds? I think, considerable; though it will probably come to rest on two or three pieces of verse, and a still vaguer accomplishment in prose.

He brought into French verse something of that "gipsy way of going with nature, as with a woman"; a very young, very crude, very defiant and sometimes very masterly sense of just these real things which are too close to us to be seen by most people with any clearness. He could render physical sensation, of the subtlest kind, without making any compromise with language, forcing language to speak straight, taming it as one would tame a dangerous animal. And he kneaded prose as he kneaded verse, making it a disarticulated, abstract, mathematically lyrical thing. In verse, he pointed the way to certain new splendors, as to certain new *naïvetés*; there is the "Bateau Ivre," without which we might never have had Verlaine's "Crimen Amoris," And, intertangled with what is ingenuous, and with what is splendid, there is a certain irony, which comes into that youthful work as if youth were already reminiscent of itself, so conscious is it that youth is youth, and that youth is passing.

In all these ways, Rimbaud had his influence upon Verlaine, and his

> ❝ He could render physical sensation, of the subtlest kind, without making any compromise with language, forcing language to speak straight, taming it as one would tame a dangerous animal. ❞

influence upon Verlaine was above all the influence of the man of action upon the man of sensation; the influence of what is simple, narrow, emphatic, upon what is subtle, complex, growing. Verlaine's rich, sensitive nature was just then trying to realize itself. Just because it had such delicate possibilities, because there were so many directions in which it could grow, it was not at first quite sure of its way. Rimbaud came into the life and art of Verlaine, troubling both, with that trouble which reveals a man to himself. Having helped to make Verlaine a great poet, he could go. Note that he himself could never have developed: writing had been one of his discoveries; he could but make other discoveries, personal ones. Even in literature he had his future; but his future was Verlaine.

-----

[1] Here is the famous sonnet, which must be taken, as it was meant, without undue seriousness, and yet as something more than a mere joke.

VOYELLES

> A noir, E blanc, I rouge, U vert, O bleu,
>   voyelles,
> Je dirai quelque jour vos naissances
>   latentes.
> A, noir corset velu des mouches éclatantes
> Qui bombillent autour des puanteurs
>   cruelles,
> Golfe d'ombre; E, candeur des vapeurs et
>   des tentes,
> Lance des glaciers fiers, rois blancs,
>   frissons d'ombelles; ▶

The Secret of Rimbaud *(continued)*

I, pourpres, sang craché, rire des lèvres
  belles
Dans la colère ou les ivresses pénitentes;

U, cycles, vibrements divins des mers
  virides,
Paix des pâtis semés d'animaux, paix
  des rides
Que l'alchemie imprime aux grands
  fronts studieux;

O, suprême clairon plein de strideurs
  étranges,
Silences traversés des mondes et des
  Anges:
—O l'Oméga, rayon violet de Ses Yeux!

Coincidence or origin, it has lately been pointed out that Rimbaud may formerly have seen an old A B C book in which the vowels are colored for the most part as his are (A, black; E, white; I, red; O, blue; U, green). In the little illustrative pictures around them some are oddly in keeping with the image of Rimbaud. ∾

Henry Miller on Finding Rimbaud

The following passage is excerpted from The Time of the Assassins: A Study of Rimbaud, *by Henry Miller (New Directions, 1946).*

It was in 1927, in the sunken basement of a dingy house in Brooklyn that I first heard Rimbaud's name mentioned. I was then thirty-six years old and in the depths of my own protracted Season in Hell. An absorbing book about Rimbaud was lying about the house but I never glanced at it. The reason was that I loathed the woman who owned it and who was then living with us. In looks, temperament and behavior she was, as I later discovered, as near to resembling Rimbaud as it is possible to imagine.

As I say, though Rimbaud was all the engrossing topic of conversation between Thelma and my wife, I made no effort to know him. In fact, I fought like the very devil to put him out of my mind; it seemed to me then that he was the evil genius who had unwittingly inspired all my trouble and misery. I saw that Thelma, whom I despised, had identified herself with him, was imitating him as best she could, not only in her behavior but in the kind of verse she wrote. Everything conspired to make me repudiate his name, his influence, his very existence. I was ▶

> 66 In fact, I fought like the very devil to put him (Rimbaud) out of my mind; it seemed to me then that he was the evil genius who had unwittingly inspired all my trouble and misery. 99

Henry Miller on Finding Rimbaud
(*continued*)

then at the very lowest point of my whole career, my morale was completely shattered. I remember sitting in the cold dank basement trying to write by the light of a flickering candle with a pencil. I was trying to write a play depicting my own tragedy. I never succeeded in getting beyond the first act.

In that state of despair and sterility I was naturally highly sceptical of the genius of a seventeen-year-old poet. All that I heard about him sounded like an invention of crazy Thelma's. I was then capable of believing that she could conjure up subtle torments with which to plague me, since she hated me as much as I did her. The life which the three of us were leading, and which I tell about at great length in *The Rosy Crucifixion*, was like an episode in one of Dostoievsky's tales. It seems unreal and incredible to me now.

The point is, however, that Rimbaud's name stuck. Though I was not even to glance at his work until six or seven years later, at the home of Anais Nin in Louveciennes, his presence was always with me. It was a disturbing presence, too. "Some day you will have to come to grips with me." That's what his voice kept repeating in my ears. The day I read the first line of Rimbaud I suddenly remembered that it is was of *Le Bateau Ivre* that Thelma had raved so much. *The Drunken Boat*! How expressive that title now seems in light of all I subsequently experienced!

The Drunken Boat! How expressive that title now seems in light of all I subsequently experienced!

Thelma meanwhile died in an insane asylum. And if I had not gone to Paris, begun to work there in earnest, I think my fate would have been the same. In that basement on Brooklyn Heights my own ship had foundered. When finally the keel burst asunder and drifted out to the open sea, I realized that I was free, that the death I had gone through had liberated me.

If that period in Brooklyn represented my Season in Hell, then the Paris period, especially from 1932 to 1934, was the period of my Illuminations.

Coming upon Rimbaud's work at this time, when I had never been so fecund, so jubilant, so exalted, I had to push him aside, my own creations were more important to me. A mere glance at his writings and I knew what lay in store for me. He was pure dynamite, but I had first to fling my own stick. At this time I did not know anything about his life, except from the snatches Thelma had let drop years ago. I had yet to read a line of biography. It was in 1943, while living at Beverly Glen with John Dudley, the painter, that I first read about Rimbaud. I read Jean-Marie Carré's *A Season in Hell* and then Enid Starkie's work. I was overwhelmed, tongue-tied. It seemed to me that I had never read of a more accursed existence than Rimbaud's. I forgot completely about my own sufferings, which far outweighed his. I forgot about the frustrations and humiliations I had endured, the depths ▶

> 66 I was overwhelmed, tongue-tied. It seemed to me that I had never read of a more accursed existence than Rimbaud's. 99

Henry Miller on Finding Rimbaud
(continued)

of despair and impotence to which
I had sunk time and again. Like Thelma
in the old days, I too could talk of
nothing but Rimbaud. Everybody
who came to the house had to listen
to the song of Rimbaud.

It is only now, eighteen years after
I first heard the name, that I am able
to see him clearly, to read him like
a clairvoyant. Now I know how great
his contribution, how terrible his
tribulations. Now I understand the
significance of his life and work—
as much, that is, as once can say he
understands the life and work of
another. But what I see most clearly
is how I miraculously escaped suffering
the same vile fate.

Rimbaud experienced his great
crisis when he was eighteen, at which
moment in his life he had reached the
edge of madness; from this point on
his life is an unending desert. I reached
mine at the age of thirty-six to thirty-
seven, which is the age at which
Rimbaud dies. From this point on,
my life begins to blossom. Rimbaud
turned from literature to life; I did
the reverse. Rimbaud fled from the
chimeras he had created; I embraced
them. Sobered by the folly and waste
of mere experience of life, I halted
and converted my energies to creation.
I plunged into writing with the same
fervor and zest that I had plunged into
life. Instead of losing life, I gained life;
miracle after miracle occurred, every

misfortune being transformed into a good account. Rimbaud, though plunging into a realm of incredible climates and landscapes, into a world of phantasy as strange and marvelous as his poems, became more and more bitter, taciturn, empty and sorrowful.

Rimbaud restored literature to life; I have endeavored to restore life to literature. In both of us the confessional quality is strong, the moral and spiritual preoccupation uppermost. The flair for *language*, for music rather than literature, is another trait in common. With him I have felt an underlying primitive nature which manifests itself in strange ways. Claudel styled Rimbaud "a mystic in the wild state." Nothing could describe him better. He did not "belong"—not anywhere. I have always had the same feeling about myself. The parallels are endless. I shall go into them in some detail, because in reading the biographies and the letters I saw these correspondences so clearly that I could not resist making note of them. I do not think I am unique in this respect; I think there are many Rimbauds in this world and that their number will increase with time. I think the Rimbaud type will displace, in the world to come, the Hamlet type and the Faustian type. The trend is toward a deeper split. Until the old world dies out utterly, the "abnormal" individual will tend more and more to become ▶

66 Rimbaud, though plunging into a realm of incredible climates and landscapes, into a world of phantasy as strange and marvelous as his poems, became more and more bitter, taciturn, empty and sorrowful. 99

Henry Miller on Finding Rimbaud
(continued)

the norm. The new man will find himself only when the warfare between the collectivity and the individual ceases. Then we shall see the human type in its fullness and splendor. ◁